Adventures into Mexico

Adventures into Mexico

American Tourism beyond the Border

Nicholas Dagen Bloom

ROWMAN & LITTLEFIELD PUBLISHERS, INC.
Lanham • Boulder • New York • Toronto • Oxford

ROWMAN & LITTLEFIELD PUBLISHERS, INC.

Published in the United States of America
by Rowman & Littlefield Publishers, Inc.
A wholly owned subsidary of The Rowman & Littlefield Publishing Group, Inc.
4501 Forbes Boulevard, Suite 200, Lanham, Maryland 20706
www.rowmanlittlefield.com

P.O. Box 317, Oxford OX2 9RU, UK

"The Beat Trail to Mexico" from *American and British Writers in Mexico, 1556–1973* by
Drewey Wayne Gunn, Copyright © 1969, 1974, is reprinted here by permission of the
University of Texas Press.
"Bridging the Cultural Gap" from *A Gathering of Fugitives: American Political Expatriates
in Mexico, 1948–1965* by Diana Anhalt, Copyright © 2001, is reprinted here by
permission of Archer Books.

British Library Cataloguing in Publication Information Available

Library of Congress Cataloging-in-Publication Data

Adventures into Mexico : American tourism beyond the border / edited
by Nicholas Dagen Bloom.
 p. cm. — (Jaguar books on Latin America series)
 Includes bibliographical references and index.
 ISBN-13: 978-0-7425-3744-6 (cloth : alk. paper)
 ISBN-10: 0-7425-3744-7 (cloth : alk. paper)
 ISBN-13: 978-0-7425-3745-3 (pbk. : alk. paper)
 ISBN-10: 0-7425-3745-5 (pbk. : alk. paper)
 1. Tourism—Mexico. 2. Visitors, Foreign—Mexico. 3. Americans—
Travel—Mexico. I. Bloom, Nicholas Dagen, 1969- II. Series: Jaguar
books on Latin America.
G155.M6A38 2006
917.20089'13—dc22

                                                    2005035268

Printed in the United States of America

♾™ The paper used in this publication meets the minimum requirements of
American National Standard for Information Sciences—Permanence of Paper for
Printed Library Materials, ANSI/NISO Z39.48-1992.

Contents

Acknowledgments

I would like to thank Colin MacLachlan and William H. Beezeley for lending their wise editorial guidance over the years. All of my contributors have been patient too, enduring the stately development of the collection.

Susan McEachern at Rowman and Littlefield proved to be a responsive editor for a project inherited from Scholarly Resources Press. Bridgette Moore guided the project through publication, and the copyediting skills of John Shanabrook brought clarity to our prose.

The New York Institute of Technology has been a pleasant academic home for the past two years, and I thank the faculty and administration for their continuing support. Gerri Brown provided timely and accurate retyping of certain published materials. I would like to thank Archer Press and the University of Texas Press for permission to republish sections of previously published books.

My parents' charming descriptions of their misadventures and joys in San Miguel de Allende made me consider Mexico a potential travel destination in the first place. Adventures into Mexico with my wife, Leanne Bloom, ultimately inspired this book project, but words can never convey the thrill we felt as we wandered into yet another stunning Mexican city.

Introduction

A cast of American characters and Americanized places fills these pages. Here are the artists, writers, retirees, students, beatniks, communists, homebuyers, realtors, racists, philanthropists, art dealers, and sun worshippers. Here too are the gated communities, the Americanized Mexican neighborhoods, the beach resorts, nightclubs, colonial gems, and cantinas frequented by traveling and expatriate Americans. This collection proudly features a collage of American types and spaces, some of dubious merit, others of notable spirit.

These places, and the American tourists and expatriates who inhabit them, are not static. Every decade has brought changes to the identity of these Mexican destinations and to the tourists themselves. Adventurous American tourists and students, blacklisted fellow travelers, and a few beatniks in the 1950s have been replaced by a stunning range of American visitors today. Small and informal American communities have become structured, self-sustaining colonies. A legacy of growing American involvement in Mexico can now be tracked, evaluated, and critiqued.

This American passion for Mexican spaces is no longer a minor trend. Millions of Americans visit their southern neighbor every year, making Mexico one of the most popular foreign destinations for American travelers; hundreds of thousands of Americans also live in Mexico on a seasonal or semi-permanent basis. Study of this movement is by no means proportional to its magnitude.

Mexican migrants and the controversial, honky-tonk border zones between Mexico and America have been treated with greater seriousness than American adventures deeper into Mexico. Most scholars are dazzled by the "asymmetry" apparent at the border because "nowhere else does a poor Third World country like Mexico share a common border with a wealthy, powerful neighbor."[1]

Urban geographer Lawrence Herzog heralds the rise of a massive urban region that he calls a "transfrontier metropolis" that not only blends the architectural traditions of both nations but has become the most dynamic economic region within both countries. Herzog, like many others, has also documented and analyzed the costs and benefits of the *maquilador* system on the Mexican side of the border; before the rise of capitalist China, the *maquilador* served as one of the most ubiquitous economic bogeymen in both popular and academic circles.[2] The millions of migrant laborers flowing over the border have attracted attention not only from law enforcement (and disgruntled Americans) but also from scholars who have noted a "militarization" of the border region in the pursuit of immigration control.[3] Many scholars, while acknowledging the problems of exploitation and national inequality, have discovered an exciting hybrid culture emerging. Oscar Martínez writes that "two systems have blended to produce an order that is quite distinct from the structures of the two parent societies." Languages, families, cuisines, and musical styles blend at the border.[4]

The border is thus not only the region of Mexico most accessible to the American traveler, but decades of academic and popular coverage have made the border zones a primary image of Mexico in the American imagination. This collection is specifically designed to move beyond the border by following those Americans who travel deeper into the heart of Mexico.

The fact that Americans, even deep within Mexico, are primarily tourists or temporary expatriates has not furthered the case for careful study of Americans in Mexico. Historians have dealt seriously with the influence of American business and political elites in Mexico during the nineteenth and twentieth centuries, but the post-1945 American experience within Mexico has not been limited to the business or diplomatic worlds. Tourism—including both package jaunts and longer-term "pleasure" colonies—has become increasingly popular, but at the same time, tourism is difficult to analyze and, until recently, has been much derided.

Tourism is still treated by many of its critics as a virulent disease on a par with sexism and racism. Tourism, it is said, has infected not only Mexico but the globe with dependency, subservience, mass culture, "airplane" art, and fast food. As with many intellectual fads, this hyperbole does contain a kernel of truth. Tourist sites and promotions do indeed tilt toward the unequal, the homogeneous, and the shallow. To accept this formulation of tourism as the final word, however, is a mistake.

Scholars have since the 1960s noted that tourism is a complex form of human behavior with spiritual, social, cultural, and economic dimensions. The great innovator in tourism studies, Dean MacCannell, wrote in 1967 that "tourist attractions and the behavior surrounding them are . . . one of the most complex and orderly of the several universal codes that constitute modern society."[5] Much human activity now blends into the tourism industry; where ordinary life ends and tourism begins is becoming difficult to distinguish.

Within Mexico, for instance, tourism has exercised and will likely continue to exercise a complex effect upon both the tourists themselves and the places that they visit. Some cities, such as Cancún, do indeed fit neatly into a stereotypical vision of touristic, "other directed" landscapes because they have grown up specifically for the tourist trade and are almost entirely synthetic, but many more destinations evolve gradually. Cities such as San Miguel de Allende and regions such as Oaxaca have been able to preserve signal elements of their authentic nature long after the tourism wave broke over them. Tourism can even help some communities rediscover and protect cultural sites and traditions. UNESCO World Heritage designation, for instance, has helped save many historic districts in Mexico, because formal recognition has become an essential part of tourism-related marketing strategies.

Nor can we really expect the tourist stereotype to retain a stable identity. Most travelers in Mexico and elsewhere are indeed inflamed with standardized consuming fantasies, but others seek out unspoiled spots, learn languages, and appreciate local customs: "Many tourists prefer places that are exaggerated for their attractiveness. . . . More sophisticated travelers, offended by the obvious, seek subtle attractions in the everyday world."[6] Factors such as national origin, age, gender, length of stay, and class status further complicate the picture. Tourism today is a phenomenon of great intricacy both in Mexico and across the globe.

Tourism can trace its modern roots to a distinctly upper-class tradition. Those British sons of the aristocracy who traveled on a grand tour of Europe in the seventeenth and eighteenth centuries did so because such leisurely transit had become an essential sign of high social and cultural standing. Dr. Samuel Johnson remarked, for instance, that "a man who has not been in Italy is always conscious of an inferiority."[7] The association of tourism with high society in its early days gave a patina to the notion of tourism that has never entirely evaporated.

Because it served as a sign of their wealth, these tourists not only traveled and studied at a leisurely pace, but during their sojourns they spent freely on sometimes frivolous desires. Usually these young men were accompanied by tutors who did their best to ensure that these journeys had more than a recreational function. The weakness of the British educational system—aristocratic young men learned surprising little at Oxford—was thought to be remedied through direct social contact with foreign courts, culture, and social rituals. Those locals with sharp eyes cultivated the lodging, feeding, and entertaining of these select voyagers.[8]

A burgeoning middle class in England, and the industrial revolution in the United States, produced ever more travelers. During the nineteenth century, Thomas Cook devised his package tours, Baedeker guides multiplied, and the steamships and railroads cut their rates. Women, who had traveled in small numbers before, joined with men in this new tourist wave. "Unlike the privileged travelers of a bygone age, modern tourists were in neither the position nor the humor to squander their resources; they needed the guidance, the advice, the solicitude offered them by the new firms."[9] Limited, short-term access to Paris and other continental destinations became reason enough to travel, even if the modern tourist moved in large crowds and met few of the locals.

Americans also cultivated their own tourist sites during the nineteenth century. While most eighteenth- and early-nineteenth-century Americans had looked primarily to Europe for inspiration, nineteenth-century American tourists began to find cultural, national, and spiritual interest in domestic destinations such as Niagara Falls and Yellowstone Park. By the second half of the nineteenth century, railroads were bringing Americans and others face-to-face with previously distant natural wonders.

The rise of mass tourism in Europe and the United States, however, created a subtle form of class conflict, as those of greater means and education generally ridiculed those who lacked the means for anything but a package tour. The rise of mass tourism "ensured that tourists who sought to be distinctive were reacting against other tourists as much as in response to what they were visiting."[10] This tradition of the "snobbish anti-tourist" is now seen by many scholars as an essential part of tourism (and strongly conditions the attitudes of many Americans in Mexico today).[11]

Nevertheless, the notion of the tourist remained exalted in the nineteenth century, because a tourist, while not always of a high social class, almost always possessed ample means, education, and leisure hours. Travel writing was a particularly popular activity: "the traveling class was a reading class, and travel was seen as a preeminently literary activity."[12] In a rapidly industrializing world, the great mass of workers in Western industrial society did not have the means, education, or time for extended travel—working-class travel was limited to amusement parks and short jaunts by streetcar or railroad. Those of the lower economic classes who did travel long distances, often as migrants, generally faced an uncomfortable and dangerous journey. The connection between tourism and social standing thus remained.

The tourist as a source of wealth to others became far more noticeable with the growing number of tourists in the nineteenth century. The social identity of the tourist had been slightly blurred, but the economic impact of tourism became crystal clear. Popular destinations in both Europe and the United States began to cater to the tourist. In Europe, towns and cities reshaped their old ruins and districts for tourist eyes, created new restaurants with fare tasty to visitors, and encouraged clever craftsmen to adapt ancient arts to visitors' desires. In the United States, destinations such as Niagara Falls became increasingly commercialized. That the individual tourist now might not be so rich, or well mannered, or culturally or spiritually concerned was less important than the fact that the tourist wave as a whole promised steady sales.

During the twentieth century, the association of tourism and a certain class standing further diminished as a result of the uniformly higher standard of living achieved in the West. The automobile, in particular, "popularized travel, spreading the advantages of tourism from society's elite to the masses. No longer did the railroads and steamship lines and their resorts, dictate travel tastes."[13] Affordable airline travel, initiated in the 1950s, further expanded international movement. Longer vacations and larger pensions enlarged the group of tourists and long-term expatriates over the course of the twentieth century so much that tourism emerged as a pillar of industrial society.

Popular destinations have accentuated their characteristics in similar and often predictable ways, and many have been overwhelmed by the tourist trade. Many cities and rural areas, through prescient regulation and their scale, have been better able to absorb tourists without unduly taxing their resources or authentic culture. The package-tour industry and low cost of world travel has, however, opened even formerly exclusive districts such as the French Riviera and the Swiss Alps to the mass tourist.

Contemporary tourists are themselves mostly blind to the fact that tourism is losing its exalted standing. Tourists, even if they are working class back home, take on an air of the upper-crust traveler that is reminiscent of the grand tour. Travel is an ideal opportunity to play at being a gentleperson because the seemingly elaborate service that accompanies it, often in a poorer land, magnifies a person's sense of status. Much of the world is happy to play along in this theater of subservience and to secretly laugh at the pretensions of such visitors. The economic power of the mass tourist is, after all, more striking than before with its power to transform impoverished backwaters into booming destinations overnight. The slipping class status of the tourist matters less than the fact that mass tourism is the world's leading industry.

The sense of superiority that can come from the travel experience is only one of what might be seen as the potential benefits derived from tourism; the stimulation of the exotic and contact with the "other" is just as powerful a force in driving foreign travel: "In tourism we are freer to explore the unexpected, to face experiences directly and immediately through our senses, unedited by other minds."[14] Americans, for all their success and world power, are particularly susceptible to exotic longings. As affluent and safe as the United States may be, it is growing in predictable ways.

The national mass culture initiated in the early twentieth century in the United States has accelerated a drive toward a national way of life that threatens local and regional characteristics. Many old downtowns, small towns, and urban neighborhoods still preserve a unique flavor rooted in the environment, local materials, and building traditions of their particular region, but most new suburbs—from one end of the country to another—are more similar to each other than to their respective locales. Drive to Boston or New Orleans and you will only find that the new suburbs of these cities share the same standardized housing tracts, television programs, fast-food restaurants, and shopping malls.

American tourism has also become such a well-oiled business that the attractions of that business, while technologically astounding, are unsurprising. Synthetic theme environments—from Busch Gardens to Chi-Chi's—may pique interest in other cultures but are so deliberately familiar and staged that the sense of foreignness is obliterated. Nor does the travel experience in America add inspiration. Many domestic destinations are overly commercialized or crowded, and the march of highways has paid truth to John Steinbeck's prediction that "when we get thruways across the whole country, as we will and must, it will be possible to drive from New York to California without seeing a single thing."[15]

Given all this, a day inevitably arrives in the lives of many Americans when they yearn for a different way of seeing, thinking, eating, and traveling. Some want only a quick alteration in their world view, that is, a vacation; some seek a more dramatic shift in their frame of reference; and others need, for political or personal reasons, an escape from the world they inhabit.

There are countless options for those weary of the United States. That tourist destinations around the world tend toward uniformity does not mean that they fail to offer a sufficiently exotic experience to the American traveler. Other continents beckon, and Europe, Asia, and Africa attract a fair share of American tourists. Canada has also become increasingly tourist oriented during the past decades. The growth in American travel to Mexico since the end of the Second World War also merits deeper consideration.

There were in the past many reasons for Americans to avoid anything more than a short taste of excitement along the Mexican border. This neighboring country was politically unstable and often anti-American; personal safety there was questionable, food safety dubious, and travel difficult. These disturbing factors have subsided (although they have not disappeared) during the last fifty years to the point that Mexico has become the first or second most popular international destination every year for American international travelers. A drive to the border or a short jump on a plane and an American can be free of the chains of the quotidian.

Few destinations for Americans anywhere in the world now compare with Mexico for its unique combination—a wonderful calculus—of propinquity, value, and exoticism. Mexico, while sharing a sprawling, red-light, polluted border with the United States, still boasts further south a magnificent colonial and nineteenth-century urban fabric, a noticeable and often picturesque Indian presence, gorgeous beaches, a vibrant street culture, colorful markets, a unique linguistic pattern, a strong leftist tradition, and mañana attitudes.

Americans are usually pleased to find that in Mexican cities "the downtown still retains functional importance and is a locus of social movement, business decisions, and political concerns." The central plazas of Mexican cities remain lively places in which to experience Mexican public life and to see and be seen. Although there are American-style, middle- and upper-class suburbs growing on the outskirts of Mexican cities, most Mexican cities also include "a large proportion of urban space devoted to squatter settlements" (unknown in the well-regulated United States) that have minimal services but also a great deal of creative and comparatively exotic self-building.[16]

The tourism industry has by no means taken the spirit out of all of Mexico's cities and towns. Even Acapulco is still a zesty Mexican place after a half century of Americanized tourism development. The natural wonders of Mexico inspire too, including the mountains and the beaches, the pleasant climate in the high altitudes, and the warm winters on the coasts. Political instability and decades of one-party leftist rule during the twentieth century undermined economic development, thus preserving a preindustrial character in much of the country (as well as low prices for first-world travelers).

What were liabilities to many Mexicans in creating the good life—an underdeveloped economy, for instance—have in the meantime enhanced the charms of Mexican travel for Americans. Americans in Mexico can reasonably expect to encounter bustling streets and markets, Native Americans in abundance, and a comparatively old fashioned, exotic national culture. They can also expect to eat and stay cheaply; to buy at will without fear of breaking their budget; to purchase a second home, again without worries over cost; and to be massaged or otherwise served at low cost. Americans find unpleasant surprises, too. Sickness, robbery, rudeness, confusion, pollution, widespread poverty, and corruption also taint the American experience in much of Mexico, but the threat of these has much diminished.

For the writers and artists who have sought a refuge in Mexico, both the culture and its surprises can become rich material. The overwhelming natural beauty of the country, the funk of its open-air marketplaces, and the contrast it shows of ancient and new traditions are profound sources for stories, paintings, sculptures, and photographs. The artist still has the best experience of all those Americans who travel to Mexico because Mexico's scenery, old buildings, native scenes, cheap booze, drugs, and brothels can fuel an artist's mind and body. A dose of Montezuma's revenge or a mugging is a small price to pay for inspiration so full and cheap.

Those without a creative turn of mind may find less inspiration in their travels or new homes. The sharp edges of the Mexican experience have gradually been rubbed off, leaving behind a pleasing essence of foreign travel, but those edges are not entirely gone either. The low standard of living of the vast majority of Mexicans is at a level that may exist in pockets of the United States but is otherwise well concealed from the eyes of most middle-class American citizens. The Mexican government's failure to provide safe water, sanitary systems, and food standards may affect all in Mexican society, but these deficiencies push even harder at the brittle tolerance of the tourist and expatriate. The neglect of the law, the informal nature of life (including the mañana attitude), and the refusal of the locals to learn English can become a hindrance to the achievement of the level of service Americans demand. Many Americans thus seek out the tourist zones or gated subdivisions in Mexico where they think that they can insulate themselves from the uncomfortable aspects of Mexican society. Rarely is this state of perfect isolation achieved.

Given the oftentimes glaring contrast between American expectations and Mexican realities, the articles in this collection are an attempt to capture and collectively represent the spirit of interaction between American travelers and the Mexican places and people they visit and meet.

The first set of essays focuses directly on this tourist experience, as historian Dina Berger begins with a spirited look at the development of Mexico City nightlife in the years following World War II. Literary analyst Rebecca Schreiber then takes us into the critical mind of African-American writer

Willard Motley through his early and unflattering portrait of the 1950s Americanization of Mexican resorts. Rebecca Torres and Janet Momsen outline the story of Cancún's development and offer a critical portrait of its current physical and social geography.

A second set of essays treats longer cultural adventures undertaken by Americans. Drewey Wayne Gunn tracks the strange journeys of beatniks in 1950s Mexico. Geographer Richard Wilkie offers a personal memoir of the heyday of Mexico City College in the 1950s with an eye to its unique educational environment and links to Mexican experiences, and Michael Chibnik, an anthropologist, takes us into the world of American folk-art dealers in Oaxaca.

The third and final set of essays analyzes longer-term American communities in Mexico. The ways of life in 1950s Mexico City of an expatriate leftist community (who had ample time to explore their new surroundings) are detailed in Diana Anhalt's intimate historical essay. The social development and spatial organization of the Lake Chapala Riviera is the theme of geographer David Truly's article. Finally, I discuss the mix of private splendor and public spiritedness that has made San Miguel de Allende a growing tourist and expatriate destination.

These diverse essays illustrate that there has been, and there is still today, more than one way for an American to interact with the Mexican environment. It is my hope that, on a practical basis, this combination of inspiring stories and embarrassing critical portraits might celebrate the spirit of American travel while also encouraging greater cultural sensitivity by American travelers as they continue to explore Mexico—beyond the border.

Nicholas Dagen Bloom
Old Westbury, New York

Notes

1. Ramón Ruiz, *On the Rim of Mexico: Encounters of the Rich and Poor* (Boulder, Colo.: Westview, 1998), xi.

2. Lawrence Herzog, *Where North Meets South: Cities, Space, and Politics on the U.S.-Mexican Border* (Austin: Center for Mexican American Studies, University of Texas, 1990), 5.

3. Timothy Dunn, *The Militarization of the U.S.-Mexico Border, 1978–1992* (Austin: CMAS Books, University of Texas, 1990).

4. Oscar J. Martínez, *Border People: Life and Society in the U.S.-Mexico Borderlands* (Tucson: University of Arizona Press, 1994), 304.

5. Dean MacCannell, *The Tourist: A New Theory of the Leisure Class,* (New York: Schocken Books, 1976), 46.

6. John Jakle, *The Tourist: Travel in Twentieth-century North America* (Lincoln: University of Nebraska Press, 1985), 23.

7. Samuel Johnson quoted in Michael Foss, ed., *On Tour: The British Traveler in Europe* (London: O'Mara, 1989), 197.

8. Christopher Hibbert, *The Grand Tour* (London: Thames Methuen, 1987), makes this interesting point about the weakness of British education and the hope placed in the practical side of the grand tour.

9. James Buzard, *The Beaten Track: European Tourism, Literature, and the Ways to Culture, 1800–1918* (New York: Oxford University Press, 1993), 48.

10. Jeremy Black, *The British Abroad: The Grand Tour in the Eighteenth Century* (New York: St. Martin's, 1992), 4.

11. James Buzard fully describes the rise of the mass tourism industry as well as the reaction against it. He also provides detailed analysis of the growing travel-writing field.

12. William Stowe, *Going Abroad: European Travel in Nineteenth-century American Culture* (Princeton, N.J.: Princeton University Press, 1994), 13.

13. Jakle, *The Tourist*.

14. Jakle, *The Tourist*, 2.

15. John Steinbeck quoted in Jakle, *The Tourist*, 190.

16. Herzog, *Where North Meets South*, 80–88.

PART I

Short Visits

CHAPTER ONE

"A Drink between Friends: Mexican and American Pleasure Seekers in 1940s Mexico City"

Dina Berger

On the lam from the law, numbers-racket king Joe Bascom fled from the United States to Mexico to find his partner who set him up for a fall. Upon arriving in Mexico City, where he changed his name to Humphrey Fish, Bascom performed a series of comedic follies to disguise himself from police by dressing as a Mexican bullfighter, a Mariachi band member, and an Indian *tortillera*. As played by actor Bobby Clark, Bascom was one of the many zany characters in the musical comedy *Mexican Hayride* written by brother-and-sister team Dorothy and Herbert Fields.[1] Described by critics as Broadway's "flashiest and most opulent show of the moment"[2] with a story that "allows for a lot of good will between sister republics,"[3] *Mexican Hayride* centers on a plot in which Clark's character Humphrey Fish (Joe Bascom) is mistakenly chosen as guest ambassador of goodwill with the toss of a sombrero at a bullfight. Like a tourist guidebook, scenes in this play follow contest-winner Fish to the Plaza de Toros, the Merced market, the National Palace, Chapultepec Castle, the canals of Xochimilco, and silver-rich Taxco. Produced by Michael Todd for no less than $263,000, and with a score composed by Cole Porter, this musical opened in early 1944 at Manhattan's Winter Garden Theater and closed nearly a year later when the Majestic Theater in Boston picked it up for an additional three-month run.

Whereas the writers' decision to set the overall production in Mexico offered Clark's character unique comedic opportunities, their decision to set particular scenes in Mexico City offered them an opportunity to promote a holiday south of the border. Two scenes of particular interest take place in the capital city's most fashionable venues: the ultra-deluxe Hotel Reforma and its plush nightclub, Ciro's. Opened to pleasure seekers the same year that the Fieldses penned this play, Ciro's had quickly earned a reputation as the smartest nightclub in the Americas. It played such a central role in putting Mexico City nightlife on the map that the Fieldses included a scene in which Clark's character meets Ciro's founder, American A. C. Blumenthal, played by Larry Martin.[4] More than a musical comedy about a racketeer and his many disguises, *Mexican Hayride* allowed Mexico City to play its own role as a lively and cosmopolitan capital in the early 1940s.

Just a few years earlier, however, writers would not have cast Mexico City in such a starring role because, as Anita Brenner bluntly wrote in *Your Mexican Holiday*, it "had no nightlife."[5] Mexico City had long been referred to in travel diaries as the "Paris of the New World" for its elegance and timeless beauty. But by the 1920s, as nightlife became popular in major cities such as New York, Havana, Paris, Berlin, and Hollywood, Mexico City offered patrons little of what was en vogue: floor shows, supper clubs, dancing, and provocative cabaret acts.[6] Moreover, before the 1940s, U.S. tourists infrequently chose Mexico City as their holiday destination. An embittered past wrought with war, invasion, and expropriation characterized relations between the United States and Mexico. And events in Mexico such as revolution, coups d'état, religious rebellion, political assassination, and border banditry only made matters worse. Mexico had earned itself a reputation in the American imagination as backward, unruly, and dangerous—so much so that U.S. tourists opted instead for tours in major U.S. cities, the Canadian wilderness, and tropical Cuba.[7]

But on the eve of World War II, Mexico's reputation in the United States dramatically shifted from that of an unruly to a good neighbor, mirroring broad changes in foreign relations between the two countries in light of the impending world war. Suddenly, Americans began to replace their distrust of Mexico with goodwill and to embrace Mexico as the "Faraway Land Nearby."[8] The meaning of a vacation in Mexico now became tied to a larger, almost spiritual purpose: to foster good relations and to spread democratic values. This shift reflected the new partnership forged between Mexico and the United States during the war, a partnership in which Mexico supplied the United States with wartime goods, *bracero* labor, and a united front in the fight for democracy. In turn, the United States became Mexico's greatest consumer market and helped usher in what many describe as Mexico's "economic miracle." By the close of World War II, the benefits of this new geopolitical relationship were clear: the number of U.S. tourists traveling to Mexico boomed as did the bank accounts of many Mexicans.

In anticipation of the boom, Mexico's tourism developers and promoters—presidents, government ministers, industrialists, and entrepreneurs—had already begun to improve the tourism infrastructure. These same individuals funded at unprecedented rates after 1936 the widespread construction of highways, hotels, and other tourist services.[9] By the early to mid-1940s, entrepreneurs had opened Ciro's, Bricktop's Minuit, Bar 1-2-3, Sans Souci, and other premier nightclubs in Mexico City not only in anticipation of increased numbers of U.S. tourists but also in response to an increasing demand for nightlife by nouveau-riche and middle-class Mexicans, as well as recent European émigrés, who sought modern, nighttime fun. Against a backdrop of live big bands, Havana floor shows, and local entertainment, pleasure seekers dined at the same supper clubs, swayed their hips to the same orchestras, and ordered the same *jaibols*.

More than just a hodgepodge of places or faces, this new nightlife characterized Mexico City's emerging image as a cosmopolitan metropolis. Like a World's Fair exhibition, Mexico City nightlife was showcased by tourism promoters as one of the nation's greatest attractions for U.S. pleasure seekers. In tourist guidebooks and magazines, promoters celebrated the city's modern nightlife, featured its premier nightclubs, and tempted readers with delicious gossip about the film and music celebrities one might spot when out. At the same time, the well-to-do in Mexico City exhibited their own progress by forging a new, "nightlifeing" movement. This movement among the local, urban elites of Mexico City reached such popularity by 1945 that it warranted its own magazine, *Noctámbulas*, replete with snapshots of glamorous nightlifers at featured clubs. But in contrast to temporary fair exhibits whose displays historically created the illusion of progress in Mexico,[10] Mexico City nightlife by the 1940s had become a permanent fixture in the urban landscape, and it reflected real progress designed not to attract foreign investment but to attract pleasure seekers willing to pay for this leisure-time activity.

As a hallmark of modernity, the same nightlife then promoted cultural understanding between Mexico and the United States. Following World War II, tourists flocked to Mexico City where they could simultaneously experience antiquity and modernity: pyramids by day and martinis by night. Meanwhile, swanky nightclubs emerged as familiar, shared, and potentially interactive spaces for Mexican and American pleasure seekers who helped bridge the gap of long-held misunderstandings between Mexico and the United States. Whereas government leaders and industrialists forged a political and economic partnership between Mexico and the United States during the 1940s, pleasure seekers from both sides of the border forged a social and cultural one, proving that interactions between nations do not always occur in official capacities and with state pomp. Rather, through nightlife, representatives from Mexico and the United States interacted outside formal geopolitics and on the dance floor.[11]

Mexico's Reputation Before *Mexican Hayride*

By 1946, Mexican and American nightlifers had become partners in pleasure. And the partnership mirrored a growing political and economic friendship between the nations. This good neighborliness reached a high point when President Truman visited Mexico City in March 1947, the first U.S. president to do so. During his three-day visit he laid a wreath at the foot of the monument to *Los niños heroes* (young cadets who chose to die rather than surrender to U.S. troops during the U.S. invasion of Mexico City in 1847), and returned to Mexican President Miguel Alemán flags captured by U.S. troops during that war.[12] In no small way, Truman's visit worked to symbolically heal Mexico's wounds caused by the war and by the subsequent loss of nearly half its national territory following the Treaty of Guadalupe Hidalgo in 1848.

Yet the troubled past between these two neighbors ran much deeper than the U.S.-Mexican War or even the oil expropriation that followed nearly a century later. Instead, there was a cultural disconnect between the nations. Whereas Mexico's national memory associated Americans with a history of direct foreign investment and military invasion, the American public associated Mexico with banditry and backwardness. Nineteenth-century American travelers to Mexico may have been impressed with the Porfirian persuasion of order and progress, but they were disappointed and surprised to find that the capital city's finest hotels were far from first-class[13] and that the peasants were still using nonmechanized farm equipment.[14] Political events in Mexico throughout the early twentieth century had only affirmed Americans' prevailing beliefs about U.S. superiority and Mexican inferiority, and especially their belief in the inability of Mexicans to peacefully govern themselves. Americans needed only look at one of the many political cartoons of the time to learn the official view of the Mexican Revolution (1910–1917). In a 1916 *Chicago Tribune* cartoon drawn by John T. McCutcheon, Uncle Sam appears as a father figure in a room with children who represent the Latin American nations.[15] Behind Uncle Sam, under a banner that reads "Civilization Follows the Flag," stand the well-dressed and well-behaved boys who symbolize cooperative nations like Cuba, Panama, and Nicaragua. In contrast, Uncle Sam, the American icon of liberty and freedom, is firmly attempting to give an unshaven and unkempt Mexican bandito a "pacification pill," most likely a large dose of democracy. Behind the struggling bandito, who pulls on Uncle Sam's beard, is a wall marked with dirty palmprints, presumably owing to the Mexican, and on the floor lies a spilled liquor bottle containing "Lawlessness."

Such depictions of Mexico not only reflected criticisms of an invasive U.S. policy in Latin America but also reflected widespread public opinion in America.[16] When Mexican President Portes Gil, under a recommendation from former president Plutarco Calles, organized the first tourism commission in late 1928 to study the viability of the Mexican tourism industry,[17] he was probably not surprised to read that, according to one mayor of a Louisiana town, U.S. tourists in search of a pleasure holiday dared not venture south of the border for fear "that [if] should they go to Mexico and do the least offense, they will be immediately put in jail and held for ransom."[18] With the exception of educational excursionists, artists, and journalists making cultural pilgrimages,[19] and a few thousand adventurous sorts, pleasure travelers from the upper and middle classes rarely before the 1930s envisioned a vacation in Mexico.

In addition to constructing good roads, first-class hotels, restaurants, nightclubs, and a guidebook industry, Mexican tourism developers and promoters also worked diligently to reverse their nation's unflattering image in the American tourist's imagination. By the late 1920s and early 1930s, during the Mexican tourism industry's most formative years, its advocates embarked on a pro-Mexico campaign using written and oral press, namely lectures, given by friends of Mexico from academia and business. In 1929, Dr. Lincoln Wirt lectured on the lure of Mexico, describing it as something quite distinct from the "dirt, flies, poor water, bandits and hostility" found in border towns.[20] Instead, relaying his recent experience as one of eighty-five participants in Professor Hubert Herring's "Seminar on Cultural Relations with Latin-America," he said he was astonished to find Mexico City beautiful and clean.

While these initial efforts helped to recast Mexico in a better light, war in Europe, as noted above, served as the real catalyst for the transformation of its image. In public lectures throughout the United States, advocates spoke about true *Pan-Americanism*, namely a shift in U.S. foreign policy from "dollar" or "gunboat" diplomacy to a diplomacy founded on understanding and a respect for cultural differences.[21] Tourism, many of these Pan-Americanist advocates argued, was the ideal vehicle for cultivating mutual understanding and cooperation between nations, especially given that travel had by the late nineteenth century become inextricably linked to U.S. national identity.[22] Capitalizing on this fact, one of Mexico's most

ingenious tourism promoters, J. J. March, wrote the following in a press release distributed to U.S. readers in 1942:

> Travelling is an American custom, so deeply rooted in the national way of living
> that no one could imagine a "sedentary" America. As a matter of fact, the habit
> of travelling has counted to some extent for the brilliant, steady progress and
> prosperity of your dynamic country. . . . [War] won't counteract America's travel
> mindedness, but perhaps it will [increase] the sort of travelling toward a spiritual
> sense not well discovered so far. Individual Panamericanism—that is, you, and
> the wife and children visiting us—implies no sacrifice of that recreational angle
> that is to be ranked on top of your vacation plans and schedules this year.[23]

In statements such as these, promoters not only played on the patriotic heart-
strings of Americans who valued travel as an expression of democracy but
they also put a new twist on a familiar slogan, "See America First," used in
advertising as early as 1906 to encourage national tourism in the United
States.[24] By encouraging pleasure travelers to "See America First, Old Mexico Next," and to "See America First, Start in Romantic Mexico,"[25] Mexican
tourism advocates promoted to their American audience the two main characteristics of a holiday in Mexico: its antiquity value, especially compared to
that of contemporary U.S. cities, and its Pan-American identity.

By 1940, tourism to Mexico, and to Latin America in general, had become
an important medium by which to foster this emerging Pan-Americanism.
Just as Carmen Miranda played the role of Brazilian emissary of goodwill
through song and dance in Hollywood, tourists expressed their "individual
Pan-Americanism" and acted as cultural diplomats by touring the beaches,
rural villages, and cities of their southern neighbors. One such cultural diplo-
mat, Dorothy Reinke, traveled south following President Franklin D. Roosevelt's advice to take part in the new inter-American travel movement.
Dorothy, a twenty-eight-year-old nurse from Oklahoma City, drove coast-to-
coast through Mexico with a girlfriend. In a 1941 letter addressed to Mexican
President Manuel Ávila Camacho, she described her experience as one that
was transforming for her, "a sister from the north." She wrote that not only had
she found Mexicans kind and friendly and the climate and food far superior to
anything in Canada, she had also met Roberto, who showed her that romance
could transcend language and cultural differences. Much to her surprise, she
had found love and goodwill inside a package labeled "Mexican Vacation."[26]

As guests in Mexico, American visitors like Dorothy acted as informal
diplomats who spread American values; and as host to thousands of guests,
Mexico too imparted its own values, history, and character, while turning
quite a profit in the process. The benefits of travel to Latin America became

so much a part of "good neighbor diplomacy" that Roosevelt decreed 1940 the "Year of Inter-American Travel." And when the Pan-American Union held its first Inter-American Travel Congress in San Francisco, board members named Mexico City the conference host for 1941. As an expression of "American brotherhood," Mexican President Lázaro Cárdenas responded by declaring a Tourist Biennial for the years 1940 to 1941, which acted as a call to arms and created a united front among tourism interests who helped make Mexico the perfect host to thousands of guests.[27]

Nightlife on Display

As tourists considered the benefits of "rediscovering America," they demanded to see more than pyramids and colonial monuments—they sought pleasure that could only be found in modern forms of entertainment like floor shows, dining, and dancing. In short, they wanted nightlife, which was something that New Yorkers and urban tourists had begun to participate in by the early twentieth century when Victorian practices of home entertainment gave way to the more liberating ones of a public social life.[28] Since the 1920s, Hollywood had also helped to glamorize and normalize nightlife. Screenwriters set countless plots in nightclubs, and celebrities of stage and screen created an allure around West Hollywood's nightclub scene by frequenting such fashionable hotspots as Cocoanut Grove, the Hollywood Brown Derby, Café Trocadero, Ciro's (that is, the original Ciro's), and Mocambo, where fans lined the streets to stargaze and to request an autograph from one of the many trendsetters.[29] By way of contrast, nightlife was not easily found in Mexico's capital city before the 1940s. One travel writer of the time, folklorist Frances Toor, emphasized in her 1930s guides that tourists should not expect to find much in the way of entertainment in Mexico City.[30] She warned American visitors to Mexico City that amusements in the capital were wholesome and limited. And among the sparse nightspots in the capital, she wrote, few had floor shows. Toor described those nightclubs that did have floor shows as staging shows "of [an] indifferent quality" and "much simpler than those found in the United States."[31] Likewise, Herbert Cerwin noted in his 1947 memoir, *These Are the Mexicans*, that nightlife in Mexico City, even by 1940, hardly existed. Apart from official receptions organized by the government, he wrote, entertaining in Mexico City took place at home.[32] And another guidebook writer remarked that the inhabitants of this capital city "went to bed early."[33]

As travel writers commented on the lack of nighttime diversions in Mexico City, tourism developers recognized the pressing need to create a vibrant nightlife not only to satisfy tourists but also to elevate the city's image from ancient to modern. As early as 1929, tourism pioneer A. L. Rodriguez, who worked for the short-lived Tourism Department of the Bank of Mexico, explained to members of the state-sanctioned Pro-Tourism Commission that it was useless to talk about Mexico's inherent attributes, such as its climate, landscape, pyramids, and colonial architecture, if modern services like nightlife were not developed.[34] And writing nearly a decade later, one journalist argued that entrepreneurs had a duty to create Mexico City nightlife in order to wear "the face of a good friend and good neighbor."[35] But it was more than just a matter of wearing a friendly face or providing modern services: the creation of nightlife—a leisure form that mirrored international trends—further provoked a long-standing debate about the nature of Mexico's national character, a character then in the process of being reinvented.

In the midst of a widespread nationalist movement following a revolution that had rebuked imported political, economic, and cultural models, tourism advocates had little desire to merely imitate the kind of nightlife found elsewhere. Another Mexican tourism pioneer, José Quevedo, head of the government's Department of Tourism from 1936 to 1937 and president of the National Tourist Committee, broached this very subject at a meeting of tourism interests in 1936. Quevedo argued that tourism placed Mexico in a cruel paradox.[36] He argued that as towns and cities in an effort to appeal to tourists introduced new diversions modeled on "the foreign," Mexican customs and traditions slowly degenerated. If tourism developers continued to follow this trajectory, he feared, the nation's soul would die.

In addition to their fear of the potential loss of what Quevedo believed to be "authentic" Mexico, tourism advocates also had little desire to place an official stamp on venues of debauchery as they worked to create a refined Mexico for tourist consumption. As such, members of tourist organizations, such as the privately funded Mexican Tourist Association (AMT), founded in 1939, argued that nightlife should not only consist of cabarets, and similar nightclubs, but it should also offer spectacles like the theatre, opera, and symphony orchestra.[37] In short, they advocated high culture.

Due to these and other debates among tourism promoters, the nature of Mexico City nightlife, and the development of tourist sites in general, teetered on a fine line that separated attractions that were unique to Mexico and those that were familiar to tourists. Early tourism promoters like Quevedo whose development strategies were highly nationalistic believed that Mexico's particular qualities—its pyramids, colonial architecture, mild climate, beaches, and Indian villages—were enough to attract tourists. His idealism, however, soon gave way to the more internationalist stance taken by tourism promoters in the early 1940s, when many of them realized that in order to attract ordinary American tourists, Mexico needed to offer its guests a healthy balance of sites that were not just particularly Mexican but also universally modern. Thus, tourism promoters worked to reproduce what John Urry refers to as "objects of the tourist gaze."[38] Behind this gaze, Urry argues, lies tourists' desires to see attractions that are unique and typical on the one hand and familiar and ordinary on the other. Ironically, even venues such as nightclubs, that are more or less familiar to tourists, seem unfamiliar and extraordinary in the context of a vacation and even more so in a place like Mexico.[39] In an effort to satisfy what they believed to be tourists' desire for familiar and modern attractions—one of which was nightlife—tourism promoters saw to it that boring nights in Mexico City became a relic of the past, and the capital city soon earned a reputation as an "authentic metropolis."

Mexico City Transformed

By the end of World War II, American and Mexican travel writers alike were touting what they argued to be a transformed city. Writing for Mexican readers of *MAPA*, a Spanish-language publication of the Mexican Automobile Association, one writer attributed Mexico City's new reputation to the opening of splendid and modern nightclubs, not to mention first-class restaurants and a state-of-the-art horse track.[40] And Frances Toor proclaimed to U.S. readers in her 1946 *New Guide to Mexico* that "there never [would] be a dull moment for anyone in Mexico City."[41] She compared Mexico City to New York City because smart cabarets and supper clubs like Ciro's, Minuit, San Souci, and El Patio offered superb entertainment with elegant orchestras and exciting Cuban floor shows.

Likewise, Mexican-authored tourist literature for U.S. readers showcased Mexico City nightlife in an effort to construct an image of urban modernity, familiarity, and cosmopolitanism. One of the first publications to do so was the influential *Pemex Travel Club Bulletin*, produced by the state-run oil company *Petróleos Mexicanos*. Written expressly for U.S. motor-tourists, this magazine advertised Mexico City's growing but still humble nightlife in an article from 1940 titled "Mexico City After Dark." Here an anonymous staff writer wrote enthusiastically about the variety of cosmopolitan fare available in the capital city, which was perhaps a slight exaggeration.[42] Nevertheless, the author emphasized that from "top-flight" formal places like the Tap Room in the Hotel Reforma to more risqué entertainment for the bachelor at Waikiki, Mexico City offered pleasure seekers endless fun to fit any budget. The thrill for tourists was an urban experience with a "truly foreign flavor."[43]

A few years later, after the opening of numerous nightclubs, the *Pemex Travel Club Bulletin* featured a more substantial essay on Mexico City nightlife titled "Life in Mexico," adopting its title from a widely read nineteenth-century journal kept by Fanny Calderón de la Barca, wife of the first Spanish ambassador to Mexico.[44] In this essay, the author focused readers' attention on hallmarks of modernity found in Mexico City, namely its modern buildings, glamorous urbanites, and thriving nightlife. Constructing a text around a day in the life of a typical female American tourist, the writer gave readers a glimpse into the social world of Mexico City. In just one morning, the tourist breakfasted at Sanborn's,[45] saw the pyramids, and lunched at a popular French restaurant where she spotted the Mexican minister of foreign affairs, Ezequiel Padilla, and Mexican film star Mapy Cortes. After an afternoon wearing her finest clothing at the horse races, she changed to prepare for her night out, choosing a semiformal sequined suit and hat rather than an evening gown. Accompanied by a group of friends, she sipped cocktails and danced at a nightclub with a French atmosphere, continued her whirlwind of nighttime fun in a supper club where she ate exquisite food and listened to a live orchestra, and ended her evening by slumming at a "plebeian club" where she caught an exciting floor show.

Finally, in response to the post–World War II tourist frenzy, writer Severo de la Mancha contributed a thirteen-page layout to the *Pemex Travel Club Bulletin* titled "Nightlife in Mexico City."[46] With a cover page that featured ordinary yet elegant women dining at Ciro's, the photographs accompanying de la Mancha's text showed prominent nighttime movers and shakers at Ciro's, such as famed actor and singer Jorge Negrete, animation-mogul Walt Disney, and a host of Mexican starlets walking the red carpet. In contrast to images reminiscent of what readers would find in *Variety*, the text of "Nightlife in Mexico City" emphasized the accessibility of Mexico City nightlife to the average American tourist, who by this point came from the upper and middle classes. Rather than just suggesting familiar nightclubs, de la Mancha encouraged his readers—that is, potential American tourists—to partake of the more unique side of Mexico City nightlife by visiting the Plaza Garibaldi. Then as now, tourists and locals alike visited Garibaldi at night to hire or simply browse the countless mariachis available for serenade. This, the author argued, was for the tourist who desired a real Mexican experience.

In these respects, nightlife functioned as the great equalizer or, better yet, as a common denominator in the universal formula for urban cosmopolitanism. Guidebook authors Bowman and Dickinson in 1936 defined urban cosmopolitanism as the part of a city that is understandable and that makes both visitors and residents feel at home.[47] Like the notion of modernity, cosmopolitanism, as defined by those urban markers that everyone understands, is always changing. If, among other things, the wide avenues of the Paseo de la Reforma and the elaborate building facades of the Palace of Fine Arts defined cosmopolitanism in Mexico City at the turn of the century, then plush hotels and swanky nightclubs characterized it by the mid-twentieth century. Indeed, hotel construction in the capital city boomed. Whereas in 1935 Mexico City had a total of twenty-two officially registered hotels offering a total of 1,596 rooms,[48] by early 1942 it had fifty-five registered hotels with a total of 3,582 rooms.[49] Hoteliers constructed an additional 1,500 rooms in 1944, and they built eleven new hotels providing another 4,420 rooms by 1946.[50]

Mexico City also experienced at this time a remarkable upsurge in night-club construction and in the renovation of former venues. In the late 1930s, guidebook authors reluctantly listed, at most, eight cabarets in Mexico City that seldom offered floor shows but did offer dancing, food, and drink. Frances Toor, for example, provided a list of cabarets in 1938 with a disclaimer that prepared tourists for the disappointment they were sure to find. But the opening of a Mexico City Ciro's in 1943 ushered in a new era of exquisite nightlife. Described as the first "smart" nightclub in Mexico City, Ciro's enjoyed a built-in reputation of glamor and refinement from its parent club in Hollywood. At the original Ciro's on Sunset Boulevard, frequented by the likes of Desi Arnaz, Lucille Ball, Gary Cooper, and Lana Turner, everybody that was anybody enjoyed an evening of food, drink, and entertainment. It was no accident then, that American A. C. "Blumy" Blumenthal opened a nightclub in Mexico City by the same name. A reputed Jewish mafioso and drug trafficker from New York City,[51] Blumy created his own version of Hollywood south of the border. After renting the space from Hotel Reforma owner and tourism pioneer Alberto J. Pani, Blumy hired Diego Rivera to execute murals titled *Vino, mujeres y flores*, *Champagne*, and *La dama del sombrero* on the walls of the main dining room, and he also purchased three of Rivera's oil paintings.[52] Blumy then hired interior designers Fontanals and Chauvet to decorate the club in a style that offset Rivera's art. They did so by furnishing the main room with marble-covered furniture, curtains in "electric green," and "bougainvillea red" carpets.[53] Described as a "distinct, refined, elegant nightclub for Mexico and all of the Americas," Ciro's sported its own smart "set" made up of Mexican and American celebrities as well as those of prominence among the local elite, European immigrants, and American tourists. Years later its distinction appeared too much for many: despite its allure for ordinary American tourists, it came to earn a reputation as a hoity-toity club that snubbed less prominent patrons.[54]

Following the opening of Ciro's, nightclubs that offered cabaret acts, Cuban floor shows, big band orchestras, dance floors, dining, and cocktails flourished in Mexico City. By 1947, the average guidebook listed a nightclub directory with no fewer than twenty venues. From swanky and plush clubs like Sans Souci and Bricktop's Minuit, to the "semi-hemi" like Astoria and Los Tarzanes, and from middling clubs like Chapultepec and Rossignol to the proletariat ones like Bagdad and Mi-Ra-Bu, Mexico City nightclubs were showcased by guidebooks as the city's main attraction.[55] With the exception of the deluxe, first-, and second-rate nightclubs, guidebook authors encouraged tourists to hire a trustworthy guide when venturing to the least luxurious, and potentially dangerous, venues. The practice of slumming, popular the world over, provided nightlifers with a more titillating experience. Visits to the rougher and more colorful spots like Tenampa and Leda, where pleasure seekers traded whiskey and gin for tequila, were in such demand that the well-known travel agency Wagon Lits-Cook offered an all-inclusive nightclub tour for sixty-five pesos that took tourists to dodgy, semi-formal, and more luxurious spots.[56]

A Drink Between Friends

Although this nightlife had been created in large part for tourist consumption, visitors to the city were not alone on their evening escapades through Mexico City. Urban Mexicans, including recent European émigrés, equally participated in the nightlife and created a movement that both intersected with and diverged from the ideal tourist agenda mapped out in guidebooks. As described in Salvador Novo's 1946 award-winning chronicle titled *New Mexican Grandeur*, Mexico City's nightlife, like the places described in Bernardo de Balbuena's seventeenth-century description of Mexico City that bore the same name,[57] proved to be one of the city's greatest achievements after its prestigious universities and museums.[58] Of the countless submissions to an essay contest organized by the Mexico City government, Novo's essay won the contest, its prestigious award, and subsequent publication at the 1946 Mexico City Book Fair. In this essay the author and a fictional friend paid homage to Mexico City's nightlife and its many exceptional nightclubs, restaurants, and theaters. As if recording his every move in one evening, Novo wrote of how he and his friend explored the city's most exclusive supper clubs, like Ciro's and Casanova, and its most inclusive dance halls, such as Pirata and Salón México. In the course of his tour, Novo implicitly argued that nightlife, and nightclubs in particular, had a modernizing effect on urban Mexicans. Like the New York residents who decades earlier shed their prudish behavior and opted for an intimate cabaret experience, working-class Mexicans, Novo noted, had traded in their sandals for shoes, their white pants and overalls for trousers and dress shirts, and their *pulque* for beer as they enjoyed a night out at a dance hall.[59]

But the most zealous Mexican pleasure seekers, who often crossed paths and perhaps shared the dance floor with their American counterparts, were the emerging Mexican urban elite and middle class who, by the 1940s, were enjoying the benefits of Mexico's new economic and political partnership with the United States. Nightlife, especially among the well-to-do, became so popular that one journalist dedicated an entire magazine to it: *Noctámbulas*, or "Nightlifeing."[60] This biweekly Spanish-language magazine founded and edited by *Excelsior* journalist Carlos Denegri, functioned as a beacon for nighttime pleasure seekers among urban elites. Whereas tourists had their guidebooks, the more well-off, and perhaps curious onlookers as well, leafed through the pages of *Noctámbulas* on which celebrities of the night offered pleasure-seeking advice to help guide their readers' evening plans. *Noctámbulas* also illustrated the existence of what one guidebook author described as "the tilting class."[61] It was this group of people, recognized broadly as the bourgeoisie, who breathed life into swanky Mexico City nightclubs at the same time as American tourists were frequenting their continental neighbor to the south in droves after World War II.

As depicted on the cover and pages of *Noctámbulas*, Mexico City's new leisure class helped to produce and reproduce this more exclusive and not surprisingly most publicized side of nightlife. Compared to its underbelly attractions, namely the "going-slumming spots," Mexico City nightlife for the glamorous and fashionable pleasure seeker set its participants apart from the rest of society. It also put the capital city on a par with other cosmopolitan metropolises. One cover of *Noctámbulas* in particular pokes fun at, as well as celebrates, the freedom with which the leisure class sought pleasure in Mexico City during the mid-1940s. Drawn by well-known caricaturist Antonio Arias Bernal, this 1946 cover is a caricature of a man dressed in a tuxedo and top hat who uses his cane to steady himself on a bus crowded with ordinary Mexicans on their way to work (see figure 1.1). Sandwiched between a hefty, casually dressed man intently reading a newspaper and an Indian woman carrying her baby wrapped in a *rebozo*, this middle-aged man has obviously been out all night and is only just returning home. Seeing his swollen-shut eyes engulfed in purple circles, a nose bright red from too much drink, party favors (streamers and confetti) still hanging from his clothes, and his white-gloved hand barely holding on to a paper horn, readers undoubtedly understood that this man had enjoyed the debaucheries of an evening out in

Mexico City. To make this point even clearer, Arias Bernal draws from an angle that allows the viewer to catch the headline of a newspaper held by another bus rider that reads: "Huelga general," or general strike, presumably by city workers. Compared to other city dwellers from nearly all walks of life, this pleasure seeker seems to live without a care in the world.

Figure 1.1. In the new Mexico City, the party could last all night long. A member of the "smart set" surrounded by morning commuters.

The pages inside *Noctámbulas* equally distinguished this group of Mexico City pleasure seekers. Contributors and correspondents updated readers on the latest crazes and trendsetters abroad through reports from Paris and New York. Also included were opinions about Mexico City nightlife by the city's chroniclers who recognized how it reflected their nation's success. In one editorial, a contributor described the nightlife as an extraordinary success not only because Mexico City's nightclubs "are considered the best in the Continent" but also because no politician had yet caused scandal in them by pulling out a .45-caliber pistol to shoot a dinner companion whom he found distasteful. Unlike the gun-toting revolutionary of yesteryear, the writer pointed out, contemporary politicians were civilized and knew how to simply enjoy an evening out.[62]

The most fascinating section in each issue of *Noctámbulas* was titled "Escándalo!" As its name implies, "Scandal!" offered readers the latest gossip about the who's who of nightlife, complete with details about the "buzz," or what people were talking about that evening. Even better, the editors accompanied the text of "Scandal!" with photographs that caught prominent nightlifers in the act at the city's most fashionable nightclubs like Ciro's, Bar 1-2-3, Tony's Bar, El Patio, Minuit, and San Souci. Taken by self-professed "journalist of the night" Carlos Bodeler, the photographs might show a close-up of film celebrities Dolores del Río and Armando Calvo out at Minuit or of not-as-famous early television actor Jack Newmark seated at a table next to Colombian Ambassador Carlos Echeverrí at Tony's Bar located in the Hotel Reforma. Snapshots of pleasure seekers at Ciro's helped to confirm its reputation as the premier Pan-American hot spot and as the "Latin American Hollywood" south of the border. Here, artists from Mexico, Latin America, and Spain might be seen hobnobbing with Mexican actors (today, telenovela stars) Gustavo Rojo and Sara Guash, Chilean singer Malú Gatica, and Spanish actress Rosita Diaz.[63]

If we judge from gossip columns and photographs found on the pages of *Noctámbulas* and described by guidebook writers, Mexico City nightlife by the mid-1940s was not only abundant, gay, and first rate, it was also international in reputation and cosmopolitan in nature. Perhaps its many creators imbued it with this flare, because its growth was owing to the combined efforts and goals of diverse groups: the many sophisticated European refugees with a taste for nightlife who arrived in Mexico on the eve of World War II; chic Mexicans who had traveled abroad or who merely sought ways to spend their wartime profits; developers who sought to lure U.S. tourists to Mexico City, especially after 1936 when the Pan-American Highway opened; and the U.S. screen and stage that popularized Mexico City nightlife and normalized in the American tourist's imagination the idea of a vacation to Mexico.

Two years after *Mexican Hayride* premiered on Broadway, MGM released a travel-brochure musical titled *Holiday in Mexico*. Hardly remembered today, *Holiday in Mexico* starred Walter Pidgeon as the U.S. ambassador to Mexico, Jane Powell as his daughter, Xavier Cugat as a nightclub owner and entertainer (with Chihuahua in hand), José Iturbi as a talented pianist, and Ilona Massey as a sultry singer. With no Mexicans starring but starring many Mexican stereotypes, this musical was set in Mexico City around a plot related to a party the ambassador is organizing with the help of his daughter. Apart from its weak plot, this Hollywood musical gave audiences a glimpse of the glamor of Mexico City nightlife. When the camera follows Jane Powell into Cugat's nightclub where she spies on her father as he sips cocktails in a packed house of elegantly dressed international nightlifers, U.S. audiences saw the excitement to which travel writing had only alluded. Watching the riveting, albeit ridiculous, performance by Cugat, accompanied by a full orchestra, rumba dancers, and the Chihuahua, the American moviegoer was surely swept away by the film's combination of glamor, refinement, and exoticism, or in other words "its truly foreign flavor." Like its Broadway predecessor, *Holiday in Mexico* used nightlife to showcase civilized Mexico and cosmopolitan Mexico City. In this way, the refined leisure activity of seeking out nightlife attractions became inextricably tied to a vacation south of the border.

The Consequences of Nightlife

At the end of this journey through the remarkable growth and popularity of a nightlife that had only began to reach its peak in the early 1950s, Mexico's national identity, according to some, stood at a cultural crossroads. Just as José Quevedo had warned tourism advocates to avoid promoting and developing imported attractions to satisfy foreign tastes and the tourist gaze, so too did many others contemplate a suspected loss of morality in Mexico City. More importantly, because nightlife had been seemingly absorbed into Mexican culture as something innately Mexican, others speculated that Mexican culture had become Americanized.

One might imagine that these fears were most prevalent by the early 1950s when in the United States general ill will toward Mexico had been almost entirely replaced with goodwill. The number of tourists vacationing in Mexico increased to 390,000 in 1950 from a humble 24,000 in 1930, only two decades earlier. Promotional campaigns of the 1930s and 1940s in U.S. mass media had succeeded in recasting Mexico as the good, civilized neighbor, which shored up a political, economic, and social partnership between these nations that remains strong today. Consumerism also flourished. In

1947, Sears, Roebuck opened its doors in Mexico City with much fanfare, including a bishop's blessing, because it allowed shoppers to buy on credit.[64] It is no surprise, then, that many argued that this new Mexican grandeur—namely, the heyday of modern nightlife set against a backdrop of Pan-Americanism—came at a cost to Mexico's uniqueness as what was once a largely provincial and rural nation. As pleasure seekers from home and abroad passed their evenings at nightclubs and bought mixed drinks for new friends, a reactionary and conservative backlash emerged that questioned what state and civil society believed to be important and desirable changes in the definition of Mexico's national identity.

In the tradition of Samuel Ramos, who in the 1930s analyzed the "authentic" Mexican character to argue for a schism in Mexican culture between nationalists and "Europeanizers,"[65] Octavio Paz asked fellow Mexicans in 1950, "What are we, and how can we fulfill our obligations to ourselves as we are?"[66] In so doing, he, like Ramos, argued for an obscured national identity. Whereas Ramos contended that Mexicans believed their character to be inferior, Paz contended that Mexicans hid behind masks in an effort to disguise their true nature in light of the rapid urban and geopolitical changes in which nightlife and tourism played a significant role. Much to Paz's dismay, the damage was irreversible. Mexican children began to consume *jotdogs* (hot dogs) and *hamburguesas* (hamburgers) while adults sipped whiskey-filled *jaibols* (highballs).

In addition to Paz's commentary, filmmakers also gave voice to this reactionary movement. One of the most poignant films to do so was the 1951 film *Siempre Tuya*. Directed by Emilio "Indio" Fernandez and starring Jorge Negrete and Gloria Marín, this film told the familiar story of Rámon and Soledad, a couple from rural Zacatecas who are forced by droughts and poverty to make an exodus to Mexico City. Unable to find regular work, Rámon auditions for a singing spot on the national radio station XEW. When he takes the stage wearing typical *campesino*, or rural, attire—white pants, hat, and sandals—an audience member shouts, "Where is your pistol?" Slightly shaken, Rámon belts out the bolero *México Lindo* and instantly becomes a star. Over the next twenty minutes of the film, he is transformed from a humble peasant into an egotistical celebrity and from a loving to a thoughtless husband. He discards his agrarian clothing for an elegant suit and trades in his rented shack for an ultramodern apartment with indoor plumbing, an elevator, and running hot and cold water. Meanwhile his wife, Soledad, remains wholly unaffected by their new wealth, and even admits to her husband that she is afraid he has lost sight of his modest roots and traditional Mexican values. She asks, "How can we live like this when people are so poor?" Angry that his wife refuses to embrace a modern lifestyle, Rámon initiates an affair with a beautiful, elegant, and wealthy American woman who introduces him to the nightlife of Mexico City. In the next few scenes, Rámon and his mistress are out at the horse races and at nightclubs where they drink whiskey and enjoy performances by Cuban rumba dancers. Opting for this modern way of life, Rámon asks his wife for a divorce but is refused, and it is at this point that he hits rock bottom. When he realizes that his stardom, wealth, and international friends have left him morally bankrupt, during a party with his uppity friends at his house he throws a cocktail glass in disgust at his own reflection in a mirror . When Rámon is enraged after being called a *pelado*, a derogatory term for someone who puts on airs of urbanity but is really just a country boy, his guests leave the house with the exception of Rámon's manager who takes revenge on him for stealing his girl by shooting him four times with a pistol. With Soledad at his side, Rámon then recovers in the hospital, and they return to the tranquility of rural Zacatecas wearing the same clothes in which they came.

Moral overtones in *Siempre Tuya* warned viewers about the dangers of the cosmopolitanism and wealth that were eating away at traditional Mexican values of family and nation, echoing broader concerns about the cultural transformations that had taken place by the 1950s. Other films, like the *cabaratera*, or cabaret genre, offered plots that expressed similar concerns.[67] Set in dance halls against the sounds of the rumba, the female protagonists in films such as *Salón México* and *Distinto Amanecer* were recently arrived rural migrants in search of work in Mexico City. With few skills but their femininity and talent for dance, the female characters in these films fell into compromising positions as hired dancers, which often led to prostitution. Like Rámon, the city bewildered these women until they eventually lost their footing. Taken together, these films sought to demonstrate how the grandeur of Mexico City often led to sin.

In the same way as Mexican filmmakers, Mexico City officials also reacted to this modernization and its perceived dangers by passing a series of laws targeting nightclubs. One of the most significant of these, enforced in 1952 by Mexico City's new mayor-elect Ernesto Uruchurtu, was a standard closing time of 1:00 a.m. for the capital city's nightclubs. How Mexican and American pleasure seekers must have reacted!

Despite this modest backlash, an active nightlife continues to be inextricably tied to the cultural milieu of Mexico City. Current advertising campaigns by the Mexico City Ministry of Tourism encourage tourists to experience Mexico's "many moods," namely, its ancient side (the pyramids), adventurous side (the rainforests), playful side (the beaches), and cultured

side (its opera, theater, and nightlife).[68] This universal understanding of a refined nightlife as a sign of progress and familiarity continues to foster understanding between Mexico and the United States, and it does so through the
leisure activities of tourists and locals alike. This is owing in no small part to
those Mexican and American pleasure seekers of the 1940s who forged this
unprecedented social and cultural partnership through their participation in
the nightlife of the city. It does not matter if these pleasure seekers ever con-
versed at their nightclubs, because the friendship between two continental
neighbors improved as hips swayed, toes tapped, and cocktails were ordered.
Still more significantly, perhaps, nightlife became part of Mexico City's cosmopolitan identity.

Notes

1. See Stanley Green, *Broadway Musicals Show by Show* (Milwaukee, Wisc.: Hal Leonard
Books, 1985), 122. Universal Studios bought the rights to the screenplay and transformed it
into a film comedy starring Abbott and Costello. Released in 1948, this picture received luke-
warm reviews at best and is described today as the duo's worst performance. The star of the theatrical production, Bobby Clark, Cole Porter's score, and the Ciro's scene were all cut from the
film version.

2. *Life*, "Mexican Hayride," February 21, 1944, 83.

3. Lewis Nichols, "Mexican Hayride," February 4, 1944, *New York Times Theater Reviews* 5,
1942–1951.

4. According to Salvador Novo, *New Mexican Grandeur*, trans. Noel Lindsay (Mexico City:
Ediciones ERA, 1967), a fellow named Goggi first opened Ciro's and modeled it after West
Hollywood's most famous nightclub by the same name. While little is known about Goggi, we
do know that by 1943 Blumenthal took over the lease of Goggi's nightclub only to close the
nightclub in 1948 when he could no longer make his contract payments. See Armando
Jiménez, *Sitios de rompe y rasga en la Ciudad de México* (México City: Oceano, 1998), 166–77;
and Pepe Romero, *My Mexico City and Yours* (Garden City, N.Y.: Dolphin Books, 1962), 58–59.
Other characters in the theatrical production that added to the overall cosmopolitan setting
included the former king of Romania, King Carol (played by Arthur Gondra), and his companion Magda Lupescu (played by Dorothy Durkee). Both sought refuge in Mexico from the
war in Europe and both were frequently spotted at the horse races at the popular and chic Hipó-
dromo de las Ámericas, owned by Bruno Pagliai.

5. Anita Brenner, *Your Mexican Holiday: A Modern Guide* (New York: G. P. Putnam's Sons,
1947), 118.

6. See Lewis A. Erenberg, *Steppin' Out: Nightlife and the Transformation of American Culture,
1890–1930* (Chicago: University of Chicago Press, 1981); James Gavin, *Intimate Nights: The
Golden Age of New York Cabaret* (New York: Limelight Editions, 1992); Peter Gelavich, *Berlin
Cabaret* (Cambridge, Mass.: Harvard University Press, 1993); and Jim Heimann, *Out with the
Stars: Hollywood Nightlife in the Golden Era* (New York: Abbeville Press, 1985).

7. See Catherine Cocks, *Doing the Town: The Rise of Urban Tourism in the United States,
1850–1915* (Berkeley: University of California Press, 2001); Marguerite S. Shaffer, *See America*

First: Tourism and National Identity, 1880–1940 (Washington, D.C.: Smithsonian Institution Press, 2002); and Rosalie Schwartz, *Pleasure Island: Temptation and Tourism in Cuba* (Lincoln: University of Nebraska Press, 1997).

8. "Mexico—The Faraway Land Nearby" is the title of a tourism brochure written in English in 1939 by Howard Phillips expressly for reproduction by the Asociación Mexicana de Turismo (hereafter AMT); see Centro de Estudios de Historia de México CONDUMEX, Fondo: Luis Montes de Oca (hereafter CEHM: LMDO), 373/34383 (17 de diciembre de 1939). For a text-only version of "Mexico—The Faraway Land Nearby," see CEHM: LMDO, 363/33550.

9. In 1936 officials inaugurated, with much pomp and ceremony, the first main section of the Pan-American Highway, which offered motorists mostly paved road from Laredo to Mexico City with strategically placed accommodations along the way. With the exception of Monterrey, where industrialists made sure to build first- and second-class hotels, motorists could stay the night in tourist courts or motels until they reached Mexico City.

10. See Mauricio Tenorio-Trillo, *Mexico at the World's Fairs: Crafting a Modern Nation* (Berkeley: University of California Press, 1996). For Latin America in general, see Ingrid E. Fey, "Peddling the Pampas: Argentina at the Paris Universal Exposition of 1889," in *Latin American Popular Culture: An Introduction*, ed. William H. Beezley and Linda A. Curcio-Nagy (Wilmington, Del.: SR Books, 2000), 61–85; and Blanca Muratorio, "Images of Indians in the Construction of Ecuadorian Identity at the End of the Nineteenth Century," in Beezley and Curcio-Nagy, *Latin American Popular Culture*, 105–21. For the United States, see Robert W. Rydell, *World of Fairs: The Century-of-Progress Expositions* (Chicago: University of Chicago Press, 1993); and Robert W. Rydell et al., *Fair America: World's Fairs in the United States* (Washington, D.C.: Smithsonian Institution Press, 2000).

11. I owe a special thanks to my colleague Greg Shaya for discussing ideas for this paper and for bringing this particular phrase to my attention.

12. Harry S. Truman, Public Papers of the President, Document 51, "Address in Mexico City," March 3, 1947, Truman Library. Documents digitized and online at www.truman library.org (last accessed October 1, 2005); Sam Dillon, "On Clinton Itinerary: Mexico City Counterpart of the Alamo," *New York Times*, May 6, 1997.

13. See Aida Mostkoff, "Foreign Visitors and Images of Mexico: One Hundred Years of International Tourism, 1821–1921" (PhD diss., University of California, Los Angeles, 1999).

14. See William H. Beezley, *Judas at the Jockey Club and Other Episodes of Porfirian Mexico* (Lincoln: University of Nebraska Press, 1987).

15. From John J. Johnson, *Latin America in Caricature* (Austin: University of Texas Press, 1980), 149.

16. For an in-depth discussion of prevailing American stereotypes of Mexicans and Latin Americans see Fredrick B. Pike, *The United States and Latin America: Myths and Stereotypes of Civilization and Nature* (Austin: University of Texas Press, 1992).

17. For an examination of the Comisión Pro-Turismo, the first government-funded tourist organization in Mexico, see Dina M. Berger, "Pyramids by Day, Martinis by Night: The Development and Promotion of Mexico's Tourism Industry, 1928–1946" (PhD diss., University of Arizona, 2002), ch. 1.

18. Letter from Alexandria, Louisiana, Mayor V. V. Lamkin to President Portes Gil, Archivo General de la Nación (hereafter AGN), Fondo presidencial: Emilio Portes Gil (hereafter EPG), Caja: 41, Exp: 2/302/104, Folio: 15140 (November 8, 1929).

19. See Helen Delpar, *The Enormous Vogue of Things Mexican: Cultural Relations between the United States and Mexico, 1920–1935* (Tuscaloosa: University of Alabama Press, 1992).

20. The speech was titled "The Lure of Mexico" and was given to the San Francisco Commonwealth Club. The transcribed speech was sent to President Portes Gil in hopes of publication in Spanish by the official press department. AGN: EPG, Caja: 9, Exp. 315/104, Folio: 14004 (September 6, 1929).

21. Dr. Osgood Hardy, professor of history at Occidental College, gave this speech titled "The New Panamericanism" to the Publicity Club of Los Angeles at the Biltmore Hotel on July 2, 1940. His speech in Spanish translation can be found at CEHM: LMDO 376/34550.

22. See Shaffer, See America First.

23. J. J. March, "A Few Words from the Editor," Pemex Travel Club Bulletin, 4:127-A (February 1, 1942).

24. Shaffer, See America First, 26–39.

25. The government's tourism department used the first slogan on tourist brochures in 1939, and the second was used by the Mexican delegation of the Hotel Greeters of America during their cross-country tour in 1944. See CEHM: LMDO, 373/34304 and AGN: Manuel Ávila Camacho (hereafter MAC), 704/621.

26. Dorothy Reinke to President Ávila Camacho, on August 12, 1941. Archivo General de la Nación, Grupo Documental: Manuel Ávila Camacho (hereafter AGN: MAC), 548.3/4.

27. "President Cárdenas' Proclamation Declaring 1940–41 Travel Years," CEHM: LMDO, 378/34756 (January 29, 1940).

28. See Erenberg, Steppin' Out.

29. See Heimann, Out With the Stars.

30. Frances Toor, Frances Toor's Guide to Mexico (New York: R. M. McBride, 1936), and Frances Toor's Motorist Guide to Mexico (Mexico City: Frances Toor Studios, 1938).

31. Toor, Frances Toor's Motorist Guide, 68–69.

32. Herbert Cerwin, These Are the Mexicans (New York: Reynal and Hitchcock, 1947), 63.

33. Sydney Clark, All the Best in Mexico (New York: Dodd, Mead, 1949), xii. This guidebook was also published under the title Mexico: Magnetic Southland, which preceded the All the Best series.

34. A. L. Rodriguez to the Pro-Tourism Commission, Archivo Histórico "Genaro Estrada" de la Secretaría de Relaciones Exteriores, Legajo: 2 (28 de febrero de 1929).

35. José Luis Velasco, "Metropolitanas: la ciudad nocturna," Excelsior (31 de mayo de 1938), 10.

36. CEHM: LMDO, 292/27012 (18 de septiembre de 1936).

37. Asociación Mexicana de Turismo. CEHM: LMDO, 353/32812 (enero de 1939).

38. John Urry, The Tourist Gaze, 2d ed. (London: Sage Publications, 2002), 3.

39. Urry, The Tourist Gaze, 12–13.

40. MAPA X, "Editorial, gran cuidad turística," vol. 116 (1 de noviembre de 1943).

41. Frances Toor, New Guide to Mexico by Plane, Car, Train, Bus and Boat (Mexico City: Frances Toor Studios, 1946), 59.

42. Pemex Travel Club Bulletin, "Mexico City after Dark," vol. 2, no. 113-A (August 1940).

43. Pemex Travel Club Bulletin, "Mexico City after Dark."

44. Pemex Travel Club Bulletin, "Life in Mexico," vol. 6, no. 151-A (August 1, 1944).

45. Sanborn's is a Mexico City landmark that was originally opened as a drugstore in 1903 by a California pharmacist, Walter Sanborn, and his brother, Frank Sanborn. It later featured the capital's first soda fountain. In 1918, Sanborn's moved to its famous downtown location in the House of Tiles (Casa de los azulejos). Historically, it was and still is a meeting place for U.S. tourists as well as for Mexican urbanites for breakfast, lunch, and dinner. In 1946, the Sanborn

family sold it to local entrepreneurs who, in partnership with Walgreen's, have since opened well over one hundred Sanborn's restaurants in Mexico. In addition to its restaurants, Sanborn's also sells merchandise from magazines to luggage. For a history of Sanborn's, see Romero, *My Mexico City and Yours*, 35–36.

46. Severo de la Mancha, "Nightlife in Mexico City," *Pemex Travel Club Bulletin*, vol. 6, no. 165-A (May-June 1946)

47. Heath Bowman and Stirling Dickinson, *Mexican Odyssey* (Chicago: Willett, Clark, 1936), 65.

48. Report prepared by Roberto López of the National Railways of Mexico. CEHM: LMDO, 281/26055 (1 de octubre de 1935).

49. Figures based on the "Mexico Hotel Directory/Directorio de hoteles de la República, 1941–1942," produced by the Department of Tourism and Mexican Tourist Association. AGN: MAC, 704/170-3.

50. *Boletín de la AMT*, vol. 6, no. 3 (1 de mayo de 1944). AGN: MAC, 704/170-2; *Boletín de la AMT*, vol. 8, no. 9 (1 de agosto de 1946). AGN: MAC, 704/170-2.

51. Jiménez, *Sitios de rompe y rasga*, 172.

52. Jiménez, *Sitios de rompe y rasga*, 169.

53. *Construcción*, "Restaurantes, cafés, bares, loncherias y cabarets," vol. 5, no. 50 (1 de junio de 1945), 167–205.

54. See Clark, *All the Best*, 137.

55. For a complete list of nightclubs see Brenner, *Your Mexican Holiday*, 394.

56. Brenner, *Your Mexican Holiday*, 394, 400.

57. Written in 1604 by Bernardo de Balbuena. See Balbuena, *La grandeza mexicana* (México City: Editorial Porrúa, 1971).

58. See Salvador Novo, *Nueva grandeza mexicana* (México City: Editorial Hermes, 1946). For an English translation, see Novo, *New Mexican Grandeur*.

59. Novo, *Nueva grandeza Mexicana*, 69.

60. Denegri made the first copy of *Noctámbulas* available to the public on January 15, 1945, and to the best of my knowledge, the publication ran through 1947. Though not complete and in poor condition, copies of this publication can be found at the Hemeroteca Nacional of UNAM in Mexico City.

61. Clark, *All the Best*, 145.

62. *Noctámbulas*, "Memorandum," vol. 2, no. 51 (4 de febrero de 1946).

63. See *Noctámbulas*, vol. 2, no. 59 (1 de abril 1946), 23–30.

64. For a study on Sears and consumption in Mexico, see Julio E. Moreno, "Marketing in Mexico: Sears, Roebuck Company, J. Walter Thompson and the Culture of North American Commerce in Mexico during the 1940s" (PhD diss., University of California, Irvine, 1998).

65. Samuel Ramos, *Profile of a Man and Culture in Mexico*, trans. Peter Earle (1934; Austin: University of Texas Press, 1962).

66. Octavio Paz, *The Labyrinth of Solitude*, trans. Lysander Kemp (New York: Grove, 1985), 9.

67. See Joanne Hershfield, *Mexican Cinema/Mexican Woman, 1940–1950* (Tucson: University of Arizona Press, 1996).

68. *New Yorker*, October 16, 2000, 135.

CHAPTER TWO

"Resort to Exile:
Willard Motley's Writings on
Postwar U.S. Tourism in Mexico"

Rebecca M. Schreiber

Best-selling U.S. author Willard Motley arrived in Mexico in 1951, and almost immediately he began to write vivid descriptions of his new surroundings. Although he had not initially intended to write a book from this material, his annotations began to appear to him as emblematic of an era, a time
when U.S. tourism in Mexico and the Mexican tourism industry itself were
dramatically changing the face of the country. Once in Mexico, he found
himself confronted at each turn by the expanding horizons of postwar economic growth. His completed text chronicled the juggernaut of leisure-
industry modernization, the sordid everyday details of its social consequences,
and the chilling transposition of U.S. racism. Motley's unflattering account,
however, eventually titled "My House Is Your House," was never published.

This essay examines two manuscripts written by Motley following his relocation to Mexico: the unpublished "My House Is Your House," and "Tourist
Town," the latter of which was posthumously published as *Let Noon Be Fair*
(1966). Motley's writings in Mexico are significant on two counts. First, they
provide the most extensive account of the pioneering years of the U.S.
tourism industry in Mexico during the post–World War II era. Second, they
convey a vivid analysis of the reciprocities between U.S. domestic and international racism. What I will examine in this essay are the ways in which
Motley's intended publishers rejected or significantly altered the content of
Motley's writing. This hostility to critical analysis reflects an early, although
still dominant, unwillingness of American cultural gatekeepers to sanction
realistic portraits of the exploitation that has often accompanied American
tourism not only in Mexico, but around the world.

In "My House Is Your House" and "Tourist Town," Motley narrated the racial and economic politics of tourism that emerged in the Mexican tourism industry as it was geared toward the United States. Motley also contrasted U.S. and Mexican racial ideologies, and excoriated U.S. imperialism, in the form of tourism, in Mexico. His attention to the racial and economic dimensions of Americanization and his scathing critique of U.S. tourism in Mexico led to his being censored by publishing houses in the United States. The perceived inflammatory nature of his work and his protracted negotiations with the publishing industry also provide an opportunity to examine the complexity of cold war cultural and racial politics in the expanded frame of U.S. ascendance.

Willard Motley was part of a distinct and influential political exodus comprised of U.S. writers and artists who left the United States during the 1940s and 1950s. Among the most crucial and least studied aspects of this exodus were the communities that developed in Mexico. The liberal administration of Lázaro Cárdenas (1934–1940) welcomed individuals seeking sanctuary from fascist governments in Spain and Germany, political opponents of Stalin's Soviet Union, and American veterans of the Spanish Civil War during the 1930s. Following World War II, the members of these exile communities were joined by other Americans, some of whom were writers and artists. As a result, key U.S. exile communities developed in Mexico City and Cuernavaca, consisting primarily of Spanish Civil War veterans, Hollywood blacklistees, and African-American writers, poets, and artists increasingly frustrated with U.S. racism during the post–World War II period. In the years between Spanish Civil War veteran and composer Conlon Nancarrow's settlement in Mexico City in 1940 and the posthumous publication of author Willard Motley's final novel, *Let Noon Be Fair* (1966), there came to be a critical mass of U.S. artists and writers living in exile in Mexico.

Americans in Mexico, and specifically tourists, were frequent subjects in the work that U.S. exiles produced between the late 1950s and mid-1960s. It may seem ironic that these individuals who traveled to Mexico as exiles, not tourists, would write about American tourism in Mexico. This choice of subject matter can in part be related to the growth of the Mexican tourism industry during the 1940s and 1950s when these U.S. exiles lived in Mexico as well as to an accompanying surge of tourists from America. However, this focus can also be explained by the uneasy relationship between the U.S. exiles and tourism. In Motley's case, his writings in Mexico narrate the tension between the demands of his editors that he take up the position of a tourist in his writings, set against his own efforts to critique the actions of American tourists in Mexico.

Working in Mexico presented the cold war exiles with a perspective from which to consider the relationship of the United States to Mexico, and to

Latin America more generally. In particular, the African-American artists and writers who chose exile in Mexico, like those who went to Paris during the 1940s and 1950s as "an overt protest against American racism,"[1] articulated links between American racism and imperialism in Mexico. Scholar Paul Gilroy argues that once in France, Richard Wright started to envision "links between the struggles against racial subordination inside America and wider, global dimensions of political antagonisms."[2] Similarly in Mexico, African-American artists and writers, including novelist Willard Motley, examined the connections between the status of African Americans in the United States and the working-class and indigenous populations of Mexico. In addition, Motley explored how U.S. racial ideologies were transposed to the Mexican context through tourism. Considering Motley's writings in Mexico offers us an opportunity to examine the conditions in which cultural work that critically linked American racism and imperialism persisted during the early cold war era.[3]

Willard Motley's writings in Mexico provide a sharp opposition to the U.S. framework from which he (and his work) emerged. Motley, the best-selling author of *Knock on Any Door* (1947), moved to Mexico after publishing his second novel, *We Fished All Night* (1951). Both of these novels, like Motley's earlier writing for *Hull-House Magazine* in the 1930s and 1940s, focused on white characters. In fact, Motley had not included African-American characters in his writings previous to his relocation to Mexico in the early 1950s. Motley wrote a number of book-length manuscripts in Mexico including *Let No Man Write My Epitaph* (1958), "My House Is Your House," and *Let Noon Be Fair*. These works, unlike the novels that Motley wrote in the United States, directly examined race relations. In the introduction to Willard Motley's published diary, Jerome Klinkowitz writes that "Race, a subject of little concern to the early Motley became by the end of his life a major personal issue."[4] In an interview published in *Ebony* magazine in 1958, Motley had in fact told a reporter that he had chosen to live in Mexico "because there is a feeling of freedom there."[5]

Motley gained new insight into race relations while living outside the United States, a perspective that transformed his work. In "My House Is Your House," Motley's nonfictional book about Mexico, he explores how U.S. imperialism operates through white supremacist ideology by an examination of white American tourists who espouse their ideas about racial segregation while in Mexico. In a chapter of "My House is Your House" titled "An American Negro in Cuernavaca," Motley explains his new understanding of U.S. racism:

> Richard Wright once made a statement, briefly criticized in the U.S., that there was more freedom in a block of France than in all of the U.S. There are overtones

of truth in the statement, economically, socially speaking, surely psychologically speaking; I'd say that there is more thought about a person's race or color in every individual family in the U.S. than there is in all of Mexico. This deadly self-consciousness about race and color in the U.S. has actually numbed an entire country. This skin disease is something everyone born there has to suffer from the day of his birth. And you never realize how psychologically sick the U.S. is from this point of view until you live in a foreign country.[6]

As Motley suggests here, he developed a more critical perspective on racial inequality in the United States as a result of living in Mexico.

This new perspective is also evident in "Tourist Town," the novel Motley wrote following "My House Is Your House," in which he fictionalizes his observations of American racism and imperialism through an examination of the social and material effects of U.S. tourism on Las Casas, a small Mexican fishing village. However, Motley's representation of U.S. racism changed between the writing of "My House Is Your House" and the writing of "Tourist Town." In the latter, he described a more complex world whereby American tourists are presented as working in conjunction with other forces, such as the Mexican elite, the Catholic Church and the Mexican government, to exploit the poorest segments of Mexican society. In "Tourist Town," Motley describes the effects of these forces on the town, as well as on its residents. Specifically, he examines the unequal relations of power among American tourists and expatriates, Mexican elites, and the Mexican residents of Las Casas, and it is the dynamics of these relations that propel his narrative. Motley's frank statements about U.S. racism, as well as the way he negatively compares the United States to Mexico, made it difficult for him to publish his work. "My House Is Your House," was never published, and "Tourist Town," which included pirated sections of "My House Is Your House," was significantly edited in its posthumous publication as *Let Noon Be Fair*.

Touring the Color Line

Willard Motley is best known for the novels he wrote before leaving the United States in 1951, notably *Knock on Any Door*, much of which was based on circumstances and events that he himself had observed while living in Chicago. By the time he had written *Knock on Any Door*, Motley was already a "self-conscious literary naturalist," according to Jerome Klinkowitz, giving "every detail from his own life and the larger life around him."[7] Once in Mexico, his fascination with literary naturalism turned to documenting the compelling social and economic transformations with which he found himself confronted. This material gradually developed into the book-length project "My House Is Your House." In the mid-1950s he set aside this project to work on a novel, *Let No Man Write My Epitaph*, which was published in 1958. He then returned to the earlier text. Motley finished the first section of the manuscript in 1960, at which time he submitted it to his agent and his editor at Random House.

Motley wrote "My House Is Your House" as the Mexican government's involvement in the development of tourism reached its peak following World War II and through the 1960s. During these years, the number of tourists who entered Mexico doubled from 300,000 in 1946 to 600,000 in 1960. It was the administration of Miguel Alemán (1946–1952) that allocated substantial resources into building the infrastructure of the tourism industry. Alex Saragoza has argued that, "Alemán was instrumental in the move to promote Mexico vigorously to foreign travelers, and in the construction of a more modern, highly commercialized approach to Mexican tourism."[8] His efforts continued after he left office in 1952, when he was hired to run the Mexican government's agency for tourism.

The rise in the number of U.S. tourists visiting Mexico was also related to a heightened demand for vacation experiences abroad by Americans after World War II. However, it was also the result of the campaigns by the Mexican and U.S. governments to promote tourism in Mexico. According to scholar Eric Zolov, tourism promotion in the postwar era was "repackaged" so as to change how foreigners viewed Mexico.[9] While Mexico had previously been perceived as underdeveloped, it was to the benefit of both the Mexican and U.S. governments to re-create Mexico as a secure and stable nation, and thus as safe for foreign capital and foreign travelers.

Following the Second World War, an important shift in emphasis distinguished publicity for Mexico's tourism industry from earlier motifs. While tourism promoters emphasized an appreciation of Mexican culture by focusing on museums and archeological sites in publicity of the 1920s and 1930s, the post–World War II form of tourism, centering on beaches and resorts, positioned Mexico as an anonymous backdrop, with Mexicans portrayed as servants. In contrast to the tourist literature of the 1920s and 1930s, postwar Mexican tourism presented Mexican locales not as extraordinary or unusual places but as familiar ones. In this sense, Mexico had thus come to function as a backdrop to a form of tourism that accented pleasure (for white Americans) through being served (by Mexicans).[10]

Unlike his earlier fictional projects, "My House Is Your House" is narrated by Motley. Most of the manuscript reflects situations and patterns he had observed, including the way in which white tourists treated Mexicans, as well as his own experience as an African American living in Cuernavaca. Motley starts "My House Is Your House" by describing the activities of American tourists in Cuernavaca. In a chapter titled "The American Verandah," Motley sets the scene where much of the racial conflict in Cuernavaca takes place. It is on the verandah of the Bella Vista Hotel, where the Americans "order drinks from the waiters who made 11 little pennies an hour," while they "complain about the dirt, how dirty the Mexicans are, how poorly their country is run."[11] Among other issues, Motley is critical of how the Americans treat their Mexican servants. In their conversations, they tell one another not to "spoil" the servants, which Motley translates as "don't pay them more than $18 a month."[12] Motley contrasts his characterizations of the U.S. tourists with the Mexicans he meets, who warmly embrace him. The title of the book itself is taken from the Mexican saying "Ma casa es su casa," suggesting the openness and generosity of Mexicans toward visitors to their country.

Motley also comments, in chapters titled "Little Texas, Cuernavaca" and "An American Negro in Cuernavaca," on the racism exhibited by white Americans toward African Americans in Mexico. In Cuernavaca, he discovers that there is a split between those white Americans who can live alongside African Americans and those who cannot. The "Texas contingent," as Motley refers to the latter group, "don't like it that Negroes have now come to Cuernavaca—and consorting with whites! That Negroes can sit on the same verandah with them in Mexico. It isn't an old Southern custom. They would like to bring their customs here." Motley, who believed that he was leaving racial prejudice behind when he entered Mexico, writes that while "we have long gone beyond thinking of color, it was to become evident that it was much on the minds of American white residents and tourists."[13] He continues, "in a dark skinned country we ironically find ourselves in a strange little microscopic world revolving around color. Had we flown across the Mason Dixon line, across the Rio Grande and into Mexico?"[14] While Motley left the United States in part to escape racial discrimination, in Mexico he found himself confronting U.S. racism through his contact with white Americans who came to Mexico not to escape persecution, but as tourists. Ironically, it is his experience as a U.S. citizen in Mexico, frequenting a hotel that caters to U.S. tourists, that exposes him to these kinds of interactions.[15]

At the same time that Motley critically observes the contingent who inhabit that "strange little microscopic world," he befriends another segment of Mexican society, namely, the Mexicans who are employed by the tourism trade in various occupations such as bellhop, bartender, and cook. (Motley socialized primarily with working-class Mexicans in Mexico rather than with Americans.[16]) He uses the perspective of the Mexican hotel employees as a means to demonstrate how citizens of Mexico, a strategic ally of the United States during the cold war, were disturbed by American racism, both within and outside the United States. In the chapter "An American Negro in Cuernavaca," Motley writes that while Mexicans didn't care what color he was, they were aware that white Americans discriminated against him. In a conversation with waiters from the Bella Vista Hotel, he is told that some of the Americans complained to the hotel management because it served African Americans. He reports that the waiters felt that the white Americans had "tried to bring prejudice to Mexico," and that they "didn't like the Mexicans either although they were visitors and guests in the country."[17] Through this example Motley draws links between U.S. racism as expressed toward African Americans and toward Mexicans. Motley writes that his conversations with the waiters were "an interesting gauge in race relations . . . giving an insight into what the Mexicans think and feel about the giant at their doorstep."[18]

While Motley directly criticizes the Americans for their racist and imperialist attitudes toward the Mexicans in whose country they temporarily reside, their racism towards African Americans is conveyed through the voices of the Mexican workers at the hotel. In fact, in "My House Is Your House," Motley employs Mexican antiracism as a counterexample to U.S. racism. In "An American Negro in Cuernavaca," Motley writes that "every Mexican boils with anger every time there's an anti-Negro incident in the United States. A dark skinned race themselves they vehemently resent the prejudice against Negroes."[19] After citing examples of friendliness and brotherhood shown to him by Mexicans, Motley writes that the racial incidents "all point to but one thing and that is that the United States has, with racial prejudice alone, made a definite enemy of Mexico; has made Mexico color conscious; conscious of its own reflection in the mirror."[20]

Motley's representations of U.S. racism in "My House Is Your House" were drawn not only from his experiences in Mexico, but also from his experiences in the United States where he returned occasionally for visits in the 1950s. In one of the chapters of "My House Is Your House," titled "The States Again," Motley describes a specific trip that he took with his mother and a friend from Mexico City to the United States. (Motley's mother and his friend were traveling to the border to renew their tourist cards, while Motley planned to continue on to Chicago and New York.) Their difficulties occurred after crossing the border into Texas. When the train pulled into Laredo, they went to town to get a hotel room for the evening. After hours of searching the town with a Mexican cab driver, they came upon a shabby hotel where they were allowed to stay. Once registered in the hotel, they went to look for a restaurant. After being denied service at a number of restaurants in town, they found a small Mexican restaurant along "skid row" where they could eat. The next day, they found the Mexican restaurant where they had been served the day before was closed. Motley remarked,

> We had nowhere to eat, aliens in our own country and I could not but think with an ironic smile: There is the church. The government buildings. The flag. How loud and in a world-wide voice they talk about American democracy— yet, once back in the States, once across the narrow little river, we had to search around corners and down alleys to find a place to sleep. The church. The government buildings. The flag. But there's no place here for a Negro to eat.[21]

Between descriptions of their stay in Laredo, Texas, Motley repeats two sentences over and over again: "This the land of my birth. This my native land," conveying his shock regarding the differences between the ways he's treated in his native and adopted countries.

In their responses to his draft manuscript, Motley's agent and editor both insisted that his depictions of U.S. racism were too controversial to be included in a book geared toward a predominantly white, middle-class readership. When Motley sent his agent, Mavis McIntosh, the first installment of his manuscript, she responded that his "sections on prejudice should be revised."[22] Motley ignored her comments, and submitted the manuscript to Random House without making any revisions to his original material. Although Robert Loomis, his editor at Random House, was initially interested in Motley's idea for "My House Is Your House," he was critical of this section of the manuscript as well. After Loomis received the first installment, he commented to Motley in a letter that "This story—your story—was confused somewhat by the inclination of the reader to look at the book as a book about Mexico when in reality, it is really a book about your own experiences."[23] Loomis challenged Motley's representations of white Americans, noting that these portrayals led to "some confusion in the reader's mind, for while you are praising your new environment, you are relentlessly criticizing the people from your former environment."[24] These images of Americans were too critical, Loomis implied, because the travel guide implicated Americans in the perpetuation of racial prejudice. In response, Motley agreed that some of the passages on American racism in Mexico could be edited, but indicated that he wanted to make sure that the editor would "leave enough to clearly show how a certain class of American goes to a foreign country and tries to import his prejudices."[25]

Part of the disagreement between Motley and Loomis lay in their differing perceptions of the book and its intended audience. Loomis was envisioning a guidebook geared toward a white, middle-class readership. Motley, on the other hand, did not think of the manuscript as a guidebook, a genre that he criticized in "My House Is Your House." In the chapter "A Gringo in Cuernavaca," Motley wrote about his view of guidebooks: "Guidebooks are the most misguiding books in the world. Written for chambers of commerce, hotel associations, for shipping lines and railroad lines and more recently for the air lanes [*sic*] they are of necessity highly colored romances bordering on fiction."[26]

Instead, Motley saw "My House Is Your House" as presenting a more realistic account of Mexican culture. This manuscript would not be a guide directing readers to traditional tourist sites, but rather, as Motley himself said, he was "trying to describe the Mexico and Mexicans the tourists never get to see—the middle and lower classes."[27] In the United States, Motley's writing had focused on the lives of the working classes, and as Jerome Klinkowitz has argued, Motley saw himself as a "social researcher, leaving his own middle-class circumstances, to seek out the deeper truth of life."[28] Motley's focus on the so-called other half of society pleased editors when he wrote novels based on the lives of white ethnic characters, such as Nick Romano in *Knock on Any Door*, but did not please them in this case when he was writing a travel book about a third-world country, geared toward first-world tourists.

Motley attempted to publish this manuscript at a time when the U.S. State Department was encouraging travel writers to learn about the countries they were writing about, as well as to present "a desire to share common interests" and "to understand significant differences."[29] Christina Klein argues that travel writer James Michener, emblematic of travel writers of the 1950s, constructed "a sentimental, racially tolerant subjectivity in his readers," at the same time that his "anti-racism constituted an integral component of the legitimating ideology of U.S. global expansion."[30] Similar to other white, liberal travel writers of the 1950s, Michener's analyses of racism can be differentiated from more critical perspectives, as articulated by Motley.

Judging by the topics of "My House Is Your House" and Motley's earlier works, it can be assumed that Motley's agent and editor were not expecting to read a manuscript that so vehemently indicted U.S. racism. From examining the correspondence between Motley and Loomis, it appears to have been Motley's criticism of American racism, as well as his unflattering comparison of the United States to Mexico, that prevented Random House from printing the manuscript. After the manuscript was rejected by Random House,[31] Motley's other agent, Elizabeth McKee, sent the manuscript to other publishers but was unable to sell it. McKee also had difficulty selling excerpts from the manuscript to magazines, although eventually the men's magazine *Rogue* accepted four noncontroversial chapters.[32]

It was Motley's descriptions of American racism and imperialism, as contrasted with Mexico's openness toward African Americans, that concerned his agent and some book editors. Similar to the work of Richard Wright and other African Americans who lived outside the United States during the early cold war era, Motley's work became more internationally focused after he relocated to Mexico. As Tyler Stovall has written about the work of Richard Wright, "To place America's racial dilemmas in an international political context at the height of the Cold War constituted for many an unforgettable sin."[33] Why would these perspectives be considered so controversial during the early cold war era? One could argue in Motley's case that it was due to the internationalism registered in a work that closely connects U.S. racism and imperialism. Set within the context of the struggle over the representation of the global dimensions of U.S. democracy, Motley's scathing indictment of the U.S. color line as ingrained at home and projected abroad was impermissible. Moreover, his narrative emphasis on the combined imposition of U.S. racial attitudes and economic expansion undermined efforts to depict the U.S. presence as an altruistic, high-minded advance of freedom and democracy. Finally, and perhaps most impermissible of all, to suggest that the leader of the free world might have something to learn from Mexico inverted the hierarchy of leadership and moral authority.

"De-scribing" the Tourist Imaginary

At the same time as he was writing "My House Is Your House," Motley started a novel titled "Tourist Town," in which he explored the effects of tourism on a small Mexican fishing village. Although Motley could not have anticipated Loomis's initial reaction to "My House Is Your House" or its eventual rejection by Random House, fiction clearly provided him with an opportunity that nonfiction disallowed. This is one way to understand why it was that Motley eventually decided to transplant segments from the controversial chapters of "My House Is Your House," which focus on U.S. racism in Mexico, into the fictional "Tourist Town." However, these and other sections of "Tourist Town" were later excised by his editor at Putnam, Peter Israel, before the novel's posthumous publication as *Let Noon Be Fair*.[34]

"Tourist Town" traces events in the fictional village of Las Casas over a period of thirty years. The incidents and characterizations in the manuscript were based primarily on Motley's experiences in and knowledge of Puerto Vallarta, Cuernavaca, and Acapulco in the 1950s and 1960s. The book comprises three sections, each of which represents a distinct period in the development of Las Casas. The first part is based on Motley's experiences in Puerto

Vallarta, where he lived for almost a year in the early 1950s before its tourism boom. The second part is drawn largely from Motley's years in Cuernavaca during the 1950s. In fact, some of the material about the U.S. tourists came directly from the opening chapters of "My House Is Your House." The third part of the manuscript was based on Acapulco, which Motley visited during its boom years in the early to mid-1960s while he was finishing the novel.[35]

The development of Acapulco and Puerto Vallarta, two coastal Mexican villages turned beach resorts, occurred after a shift in Mexico's tourism promotion that emphasized Mexico's beaches rather than its museums. During the 1920s and 1930s, the Mexican government had used indigenous and folkloric culture as a means to project a sense of national identity to potential tourists in the United States and elsewhere. As such, the state had invested money in "archeological excavations, museums, anthropological research, rehabilitation of historical buildings and neighborhoods, arts performance and production, and programs for the maintenance of folklore and popular cultural expression."[36] However, after World War II, the Mexican government started to invest in the nation's infrastructure and to support transportation networks tied to Mexico's beaches. This shifted the center of Mexican tourism from Mexico City, with its museums, to the Pacific coast, with its beaches.

One of the most significant projects of the Alemán administration was the building of a highway between Mexico City and Acapulco. The construction of this highway significantly increased the number of travelers to Acapulco.[37] In tourism promotion material published in the mid-1950s, Acapulco was proclaimed "the ultimate resort destination."[38] Acapulco's year-round population doubled during this period, after the highway from Mexico City was built. There were at this time "eight first-class hotels in addition to an uncounted number of tourist courts, inns, and pensions favored by less affluent visitors, both Mexican and foreign," according to tourism scholars Mary and Sidney Nolan.[39] In 1960, Acapulco was connected to Mexico City by a four-lane toll road, cutting two hours off the trip. By 1965, Acapulco had close to fifty thousand year-round residents, and upwards of 237 hotels.

Another fishing village on the Pacific coast, Puerto Vallarta, virtually unknown to tourists in 1955, experienced a tourism boom after Acapulco. In 1960, when the Nolans visited Puerto Vallarta, they could not envision the development of the town into a "popular resort with luxury hotels and modern transportation services," which it soon became.[40] By the mid-1960s it had become a destination for the jet set, which can be in part attributed to Hollywood's use of Puerto Vallarta as a location for *The Night of the Iguana* (1964) starring Richard Burton, a film that, ironically, offered a critical perspective on U.S. tourists in Mexico.

Motley created a broad range of characters in "Tourist Town." Of the foreigners, there are permanent residents, including U.S. artists and writers, political refugees from Spain and Germany, and seasonal visitors, including tourists. There are also foreign business investors, some of whom are permanent residents, while others either infrequently travel to Las Casas or conduct their affairs in absentia. The Mexican characters include members of the clergy, prostitutes, politicians, fishermen, businessmen, beggars, and shop owners. There is a range of social strata represented in the novel, from the very poor, primarily Indians, to the middle class and the "wealthy set."

Loomis's influence can be seen in Motley's wide-ranging portrayals of Americans and Mexicans in the novel. While Motley holds the U.S. tourists primarily responsible for the changes to Las Casas, he also indicts the town's middle- and upper-class Mexican residents, who both contribute to and benefit from tourism in their town. It is a local resident, Hector Beltran, the richest man in town and owner of its only bank and general store, who buys up all the land that the Indians live on in Las Casas so that he can develop it. (He made his money buying crops from Indians, whom he exploited by turning them into sharecroppers.) When he becomes aware that "Americans are finding us," Beltran, Tizoc (a wealthy Indian), and a general extend the boundaries of Las Casas so that the land can be sold to investors.[41] However, Motley also creates Mexican characters who are exploited by U.S. tourists and tourism. Drawing from "My House Is Your House," Motley based some of his characters in "Tourist Town" on the lower-middle-class and working-class people whom he befriended in Mexico. His observations of their lives influenced the characterizations that he developed in the manuscript. Motley does not attribute all responsibility for poverty in Las Casas to the growth of the tourism industry, citing as well the role of the Catholic Church and the Mexican government. Furthermore, in an extension of his portrayal in "My House Is Your House" of American racism, Motley does acknowledge in "Tourist Town" the presence of Mexican racism. While he describes little if any prejudice expressed toward African Americans by Mexicans, Motley does represent the bias in Mexico against the indigenous people of Mexico, who were frequently positioned on the lowest rungs of Mexican society, as well as the people of mixed ancestry.[42] He narrates the "color line" in Mexico through his characterizations of the Espinozas (Spanish), Beltran and Mario (Mexican), and Tizoc (Indian).[43]

Motley's American characters range from sympathetic expatriates to "Ugly Americans." The first American to inhabit Las Casas is a writer, Tom Van Pelt, an author from Chicago, who serves as a stand-in for Motley. Van Pelt is eventually joined by other Americans, mostly U.S.

tourists. In the opening chapter, Motley scathingly describes one of the first female arrivals:

> Near the edge of the water a woman stood before a slim-legged easel with a palette in one hand and a brush in the other. She wore a broad brimmed straw hat with farmyard animals circling it. It had come from Acapulco. A bright tire tube of fat lay exposed between the bottom and top of her swimming suit. On her feet were sandals from Cuernavaca out of which, like teeth bared, highly red-polished toenails protruded, and on her fingers were large and heavy silver rings from Taxco.[44]

Other early visitors to Las Casas are represented less critically, including American teachers, artists, writers, and retired middle-class couples.

Most of the changes to Las Casas over the course of the novel are related to the influx of American tourists and businesses. Within the first few chapters, the quaint Little Rose Hotel becomes overshadowed by the construction of larger, more standardized hotels owned by foreign investors. For example, the Hotel Tropical, a hotel with no visible ownership where things are done "American-style," opens with a huge cocktail party and becomes the center of American life in Las Casas. Meanwhile, the contents of the liquor shelf in the Candilejas cantina are filled with imported whiskeys and martini glasses, "elbowing caña and tequila off the shelf."[45] Eventually, an airport is built and later rebuilt twice. The beaches are given names. English edges out Spanish as the primary language spoken in what had been, not many years before, a remote fishing village comprised entirely of Spanish speakers. "Society" also comes to Las Casas, and it is documented in the pages of an English-language newspaper published in Mexico City. American film companies use Las Casas for on-location work. By the end of the novel a bullring is constructed, and France and Italy open consulates. Las Casas is being promoted far and wide; as Motley writes, its "radio program was beamed to Mexico City. The town was advertised in newspapers and magazines throughout the United States and in choice spots in Europe."[46] During this time, some of the locals resist the commercialization of their town, notably Mario, one of the main characters, who refuses to sell his beachfront land to investors who want to build a large hotel on the site.

Although the novel focuses on Las Casas's transformation from a small fishing village into a tourist hotspot spoiled by commercialization, there was significant disagreement between Motley and his principal editor at Putnam, Peter Israel, as to how to tell that story. The primary conflict between the two men was their disagreement over who were the main characters. In Motley's view, the main subject of the novel was the town of Las Casas itself. His representation of Las Casas as the protagonist is evident not only in the panorama of minor and major characters but also in the fact that buildings, streets, and parts of the landscape become significant elements of the novel.[47] Peter Israel disagreed with Motley, writing that while he saw "the town in the local Mexican situation as the set or framework for the book," he envisioned "the debauchers as essential characters, the stuffing, meat of the book."[48] In appealing to an American audience, Israel wanted the book to be focused primarily on the Americans (the debauchers), rather than on the economic effects of U.S. tourism or the lives of the Mexican residents.

While Motley did incorporate Israel's feedback to some extent, the editor was continually displeased with Motley's characterizations of the American tourists. After receiving subsequent sections of the manuscript, Israel commented in a letter to Motley that his American characters were less developed than the Mexicans and appeared to be interchangeable.[49] Motley responded, "Don't you think the Americans should appear and then disappear (to go somewhere else) like the monied vagabonds they are?"[50] These more superficial representations served a purpose—they enabled Motley to portray the ephemeral presence of tourists in the town.[51] A year earlier, Motley had written to Israel, "I think of the debauchers, as season goes into new season, as a new set of characters acting out the same play over and over."[52] Motley contrasted these representations with his characterizations of the permanent residents, which were more developed.

When Motley died of intestinal gangrene at age fifty-two in 1965, Peter Israel had most of Motley's autograph manuscript of "Tourist Town" in his possession. It was only four chapters from completion.[53] While the published book ends where Motley's manuscript left off, Israel made extensive revisions following Motley's death.[54] Although the story of "Tourist Town" remains to some extent, Let Noon Be Fair, the published book, differs from the manuscript in a number of important ways. For one, the structure of the story itself was revised. Motley's original "Tourist Town" had 186 chapters arranged in eight parts, while Let Noon Be Fair has 35 chapters arranged into three major parts. There were a number of chapters that Israel cut, including those that told the story of a fictionalized character, Melvin Morrison, an African-American novelist and another Motley alias, and the four parts of the novel of which Morrison was the narrator. However, before his death Motley had informed Israel that it was possible to cut these chapters, because they only framed the larger story.[55]

Israel's other cuts were the result of editorial choices he made without Motley's consultation. While Israel had written to Motley that he wanted a "rough, tough-minded angry novel . . . a no holds barred book," this criterion seems to have only applied to sex, not to racial or economic inequalities, which were important subjects in Motley's manuscript.[56] The paperback version of *Let Noon Be Fair*, published by Dell, was marketed as a novel about "a sunny paradise on the Mexican shore, where lust and greed were private affairs." The copy on the book's back cover describes the demise of Las Casas in a sensationalistic fashion, as tied to its "discovery" by those who "come in search of pleasure . . . a frantic, uninhibited orgy of thrill-seeking, where corruption flourished, desire was flaunted, and private indecency threatened to become public policy."[57] Here the destruction of Las Casas is related to the degeneracy of the tourists, notably their excessive sexual practices (which are simultaneously selling points for the novel), rather than the economic effects of the tourism industry, which Motley had detailed in his manuscript.

While the transformation of Las Casas remains in the published novel, Motley's more pointed criticisms about the economic inequalities between American tourists and the majority of Mexicans who live in Las Casas were excised by the editor. Motley's critiques were frequently constructed through the juxtaposition of conflicting elements within the same passage. However, when Israel cut Motley's 186 chapters into 35 in the published version, he also rearranged the order of events by combining references to a certain character or topic within one passage. This meant that in the published version sentences were positioned within a different context, dismantling Motley's critique. For example, in the original manuscript Motley combines a passage about Julio, a Mexican resident, with one about Bob and Cathy Matthews, two American visitors, as a way of contrasting Julio's poverty with the Matthews's carefree lifestyle. Motley writes, "The pump was working again, as the presidente had predicted, and Julio could go back to his near poverty. Cathy and Bob Matthews wandered the town, hand-in-hand, falling in love with the town."[58] In the published version, the reference to Julio has been cut and Cathy and Bob's "love" of Las Casas is combined with a passage in which Motley writes about their decision to rent a house and move there: "Cathy and Bob Matthews had fallen completely in love with Las Casas. They found a house. They moved in. It was an old comfortable house of two stories with a wide balcony and cool tile floors, renting for 12 dollars a month."[59]

In Motley's second draft of the novel, Israel edited out sections that contextualized the transformations of the town, especially those passages that contained an economic critique of tourism. For example, Israel cut a passage where Motley contrasted the growth of the tourism industry in Las Casas with the increasing poverty of Las Casas:

The season came to full swing. Every hotel was full. On the streets more women's slacks and native sandals appeared. A little village of stands, all painted baby blue, were erected on Calle Jupiter leading off from the town square. Here in these stall-like stands cheap silver bracelets, rings and earrings were sold. Another beggar had appeared on the streets.[60]

Clearly Israel was not referring back to the letters Motley had written before his death, in which he mentioned specifically that he wanted "almost constantly to show poverty living side-by-side with great wealth and waste."[61]

By the midpoint of the second draft of "Tourist Town," beggars not only exist in large numbers in Las Casas but are forcibly removed from businesses catering to the tourism trade. While their presence is noted in *Let Noon Be Fair*, Motley's analysis of the relation between tourism and poverty was for the most part excised by Israel. For example, a passage spoken by a blind beggar after he is kicked out of a restaurant was removed by Israel. In this passage, the beggar expressed "the attitudes of the natives towards the gringos":

> They had come as friends.
> We opened our arms and took them in . . .
> They tried to buy us with their money.
> Our women.
> Our respect.
> *Pinche gringos!*
> Fucking gringos![62]

Israel also edited out other examples of the locals' resistance to the growth of tourism in Las Casas. In the later sections of "Tourist Town," as the town becomes more developed and economic inequalities grow, a protest movement forms against the American tourists, specifically assailing their use of Mexican prostitutes. This movement is fronted primarily by the sons of middle-class Mexicans in Las Casas. At Maria's, a whorehouse owned by two foreigners, Zimmer and Crowe, protesters march in a picket line carrying placards that read: "Las Casas doesn't need prostitution. Las Casas needs bread," "Go home Yankees. Screw your own women," and "Las Casas has become a whorehouse."[63] Motley here uses prostitution as a metaphor for the Americans' treatment of Las Casas. However, Israel removed this section and it did not appear in the published novel.

In addition to passages that examine economic inequalities perpetuated by tourism, Israel also cut passages that refer to the racism of white Americans against African Americans and Mexicans. Motley's decision to include African-American characters in the manuscript offered him an opportunity to write about his own experiences in dealing with racist Americans in Mexico. When we compare Motley's manuscript with the published novel, it is evident that Israel removed significant sections that made reference to American racism. Not only did Israel exclude the chapters on the African-American novelist Melvin Morrison, the original narrator of the story, but he also excised references to other African-American characters. One of his largest edits cut an eight-chapter segment on Charlie Jackson, who remains the only African-American character in the published novel. As such, his character is significantly reduced by Israel's editorial decisions.

In part, Jackson serves as another stand-in for Motley because his character has many of the same experiences that Motley described in "My House Is Your House." For example, Jackson's dealings with racist Texans was excerpted from Motley's encounters in Cuernavaca. However, the appearance of Willard Motley as a character in the "Tourist Town" manuscript functions as a way to differentiate the treatment of an average African American from that of a celebrity.[64] While Jackson is not asked to a party given by white Americans in Mexico, Motley is treated differently. After a white woman recognizes him, Motley writes about himself in the third person: "Motley had arrived. He was a writer. Somehow his color wasn't so noticeable."[65] Here Motley suggests that his celebrity may have spared him other forms of racist treatment.

By including the character of Charlie Jackson, Motley was able to criticize the way in which white Americans imported their racist beliefs to Mexico, which affected how they viewed Mexicans as well. In the manuscript, it is Jackson who makes the other Americans aware of their racist treatment of Mexicans. In the following passage, edited out of the novel, Jackson reverses the usual missionary model of Anglo-Saxons traveling to far-off places to "civilize" the non-white masses: "On the veranda of HOTEL TROPICAL Charlie Jackson says to the white people, laughing, 'I'm here to humanize you. You used to send missionaries to Africa to save the blacks, now I'm here to help you. These Mexicans are people too—they're not just here to wash your clothes.'"[66]

It is telling that the only two people to laugh after the statement are Jackson and Tizoc, a person of indigenous heritage, who then asks Jackson to his table to join him in a game of dominoes. Here Motley draws these two characters together—one African American, one Mexican—through a shared understanding of U.S. racist and imperialist attitudes.

Conclusion

Making Las Casas the main protagonist of "Tourist Town" provided Motley with a dynamic narrative trope with which to describe the social and economic effects of U.S. tourism. Furthermore, Motley's decision to explore the structural changes to Las Casas provided a means to approach his interest in larger themes of U.S. imperialism and racism, which he had initially explored in "My House Is Your House."

The character of Tom Van Pelt, a white writer from Chicago, who also serves, as a writer and observer of the action, as a stand-in for Motley, comes closest in *Let Noon Be Fair* to denouncing the American population for the town's demise. In a statement that bears close resemblance to a passage from "My House Is Your House," Van Pelt remarks:

> The Americans he thought, in their privileged world. The international set, looking for anything to ease the boredom. Our women wear sandals and Mexican jewelry that would weigh a burro down, and slacks. Did you ever see that typical fat-assed gringa up-and-down the *malecon*, at the beach, shopping at the supermarket in slacks and hair curlers? And men wearing two and three cameras like burros bringing twin sacks of rocks from the beach for construction? We speak bar Spanish. We know how to ask for drink. We know how to ask for a woman: *Putas—Casa de putas—Zona Roja—Maria's?* And the silly boy's grin on the fat face below the bald head . . . "I'll pay you. Just show me where. Savvy?" . . . We are the occupation army, he thought cynically, we make Las Casas tick. It is our goddamn town, the attitude says, and we're going to do as we goddamn please. The Mexicans are just working for us. We are the ex's and the want-to-be's.[67]

Unlike the excerpt from "My House Is Your House," this passage moves from third person to first person, whereby Van Pelt, and by extension Motley, implicates himself for the changes to the town. Here the critique of U.S. tourism is perhaps more permissible because the reciprocities of domestic and international racism are not directly targeted.

In "Tourist Town," Motley indicts himself, through the figure of Tom Van Pelt, by demonstrating how "sympathetic" Americans are partially responsible for the commercialization of Las Casas and the effects of that commercialization on the town's poorest residents. Although Motley distinguishes between these sympathetic permanent residents and the American tourists who traipse in and out of the narrative, he holds all of the Americans, as well as the upper-class Mexicans, accountable for the changes to Las Casas. Toward the end of "Tourist Town," Motley encapsulates some of the effects on Las Casas of the influx of Americans and the growth of the tourism industry, effects that include the development of a slum area:

> And now there was definitely a slum area in Las Casas. It started where the hills started to climb in dirt paths. It started along the riverfront and slipped

darkly backward where, again the hills began their laborous [sic] climb as if to get away to Mexico City. Over these mountains. Out of here. Somewhere where I won't be used. It started, too, beyond and around, and in front of OLD TOWN. It started where the beach was of no value because the waves were dangerous. It started where the soil was eroded. Where there was land without irrigation; land the rich Mexicans and gringos didn't want. Land on stones. Land of cactus. It started in the hearts of men and their families who saw no future and knew a short past ago, air and sea and land that gave hope, gave home. It started when they were "discovered."

It started when they were taken over by those from the North, by those with money. It started when these hands to work had no work to do. It started small and became big.

It started with Cathy Matthews—god bless her! It started with Tom Van Pelt—god bless him! It started and continues—goddamn the others![68]

Thus, in addition to his characterizations of Americans exporting racism to Mexico, Motley's criticisms of the invasion by Americans of Mexican towns like Las Casas drew attention to the economic effects of U.S. citizens residing in Mexico, an analysis that was not developed by the other American writers who visited Mexico at the time, such as Beat writers William Burroughs and Jack Kerouac.

Unlike Motley and the other artists and writers who left the United States during the early cold war era because of racial discrimination and political persecution in the United States, Beat writers, including Burroughs and Kerouac, went to Mexico in the early 1950s as a means of "dropping out" of consumer-driven U.S. society. However, scholar Eric Zolov has argued that while the Beats' "unofficial" tourism provided a "counternarrative to the discourse of tourist travel" in the postwar era, they simultaneously "maintained a dependency on modern comforts, and displayed a certain neocolonialist arrogance towards Mexico and Mexicans."[69] As such, he suggests that the Beats were "unconscious agents of imperialist relations."[70] Aspects of this position are elaborated in a letter from Burroughs to Kerouac: "Be mighty glad to see you down here. You won't make a mistake visiting Mexico. A fine country with plenty of everything cheap. One of the few places left where a man can really live like a Prince."[71] And in a letter to Allen Ginsberg from 1951, Burroughs writes, "Old-style imperialism is done. It doesn't pay. . . . If you want to give yourself a chance to get rich and live in a style that the U.S. has not seen since 1914, 'Go South of the Rio Grande, Young Man.' Almost any business is good down here, since markets are unlimited."[72] Clearly a different social optic is at work in the worldview espoused so pointedly by Burroughs.

Although Motley's reasons for being in Mexico were quite distinct from those of the Beat writers mentioned above, he and they shared the experience of being citizens of a first-world nation, residing in a third-world country. However, Motley sought to call attention to these unequal relations of power and by extension to the imperialistic relationship of the United States to Mexico, a theme that is narrated in his final novel. He does this in part by placing himself in the story, both literally and metaphorically, noting how even his most sympathetic American characters are not exempt from developing an imperialistic relationship to Mexico. Peter Israel had insisted that Motley's U.S. characters and authorial stand-ins elicited identification and empathy on the part of Random House's English-speaking market. Instead, Motley sought to evoke a complex interplay between identification and revulsion in order to expose the subtle and not-so-subtle consequences of U.S. imperial expansion and Mexican modernization.

Notes

1. Tyler Stovall, *Paris Noir: African Americans in the City of Light* (Boston: Houghton Mifflin, 1996), 131.

2. Paul Gilroy, *The Black Atlantic: Modernity and Double Consciousness* (Cambridge, Mass.: Harvard University Press, 1993), 154.

3. Agencies of the U.S. government attempted to silence African-American activists like Paul Robeson, W. E. B. Du Bois, and others who spoke out against U.S. racism during the early cold war years because of their association with the Communist Party or so-called communist "front" organizations. Both men had their passports revoked by the U.S. Department of State so that they could not travel outside the United States. Scholarly works about the U.S. government's treatment of African-American activists associated with the Communist Party during the cold war include Gerald Horne, *Black and Red: W. E. B. Du Bois and the Afro-American Response to the Cold War, 1944–1963* (Albany: State University of New York Press, 1986); as well as Horne, *Black Liberation/Red Scare: Ben Davis and the Communist Party* (Newark: University of Delaware Press, 1994); and Kenneth O'Reilly, *Black Americans: The FBI Files* (New York: Carroll and Graf, 1994).

4. Jerome Klinkowitz, ed., *The Diaries of Willard Motley* (Ames: Iowa State University Press, 1979), xvi.

5. *Ebony*, "The Return of Willard Motley," December 1958, 58.

6. Willard Motley, "An American Negro in Cuernavaca" (from the unpublished "My House Is Your House," Willard Motley Collection, Northern Illinois University), 147–48.

7. Klinkowitz, *Diaries of Willard Motley*, ix.

8. Alex Saragoza, "Tourism," in *Encyclopedia of Mexico: History, Society and Culture*, ed. Michael S. Werner (Chicago: Fitzroy-Dearborn, 1997), 1414.

9. Eric Zolov, "Postwar Repackaging of Mexico: The Cosmopolitan-*Folklorio* Axis" (paper presented at the Woodrow Wilson International Center for Scholars, Washington, D.C., November 7–8, 1997).

10. Vacations in Mexico resort towns like Acapulco and Puerto Vallarta could also be differentiated from vacations at beach resorts in the United States because the locations in Mexico had the added benefit of being less expensive. This was due in large part to the low wages paid Mexican service workers, as noted by Motley in "My House Is Your House."

11. Willard Motley, "My House Is Your House" (unpublished manuscript, Willard Motley Collection, Northern Illinois University), 32.

12. Motley, "My House Is Your House, 111.

13. Motley, "My House Is Your House, 131.

14. Motley, "My House Is Your House, 137.

15. Motley's critical analysis of the behavior of U.S. tourists in Mexico demonstrates that the U.S. State Department was not altogether successful in its attempt to "manage" Americans who traveled abroad. During the 1950s, all U.S. citizens whose applications for passports were granted received a letter from President Eisenhower advising them to carefully consider their interactions with individuals outside the United Sates. Although it was not directly stated as such, racial prejudice in particular was viewed by government officials as a type of behavior that would work against the efforts of the United States to win the "hearts and minds" of citizens within the nonaligned countries. See Christina Klein, *Cold War Orientalism* (Berkeley: University of California Press, 2003), 110.

16. In a *Chicago Tribune* article, Robert Cromie wrote that Motley knows "no Mexican writers or artists" because he prefers "to find his friends among the lower middle-class." Robert Cromie, "New Motley Novel Near Completion," Books Today, *Chicago Tribune*, October 18, 1964.

17. Motley, "My House Is Your House," 143–44.

18. Motley, "My House Is Your House," 145.

19. Motley, "My House Is Your House."

20. Motley, "My House Is Your House," 146.

21. Motley, "My House Is Your House," 4.

22. Mavis McIntosh, letter to Willard Motley, May 5, 1960 (Willard Motley Collection, University of Wisconsin, Madison).

23. Robert Loomis, letter to Willard Motley, May 23, 1960 (Willard Motley Collection, University of Wisconsin, Madison).

24. Loomis, letter to Willard Motley, May 23, 1960.

25. Loomis, letter to Willard Motley, May 23, 1960.

26. Motley, "My House Is Your House," 122.

27. Willard Motley, letter to Robert Loomis, February 1, 1961 (Willard Motley Collection, University of Wisconsin, Madison).

28. Klinkowitz, *Diaries of Willard Motley*, ix.

29. Klein, *Cold War Orientalism*, 111, quoted in Frances J. Cooligan, "Americans Abroad," *Department of State Bulletin*, May 3, 1954, 664.

30. Klein, *Cold War Orientalism*.

31. Robert Loomis, letter to Willard Motley, July 13, 1961 (Willard Motley Collection, University of Wisconsin, Madison).

32. Willard Motley, "A Kilo of Tortillas, A Güaje of Pulque," *Rogue*, vol. 9, no. 4 (August 1964): 46–48, 57; "Give the Gentleman What He Wants," *Rogue*, vol. 9, no. 4 (October 1964): 14–16, 75; "Christmas in Mexico," *Rogue*, vol. 9, no. 5 (December 1964): 27–28, 74; "Death Leaves a Candle," *Rogue*, vol. 10, no. 4 (August 1965): 19–22, 79. Jack Conroy, in "Motley and the Novel That Never Got Written," Panorama, *Chicago Daily News*, February 26, 1966, 7,

wrote that Motley also published another chapter, about the burial of a Mexican baby, in John Edgar Webb's *The Outsider* (Spring 1963).

33. Stovall, *Paris Noir*, 221.

34. Motley's decision to integrate aspects of "My House Is Your House" into "Tourist Town" may also have been related to Motley's financial status at the time. After "My House Is Your House" was rejected by publishers and his advance was withdrawn by Random House, Motley felt a significant amount of financial pressure to write another book. Motley still owed money on a house that he had bought in Puerto Vallarta for two thousand dollars in the early 1950s, and it is evident from reading his diaries that he had so little money that he frequently went without eating. See Willard Motley's diaries between November 6, 1961, and February 19, 1965 (Willard Motley Collection, Northern Illinois University). Because of the way in which his contract with Putnam was set up, Motley would receive a check each time he turned in a predetermined portion of the manuscript. Thus he had a strong financial incentive to finish the novel as quickly as possible.

35. Willard Motley, letter to Peter Israel, August 6, 1962 (Willard Motley Collection, University of Wisconsin, Madison).

36. Saragoza, "Tourism," 1415.

37. Saragoza, "Tourism."

38. Mary Nolan and Sidney Nolan, "The Evolution of Tourism in 20th–century Mexico," *Journal of the West*, 88:17.

39. Nolan and Nolan, "Evolution of Tourism," 18.

40. Nolan and Nolan, "Evolution of Tourism," 21.

41. Willard Motley, *Let Noon Be Fair* (New York: Dell, 1966), 39.

42. Robert Fleming, *Willard Motley*, (Boston: G. K. Hall, 1973), 135.

43. It should be noted that these racial hierarchies were not explored in the work of white exiles in Mexico, who generally viewed the country as free from racism. For example, John Wexley wrote that "there was no color line drawn between the whitest descendent of Cortez or the darkest 'vaquero' riding down from the mountains wrapped in the same poncho as his Aztec ancestors." John Wexley, *The Judgement of Julius and Ethel Rosenberg* (New York: Cameron and Kahn, 1955), 149.

44. Motley, *Let Noon Be Fair*, 9.

45. Motley, *Let Noon Be Fair*, 78.

46. Motley, *Let Noon Be Fair*, 369.

47. N. Jill Weyant, "Lyrical Experimentation in Willard Motley's Mexican Novel: *Let Noon Be Fair*," *Negro American Literature Forum* 10 (1976): 96.

48. Peter Israel, letter to Willard Motley, August 2, 1962 (Willard Motley Collection, University of Wisconsin, Madison).

49. Peter Israel, letter to Willard Motley, April 19, 1963 (Willard Motley Collection, University of Wisconsin, Madison).

50. Willard Motley, letter to Peter Israel, April 25, 1963 (Willard Motley Collection, University of Wisconsin, Madison).

51. This was the effect that the book had on many readers, including Nelson Algren, who wrote in a review in *Bookweek* that the Americans tended to blend in with each other, in contrast to the Mexicans.

52. Willard Motley, letter to Peter Israel, August 6, 1962 (Willard Motley Collection, University of Wisconsin, Madison).

53. William Nelles, "From 'Tourist Town' to *Let Noon Be Fair*: The Posthumous Revision of Motley's Last Novel," *Analytical and Enumerative Bibliography*, vol. 2, no. 2, 61–62.

54. Motley wrote the autograph manuscript for "Tourist Town" between November 2, 1962, and February 18, 1965. The manuscript of 1,822 pages is organized into 186 chapters. According to Craig Abbott and Kay Van Mol, "Since Motley's agent and editor received parts of the novel as the autograph draft was completed, the second draft was being typed as the first was being written." Craig Abbott and Kay Van Mol, "The Willard Motley papers at Northern Illinois University," *Resources for American Literary Study*, vol. 7, no. 1 (Spring 1977): 7.

55. Willard Motley, letter to Peter Israel, January 3, 1965 (Willard Motley Collection, University of Wisconsin, Madison).

56. Peter Israel, letter to Willard Motley, August 23, 1962 (Willard Motley Collection, University of Wisconsin, Madison).

57. Motley, *Let Noon Be Fair*, back cover.

58. Willard Motley, "Tourist Town" (unpublished manuscript, final typescript, Willard Motley Collection, Northern Illinois University), 70.

59. Motley, *Let Noon Be Fair*, 44.

60. Willard Motley, "Tourist Town" (unpublished manuscript, second draft), ch. 58, p. 12.

61. Willard Motley, letter to Peter Israel, August 6, 1962 (Willard Motley Collection, University of Wisconsin, Madison).

62. Motley, "Tourist Town" (second draft), ch. 78, p. 10.

63. Motley, "Tourist Town" (final typescript), 1096.

64. Israel edited out the Motley character from the final version of his manuscript. See Motley, "Tourist Town" (final typescript), 614, 750–52.

65. "Tourist Town" (final typescript), 750.

66. "Tourist Town" (final typescript), 756.

67. Motley, *Let Noon Be Fair*, 306.

68. "Tourist Town" (final typescript), 788–89.

69. Zolov, "The Postwar Repackaging of Mexico," 19.

70. Zolov, "The Postwar Repackaging of Mexico," 21.

71. William S. Burroughs, letter to Jack Kerouac, in *The Letters of William S. Burroughs*, ed. Oliver Harris (New York: Penguin, 1994), 56. Quoted in Manuel Luis Martinez, "With Imperious Eye: Kerouac, Burroughs, and Ginsberg on the Road to South America," *Aztlán* (Spring 1998): 36.

72. William S. Burroughs, letter to Allen Ginsberg, in Harris, *Letters of William S. Burroughs*, 78. Quoted in Martinez, "With Imperious Eye," 51.

CHAPTER THREE

"Gringolandia: Cancún and the American Tourist"

Rebecca Torres and Janet Henshall Momsen

Cancún has been constructed as a Caribbean resort offering sun, sea, and sand in an artificial reproduction of the Yucatan physical environment and the region's Mayan heritage. This simulacrum consists of pyramid-shaped hotels stuccoed with fake Mayan hieroglyphics, Jet Ski "jungle" tours in the lagoon mangroves, Mayan waiters dressed in "authentic" Mexican garb, and caged jaguars on display outside tourist restaurants. This artificial cultural landscape is packaged expressly for the American mass-tourist gaze and consumption (Urry 1990), and is embedded in shopping malls dominated by American fast-food outlets and the widespread use of Spanglish (Boxill and Hernandez 2002). The result is "Gringolandia"—a transnational *hybrid-space* incorporating elements of Mexican, American, and Mayan culture. This landscape may be playful and fashionable, but it is also inauthentic and unequal.

A generation ago, Quintana Roo was one of the most inaccessible regions of Mexico. It was a frontier zone largely inhabited by marginalized indigenous people who lived by subsistence cultivation, chicle collecting, and smuggling. The tropical forest enclave of Quintana Roo, a space of refuge for the "rebellious Maya," seemed excluded from the growing economic, social, and political relations that increasingly bound the United States and Mexico. Through flows of investment, trade and early travelers, political intervention, and the growth of expatriate artist communities and intellectual enclaves, the United States and Mexico had become increasingly interconnected during the nineteenth and twentieth centuries. With the notable exception of early-twentieth-century logwood and chicle extraction and the henequen trade, Quintana Roo remained largely outside these ties to the United States (Konrad 1991).

Tourism was not entirely new to the Yucatán region at the time of Cancún's inception as a resort in the early 1970s. Before Cancún, the most important tourism center on the peninsula was the beautiful colonial city of Merida, with a mere 575 rooms and seventy thousand international visitors in 1970 (Enríquez Savignac 1972; Fondo Nacional de Fomento al Turismo [FONATUR] 1971). The "cradle" of Quintana Roo tourism was the tropical Island of Cozumel, which began attracting adventurous tourists seeking exotic locales in the early twentieth century (Arnaiz Burne and Dachary 1992; Dachary and Arnaiz Burne 1996; Martí 1985). By 1970, Cozumel had 307 rooms and was attracting approximately 36,300 foreign tourists each year to its world-renowned sail-fishing tournaments, tropical reefs, and Mayan ruins. Isla Mujeres, a small, sleepy island near Cancún and site of a minor Mexican naval air base, had its own nascent tourism industry dating back to the early 1950s (Arnaiz Burne and Dachary 1992). By 1970 Isla Mujeres, with 139 rooms, was attracting a total of 8,100 foreign tourists each year. The limited growth of tourism in all of these locales was due primarily to a lack of modern infrastructure, room capacity, promotion, communications, and transportation. Only the most intrepid "alternative" travelers would venture to these remote destinations—a far cry from today's typically pampered Cancún mass tourist.

The advent of large-scale tourism development in Cancún during the early 1970s ended the relative isolation of the region. Thirty years later, Cancún has become Mexico's largest tourist destination and receives over 3 million visitors a year—the majority of whom are American. The region has become a place of escape, leisure, consumption, and retirement for American tourists and expatriate settlers—an estimated 4,500, according to the U.S. Consulate (Belt 2004). Quintana Roo has been "redefined as a tropical paradise, a land of broad, sandy beaches and pristine forest" (Pi-Sunyer and Brooke Thomas 1997, 195), as the "Mexican Caribbean," or more recently, the "Riviera Maya."

The tourist resort of Cancún itself was built as an exclusive enclave separate from the town, and efforts to keep the worlds of the visitor and the native apart continue. Resort planners were careful to segregate tourist space from the living space of local residents, the intention being to avoid *Acapulquización*, in which ghettoes and their waste-flows intermingle with beach-side resort hotels, resulting in a loss of exclusivity for the resort. However, as tourists venture outside the Zona Hotelera, or tourist zone, and beyond the beach in a search for new forms of entertainment, shielding these tourists from the poverty of the local people becomes more challenging. Paz Paredes (1995, 13), a *Secretaría de Turismo* (SECTUR) official, notes that "it was easier before to take a group to a Caribbean island [and] place them in a Club Med without them seeing the misery and social problems."

Cancún has been radically transformed over the past fifteen years from a strictly "sun and sand" tourism bubble into a postindustrial, urban tourism space offering a "kaleidoscope" of activities (Hiernaux-Nicolás 1999; Torres Maldonado 1997). One pronounced consequence of Cancún's transformation into a postindustrial urban tourism center catering to mass tourists has been a major increase in the number of middle-class American families that vacation in Cancún. There have been numerous attempts to develop family oriented tourist attractions and facilities in Cancún to cater to the changing tourist profile. One local fast-food chain owner observed, "In Cancún, more than 5 years ago we realized that we were experiencing a change from an exclusive resort to a mass-tourist destination catering mostly to North Americans" (Charles 1995, 47). One clear example of this trend is México Mágico, a mega-project including a carnival-like amusement park in the hotel zone, that proved to be a miserable failure. The remaining vestiges of the park on the lagoon—carnival rides shaped liked huge Mexican sombreros and chili peppers—are an eyesore and a testimony to bad taste and a poorly conceived idea. Sadly, a portion of the Nichupté lagoon had been filled in to complete this project. The American franchise "Wet 'n Wild" water amusement park also opened in Cancún (during 1997) and is reportedly struggling to remain viable. Other family oriented attractions, a go-cart track and an equestrian center, both of which are located near the airport, are also marginally profitable.

Many of today's tourists, attracted by the cheapness of Cancún, come on package holidays and spend very little money. American "breakers"—waves of American high-school and college students—have become the object of intensive marketing campaigns designed to fill empty rooms at discounted rates during the low-season months. The issue of marketing to "breakers" has become highly contentious and a source of growing tension between Cancún residents and the local businesses that profit by the presence of the "breakers." "Spring breakers from the United States who crave Cancún's white beaches and laidback atmosphere grudgingly accept that the paradise happens to be in Mexico" (Adams 2001). This type of tourism is already bringing the problems of environmental degradation and devaluation of the attractions of the resort (Arnaiz Burne and Dachary 1992; Dachary and Arnaiz Burne 1996). Unfortunately, for many Americans Cancún has become synonymous with spring break. In summer 2003, the creators of MTV's *The Real World* series released what was touted to be the first reality movie, *The Real Cancún*, which documented sixteen American college spring breakers during their week of debauchery in Cancún. The movie follows a long line of Cancún spring break "Gone Wild" videos and annual MTV specials that have helped to promote Cancún as among the top destinations for American college students. This dubious distinction undoubtedly fills rooms in Cancún's mammoth hotels during the slower spring and summer months, but it has driven away many discriminating and higher-paying tourists. Locals have also tired of the spring breakers' antics, which one year included stealing the enormous Mexican flag that flies over the tourist-zone strip.

Quintana Roo: Design for "Gringolandia"

For centuries Quintana Roo has been a space of exile, imprisonment, isolation, and refuge, due in part to the region's marginalized tropical-forest enclave status in the larger Mexican national context. The isolated barrier island of Cancún, situated in the northeastern corner of the Yucatán Peninsula in what would become the state of Quintana Roo in 1974, was selected by the Mexican government as the site for the nation's first master-planned resort, or "Tourist Integral Center." The Cancún experiment took on national importance because it represented the cornerstone of a new, externally oriented, state-driven economic development strategy: planned tourism development (D. Cothran and C. Cothran 1998; Clancy 1999, 2001).

Tourism has long been a major source of foreign exchange for Mexico, and in 1967 the Federal Program for Tourist Development, which had been focused on the Pacific coast and central Mexico, was extended to the Yucatán Peninsula. This was a deliberate attempt to tap into the lucrative market for Caribbean vacations and to bring economic growth to a depressed, peripheral region of the state. It was felt that the area had great potential for tourism for four reasons: it had the same climatic and coastal resources as the Caribbean island resorts; it had archeological sites; there was an abundant supply of cheap labor; and it was closer to the southern and south-eastern United States than any other Caribbean resort except the Bahamas (Lee 1978). Cancún was established specifically as a growth pole for the poor and thinly populated territory of Quintana Roo on the Yucatán Peninsula.

Quintana Roo became a state of Mexico in 1974, and its population grew fivefold between 1970 and 1996. The coastal village of Cancún, which had six hundred inhabitants in the 1960s, has become one of the world's leading tourist destinations, attracting over 3 million tourists in 2000, of whom 58 percent were from the United States (Caribbean Tourism Organization 2002). Of foreign hotel guests in Cancún in 2000, 78 percent came from the United States (Caribbean Tourism Organization 2002), underlining the resort's nickname of "Gringolandia." The hotel area of Cancún remains quite separate from the town of Cancún. In the hotel sector are manicured golf courses and gardens, despite local water shortages. Beaches are populated by tourists and by touts with many ways of extracting additional tourist dollars. Many of Cancún's over 120 tourist hotels were built with a supposedly Mexican theme, but the Las Vegas or Disneyland "virtual reality" (MacCannell 1999) of the resort is now overwhelming. Bartlett (1998, 52) aptly captures the feel of the circus-like spectacle of this overbuilt Cancún, or "Gringolandia":

> Cancún is in Mexico, but not really Mexican. It is Caribbean, but not really of the region. Her soul sisters are places like Las Vegas and Orlando and Hollywood Boulevard, with perhaps a touch of Myrtle Beach: places where the Hustle also goes on night after night, endless finger-snapping, jive-talking, hip-hopping palaces of fun, American style.

Mass tourism has only encouraged the spread of American fast-food outlets and American-style clubs and bars.

On the far periphery of the town live the poor, often rural immigrants who provide unskilled workers to the tourism industry: the maids, porters, and kitchen staff. They work in the luxurious surroundings of international hotels and restaurants but live in squalid shantytowns with few facilities and out of sight of tourists. Local fishermen have also been banished to the other side of Cancún. This spatial separation between American tourists and local tourism workers within Cancún is mirrored in regional patterns as well. American tourists and the wealth and infrastructure associated with their presence remain concentrated in the Riviera Maya (a coastal tourism development extending from Cancún south to Tulum), which is separate from the impoverished Zona Maya interior of the state.

Cancún's economic landscape is complex, with control shared among the Mexican state (through FONATUR); international entrepreneurs and franchises;[1] domestic and foreign tour operators; and Mexican entrepreneurs and franchises.[2] Cancún has also developed a complicated labor market. Immigrants from other Mexican states and from abroad typically occupy the middle-to-high-end employment ranks. The Quintana Roo rural periphery enters this landscape to provide the essential low-end labor. Rural workers migrate both permanently and on a temporary basis to provide labor for construction, food service, cleaning, domestic work, and room service. This group extracts the least value and benefit from the resort, but it is upon their backs that the resort has been built, and it is through them that the resort is sustained. This abrupt transition from the "empty quarter" region of Mexico to a mass-tourism mecca serving the pleasure periphery of North America, and to an increasing degree Europe, has inserted the region into the global capitalist sphere.

Overall, the region's dependency on tourism has resulted in a landscape of uneven development deeply marked by disparities between urban and rural spaces. Seduced by the success of the resort, Mexican authorities failed to enforce the environmental and social carrying capacities established in the original master plans (Enríquez Savignac 1972; FONATUR 1971). The lagoon, for instance, provides an attractive backdrop for the hotels but is now heavily polluted (Skillicorn 1997). Cancún has become Mexico's leading resort (D. Cothran and C. Cothran 1998), and it now exhibits all the classic signs of an overbuilt mass-tourism destination: loss of exclusivity, excess room capacity, heavy discounting, and reduced per capita tourist expenditures.

Cancún's tourism development has affected all aspects of life on the Yucatán Peninsula. The region's economic landscape is highly dependent upon tourism, which accounts for approximately 75 to 80 percent of the gross domestic product (GDP) of the state of Quintana Roo (Arnaiz Burne and Dachary 1992; Castro Sariñana 1995; D. Cothran and C. Cothran 1998). As Castro Sariñana aptly puts it: "Our economic future depends almost entirely upon only one activity: we are mono-producers in the area of tourist services" (1995, 42). Tourism industry benefits remain concentrated in the resort, with planned tourism development having failed to stimulate local agriculture and industry (Torres Maldonado 1997; Torres 2003)—linkages that might have produced a more even regional development. While tourism development has created many jobs, it has also served as a catalyst for rural-to-urban migration resulting in a transfer of labor from the countryside and thus in increased urban squalor and poverty. Other effects of tourism development in the region include environmental degradation (Kandelaars 2000), shifts in local consumption habits, changing social values, and loss of Mayan language and cultural practices (Daltabuit and Pi-Sunyer 1990; Arnaiz Burne and Dachary 1992; Pi-Sunyer and Brooke Thomas 1997).

As tourist resorts have spread southward along the coast from Cancún, "Gringolandia" has taken over control of the coastal zone from local people. It is no longer possible to buy a freshly caught lobster from a local fisherman and grill it on an isolated beach, as it was only twenty years ago. Archeological sites are now overrun by bus tours and by villagers attempting to earn a living by selling cheap souvenirs, for which task they learn Spanglish.

Mass tourism predominates in the region, and those travelers seeking a more authentic cultural experience are forced to venture further outside of the growing reach of Cancún and the Riviera Maya. Cancún's reputation as a hedonistic beach resort is so dominant that it inhibits the development of alternative forms of tourism. Tourists who visit Cancún to luxuriate in its large resort hotels may not even consider the Yucatán when organizing their more environmentally or culturally oriented travel experiences. Additionally, Cancún probably serves as a deterrent to travelers seeking alternative tourism experiences such as cultural, heritage, ethnic, and environmental tourism. To experience Mayan culture, for example, this new breed of tourist is more likely to visit Guatemala or Chiapas than the Yucatán. Mass-tourist interest in authentic cultural experiences, such as watching a dramatization of Mayan history by Mayan-speaking villagers in a village close to the Coba ruins, is minimal (Momsen 2003). For many American mass tourists, Cancún is attractive because it is so much like home with all of the creature comforts and amenities—though with Caribbean beaches and a touch of Mexican flavor— and all at a bargain price. Cancún tourist Jessie P. James, quoted in the local Cancún edition of the *Miami Herald* epitomizes the American mass-tourist mentality, "What do I like about Cancún? It's so much like the United States that you might as well be in the United States."

Cancún's Spheres

Cancún has become a transnational city of interconnected spheres (Torres and Momsen, 2005). The *international*, or *global*, *sphere* exerts influence through Mexican elites with strong ties to the United States, through foreign professionals and entrepreneurs, and through expatriate tourism industry workers. By way of this sphere, foreign direct investment, foreign franchise and management contracts, and foreign products flow into Cancún. It must be noted that while 87 percent of all hotels surveyed for this article in Cancún were Mexican owned—with that ownership concentrated in the hands of companies or families from Mexico City, Monterrey, and Merida—profits are extracted from these hotels through management and franchise agreements (American companies and executives play a growing role in these franchise agreements), American product imports, and American airlines and air charter companies (the international visitors that fill the hotels are overwhelmingly from the United States and Canada).

The *Mexican urban sphere* consists of back and forth flows of immigrants from other parts of Mexico working in tourism-industry-related employment, and in jobs ranging from the unskilled to high-end management positions; it includes domestic tourists and Mexican elites with second homes and businesses. Significant in this sphere are domestic investment, imported agricultural products, and other goods and services. The bulk of food products in Cancún, for example, are brought in from the Mexico City Central de Abastos, which concentrates production from the entire country (Torres 2003). Profits and taxes are extracted from the resort, contributing primarily to the

Mexican urban sphere (and the lifestyle of many wealthy Mexican-Lebanese families) residing in Mexico City and Monterrey.

The third and most subordinate sphere, the *Quintana Roo rural periphery sphere*, represents a circular flow of temporary immigrants and permanent settlers who maintain ties with both Cancún and their city or village of origin. The most marginalized populations of Quintana Roo supply temporary labor to the growth pole, or resort center—while circulating back and forth between the center and their villages. Typically, these temporary laborers fill the lower paying, seasonal jobs because they do not have the training, education, or qualifications for the higher-end jobs that are occupied by urbanites from other Mexican states. The Quintana Roo countryside, to a lesser degree, supplies the tourism center with agricultural products. This supply is limited to low volumes of a few products that are provided on an irregular, highly seasonal basis (Torres 2003). The most significant value extracted from the resort by the Quintana Roo countryside are the remittances channeled back to the villages through either permanent settlers sending money to their families or through temporary laborers circulating between Cancún and their villages.

A fourth, unnamed sphere is the continuous circular flow of foreign, mainly American, tourists, second-home owners, and retirees into and out of Cancún. This sphere represents a constant pattern of influx that exerts a powerful and decisive effect on Cancún and the surrounding region. Americans in particular dominate the Cancún tourism landscape, consistently comprising the majority of all visitors. A focus on serving the United States tourist, beginning with the inception of the resort, has resulted in the current character of Cancún and its identification as "Gringolandia."

Cancún tourists behave almost as short-term migrants because they exhibit high rates of return and usually indicate a strong intention to return in the future. Indeed, according to a tourist survey we conducted,[3] 40 percent of Cancún tourists are return visitors and 90 percent indicate their intention to return in the future. The explosive growth of the time-share industry in Cancún is also reinforcing this pattern of regularity in tourist visits. Through the use of time-shares, tourists own a week in a particular hotel or condominium and return there on an annual basis. These regular tourists are becoming short-term transnational migrants. According to our hotel survey data, thirteen of sixty hotels surveyed offered time-share sale of rooms (21.6 percent). There are also purpose-built apartment blocks with time-share occupancy.

The large American expatriate community in Cancún, many of whom came initially as tourists, certainly qualifies as transnational. Some have set up as entrepreneurs by providing the specialist services that American tourists expect. Others are among the increasing number of American retirees choosing

Cancún as a place for retirement. In both these ways, visitors to Cancún are increasingly establishing permanent links. There is a long tradition in Mexico and the Caribbean of retirees and second-home owners (Henshall [Momsen] 1977) who eventually settle on a permanent basis. Often these retirees and second-home owners form enclaves, interacting little with locals but nevertheless exerting an influence on localities through their patterns of consumption, expenditures, and behavior. In the Cancún context, these new residents are often perceived more as an extension of tourism than as permanent immigrants.

American tourists bring their own set of consumption patterns, moral values, and customs. They leave behind not only tourist dollars, but with their continuous flow they restructure their host society through the demonstration effect and a variety of direct and indirect interactions with its residents. The demonstration effect and the influence of tourism are evident in nearly all aspects of life in Cancún and to a lesser extent in the surrounding Quintana Roo region. Given the large presence of American tourists in particular, this influence is manifest in the gradual Americanization of the region's consumption, dress, culture, language, and moral values (Boxill and Hernandez 2002). Shorts and beachwear are worn everywhere and not just on the beach. U.S. television channels are widely available, with bars offering large-screen coverage of American sports events. American tourists expect to have English spoken wherever they go. Young people, especially spring breakers, exploit the lack of age restrictions on alcohol consumption, often with disastrous effects. Mayan youth in the tourism poles look to foreign tourists and Mexican elites to reinvent their identities in this new Mexican-American hybrid-space. In some cases the new values, practices, and consumption patterns are brought back to Mayan towns and villages throughout the peninsula. Adolescent boys can be seen in the plazas of Mayan towns and villages wearing sagging-to-the-knees dungarees, sporting backward baseball caps, and jiving to rap music as they drink Coca-Cola from aluminum cans.

Apart from the demonstration effect, tourists have a profound impact on local economies through their consumption patterns. In Cancún, tourist consumption is dominated by American tastes and habits. While Americans are familiar with "Tex-Mex" foods, tourism literature suggests that in general Americans are more entrenched and reticent in their consumption patterns and that they reject local foods (Bélisle 1983, 1984a, and 1984b; Miller 1985; Weaver 1991). According to our tourist survey, 26 percent of all meals consumed by tourists are typically American, often fast food. Consumption of American food is even higher among American tourists alone, and approximately one-third of the meals they consume are regular American-style meals (Torres 2002b). Other meals served by hotels tend to be Americanized versions of Mexican food or international cuisine. This tourist consumption helps define tourism industry demand for food, which dictates, in part, opportunities for developing connections with local agriculture (Torres 2002b). With high levels of demand for American food, the potential to offer local products and indigenous dishes is constrained. This may explain, in part, why tourism industry linkages to local agriculture are so weak in the Yucatán region (Torres 2003). Tourist preferences for American food may therefore present an obstacle to creating connections between tourist demand for food and local agricultural production.

Migrants inevitably exert an influence on and reshape their host country's economic, social, and political landscapes. It is noteworthy that this influence appears to be even more intensified in the case of large-scale mass tourism, despite the short-term nature of the visits. This may be due, in part, to the fact that mass tourists are heavily concentrated, and over a given period their numbers can exceed that of the local population (Butler 1980). Also, unlike other transnational migration circumstances, and particularly in developing-country contexts, the tourist or short-term migrant is often richer than local residents, many of whom must depend upon the tourist for their economic survival. For this reason, the relationship between tourists and local residents is usually unequal and based on dependency. This uneven relationship contrasts starkly with other migration contexts in which the migrants are drawn to the host country for economic opportunities and are dependent upon host-country residents for employment. Unlike tourists, who possess economic power, transnational migrants in other contexts are often marginalized and struggling to improve their economic status in their host nation. In the case of tourist resorts, local residents are placed in a subservient position to the tourists they serve and depend upon. In turn, the migrants, or tourists, come to consume local places, services, and products. Tourism in Cancún, as in much of Mexico, therefore, represents a unique and powerful form of migration and one that operates differently from typical migration but exerts, nevertheless, equal or greater impact on its host-country destinations and people (Torres and Momsen 2005).

Cancún as Transnational Hybrid-Space

A sustained flow of tourists, large numbers of American expatriate settlers, and a strong American business influence have transformed Cancún into a truly transnational city.[4] Through the daily practice of tourism in the resort, the local and the global reconfigure economic, social, and political relations.

This is reinforced by the large number of the Mexican elite in Cancún who mimic American consumption patterns and behavior by shopping at Sam's Club and eating at U.S. fast-food outlets. Cancún is neither Mexican nor American. With its large U.S. expatriate community, foreign tourists, and Mexican immigrants, Cancún has unmistakably become "Gringolandia" (Torres and Momsen, 2005).

As a result, Cancún has evolved into a unique hybrid-space incorporating elements of U.S. and Mexican life, along with artificial representations of Mayan culture reconstituted for mass consumption. In this sense Cancún could be considered an example of an "other-directed architecture" (Jackson 1970, 64–65, cited in Relph 1976, 93) constructed expressly for the outside gaze of spectators. According to Relph,

> the total effect of such architecture is the creation of other-directed places which suggest almost nothing of the people living and working in them, but declare themselves unequivocally to be "Vacation land" or "Consumerland" through the use of exotic decoration, gaudy colors, grotesque adornments, and the indiscriminate borrowing of styles and names from the most popular places of the world.

The local Cancún environment has indeed been commoditized, reproduced, and packaged for global mass-tourist consumption. This is evident in the numerous instances in which the environment has been reinvented as a "spectacle" (Urry 1990; Edensor 2001) or "performing nature" (Desmond 1999) for mass tourists, instances that include the Xcaret eco-archeological nature theme park; the Cancún "jungle tours"; mass reef dives from an artificial diving island constructed above a now-barren Cancún reef; the Crococun crocodile park; Pepe's Restaurant with live tigers; and wildlife exhibits, among others.[5] Thus Cancún has been reconstructed to provide a utopian tropical paradise to the collective tourist imagination.[6]

More than any other Mexican tourist resort, Cancún's isolation in remote Quintana Roo only accentuates the impact on it of American tourists, timeshare visitors, and expatriate entrepreneurs, all utilizing American-style hotel and restaurant franchises. The reinvention of its environment and the creation of it as a hybrid-space for the delectation of its visitors has spread far beyond the original resort island, pushing local farmers and fishermen into the interior forests or to shanty towns around the tourist enclaves. The Caribbean and its white beaches are no longer enough. Cancún has become an imagined world for tourists seeking pleasure, diversion, and escape. Hiernaux-Nicolas (1999) suggests that the recent diversification of tourism in Cancún, offering a "kaleidoscope" of new activities to its visitors, has created a "postmodern city and tourist experience." Yet this postmodern differentiation is constructed within a consistent and continuing matrix of American consumption patterns and interests.

References

Adams, Lisa J. 2001. "Cancún tolerates annual invasion." *The Davis Enterprise*, March 15, A8.

Arnaiz Burne, S. M., and A. Dachary. 1992. "Cancún: El enclave turístico y sus costos. Subtema: Los impactos sociales y económicos del turismo." Caribbean Studies Association XVII Annual Conference, Grenada, West Indies.

Appadurai, A. 1990. "Disjuncture and difference in the global cultural economy." *Theory, Culture and Society* 7:295–310.

———. 1996. *Modernity at Large: Cultural Dimensions of Globalization*. Minneapolis: University of Minnesota Press.

Bartlett, James Y. 1998. "Tango tropicale." *Caribbean Travel and Life* 13 (2): 49–59.

Bélisle, F. J. 1983. "Tourism and food production in the Caribbean." *Annals of Tourism Research* 10:497–513.

———. 1984a. "The significance and structure of hotel food supply in Jamaica." *Geography* 1:219–33.

———. 1984b. "Tourism and food imports: The case of Jamaica." *Economic Development and Cultural Change* 32:819–42.

Belt, L. 2004. U.S. Consular Agent in Cancún. Personal communication.

Bosselman, F. P. 1978. *In the Wake of the Tourist: Managing Special Places in Eight Countries*. Washington, D.C.: The Conservation Foundation.

Boxill, Ian, and Edith Hernandez. 2002. "How tourism transforms language: The case of Playa del Carmen, Mexico." *Social and Economic Studies* 51 (1): 47–60.

Butler, R. W. 1980. "The conception of a tourist area cycle of evolution: Implications for management of resources." *Canadian Geographer* 24 (1): 5–12.

Caribbean Tourism Organization (CTO). 2002. *Latest Statistics, 2001*. Barbados.

Castro Sariñana, M. 1995. "Cancún: El auge y la crisis." *Foro de análisis: Cancún: El auge y la crisis*. Ayuntamiento de Benito Juárez. Cancún, Quintana Roo, Mexico.

Charles, A. 1995. "Commentary." *Foro de análisis: Cancún: El auge y la crisis*. Ayuntamiento de Benito Juárez. Cancún, Quintana Roo, Mexico.

Clancy, M. J. 1999. "Tourism and development: Evidence from Mexico." *Annals of Tourism Research* 26 (1): 1–20.

———. 2001. *Exporting Paradise: Tourism and Development in Mexico*. Amsterdam: Pergamon.

Constandse Madrazo, C. 1995. "Cancún a un cuarto de siglo de su fundación." Foro de análisis: Cancún: El auge y la crisis. Ayuntamiento de Benito Juárez, Cancún, Quintana Roo, Mexico.

Cothran, D. A., and C. Cole Cothran. 1998. "Promise or political risk for Mexican tourism." *Annals of Tourism Research* 25 (2): 477–97.

Dachary, Alfredo César, and Stella Maris Arnaiz Burne. 1996. "Turismo y medio ambiente. ¿Una contradicción insalvable?" *Revista Mexicana del Caribe* 1 (1): 133–48.

Daltabuit, M., and O. Pi-Sunyer. 1990. "Tourism development in Quintana Roo, Mexico." *Cultural Survival Quarterly* 14 (1): 9–13.

Desmond, J. C. 1999. *Staging Tourism: Bodies on Display from Waikiki to Sea World.* Chicago: University of Chicago Press.

Edensor, T. 2001. "Performing tourism, staging tourism: (Re)producing tourist space and practice." *Tourist Studies* 1 (1): 59–81.

Enríquez Savignac, A. 1972. "The computer planning of Cancún Island, Mexico: A new resort complex." Paper presented at the Travel Research Association third annual conference, August 13–16, Quebec, Canada.

Fondo Nacional de Fomento al Turismo (FONATUR) 1971. *Proyecto de Desarrollo Turístico.* Project proposal.

Henshall (Momsen), J. D. 1977. "Second Homes in the Caribbean." In *Second Homes: Curse or Blessing,* edited by J. T. Coppock, 75–84. Oxford: Pergamon.

Hiernaux-Nicolás, D. 1999. "Cancún Bliss." In *The Tourist City,* edited by D. Judd and S. Fainstein, 124–39. New Haven, Conn.: Yale University Press.

Instituto Nacional de Estadística, Geografía e Informática (INEGI). 1970. *General Census.* Aguascalientes, Mexico.

———. 1990. *Quintana Roo: Resultados definitivos tabulados básicos: XI censo general de población y vivienda 1990.* Aguascalientes, Mexico: Instituto Nacional de Estadística, Geografía e Informática.

———. 2000. *XII Censo general de población y vivienda.* Aguascalientes, Mexico.

Jackson, J. B. 1970. "Other-Directed Architecture." In *Landscapes: Selected writings of J. B. Jackson,* edited by E. H. Zube. Amherst, Mass.: University of Massachusetts Press.

Kandelaars, P. 2000. "A Dynamic Simulation Study of Tourism and Environment in the Yucatán Peninsula in Mexico." In *Tourism and the Environment: Regional, Economic, Cultural and Policy Issues,* edited by H. Briassoulis and J. van der Straaten, 59–89. Dordrecht: Kluwer Academic Publishers.

Konrad, H. 1991. "Capitalism on the Tropical-Forest Frontier: Quintana Roo, 1880s to 1930." In *Land, Labor, and Capital in Modern Yucatán: Essays in Regional History and Political Economy,* edited by Jeffery T. Brannon and Gilbert M. Joseph, 143–71. Tuscaloosa: University of Alabama Press.

Lee, Rosemary L. 1978. "Who owns the boardwalk? The structure of control in the tourist industry of Yucatán." *Tourism and Economic Change* 6:19–35.

Lury, C. 1997. " The Objects of Travel." In *Touring Cultures: Transformations of Travel and Theory,* edited by C. Rojek and J. Urry, 75–95. London: Routledge.

MacCannell, Dean. 1999. *The Tourist: A New Theory of the Leisure Class.* Berkeley: University of California Press.

Martí, F. 1985. *Cancún fantasía de banqueros: La construcción de una ciudad turística a partir de cero.* Mexico City: UNO.

Miller, L. G. 1985. "Linking Tourism and Agriculture to Create Jobs and Reduce Migration in the Caribbean." In *Migration and Development in the Caribbean:*

The Unexplored Connection, edited by R. A. Pastor, 289–300. Boulder, Colo.: Westview.

Momsen, Janet H. 2003. "Participatory Development and Indigenous Communities in the Mexican Caribbean." In *Participatory and Communicative Planning in the Caribbean*, edited by Jon Pugh and Rob Potter, 155–72. Aldershot, U.K.: Ashgate.

Paz Paredes, Sigfrido. 1995. "Tendencias mundiales del turismo: La zona del Caribe." Foro de Análisis: Cancún: El Auge y La Crisis. Ayuntamiento de Benito Juárez, Cancún, Quintana Roo, Mexico.

Pi-Sunyer, O., and R. Brooke Thomas. 1997. "Tourism, Environmentalism, and Cultural Survival in Quintana Roo." In *Life and Death Matters: Human Rights and the Environment at the End of the Millennium*, edited by B. R. Johnson, 187–212. Walnut Creek, Calif.: AltaMira.

Relph, E. 1976. *Place and Placelessness*. London: Pion.

Skillicorn, P. 1997. *Cancún Water and Wastewater Circumstance*. Briefing summary presented to the Ritz Carlton Hotel.

Torres Maldonado, E. J. 1997. "From Tropical Hell to Tourist Paradise: State Intervention and Tourist Entrepreneurship in the Mexican Caribbean." PhD diss., University of Texas, Austin.

Torres, R. M. 2002a. "Cancún's tourism development from a Fordist spectrum of analysis." *Tourist Studies* 2 (1): 87–116.

———. 2002b. "Toward a better understanding of tourism and agriculture linkages in the Yucatán: Tourist food consumption and preferences." *Tourism Geographies* 4 (3): 282–306.

———. 2003. "Linkages between tourism and agriculture in Mexico." *Annals of Tourism Research* 30 (3): 546–66.

Torres, R. M., and J. Momsen. 2005. "Gringolandia: The construction of a new tourist space in Mexico." *Annals of the Association of American Geographers* 95 (2): 314–335.

Urry, J. 1990. *The Tourist Gaze: Leisure and Travel in Contemporary Societies*. London: Sage Publications.

Weaver, D. B. 1991. "Alternative to mass tourism in Dominica." *Annals of Tourism Research* 18:414–32.

Notes

1. The proliferation of transnational hotel franchises in Cancún, for example, can be attributed to a variety of factors. Tourism industry transnational corporations (TNCs) are granted preferential treatment by the Mexican government, a treatment that is not afforded to foreign investors in other economic sectors. A unique trust mechanism (Clancy, 1999) was developed specifically to allow circumvention of Mexican foreign investment laws prohibiting the ownership of coastal lands by foreigners. To entice investment, the government also offered soft loans, discounted land prices, infrastructure, and assistance with project design (Enríquez Savignac 1972; Martí 1985; Paz Paredes 1995; Torres Maldonado 1997). The Mexican government also

directly solicited foreign investment from prominent tourism TNCs with offers of favorable franchise agreements. During the 1980s, the government offered debt swaps in which private investors were allowed to purchase national debt that could subsequently be converted into discounted tourism development investments. Some observers have suggested that the SWAP mechanism was the primary impetus behind the 1980s Cancún hotel construction boom, which has resulted in the current excess room capacity and the requirement for heavy discounting (Constandse Madrazo 1995; Paz Paredes 1995; Torres Maldonado 1997). Restaurants represent the second most important tourism industry subsector in Cancún. As with hotels, international franchise chains are outnumbered by national, regional, and local restaurants, but they represent a disproportionate share of the value invested in and extracted from the restaurant sector. While there is some foreign equity participation, restaurant ownership mirrors that of hotels, with the vast majority being Mexican—even in the case of international franchises.

2. The naive reflex assumption with respect to Cancún—one that is frequently used by critics of the resort—is that it was built by, and is dominated by, foreign capital. In fact, 87 percent of all hotels surveyed were Mexican owned—with that ownership concentrated in the hands of companies or families from Mexico City, Monterrey, and Merida (particularly wealthy Mexican-Lebanese families). Other nationalities owning hotels in Cancún were Spanish, Dominican Republican, and Japanese. Survey data, however, confirm that foreign ownership is highest among the Gran Turismo (GT) and five-star hotels. This means that while foreign equity is subordinate to domestic, a disproportionate share of the hotel industry value pertains to foreign TNCs and entrepreneurs. Foreign influence is exerted to a greater extent in the Cancún hotel industry through franchise relationships and management contracts rather than through direct equity participation. Franchise chains are often associated with foreign transnational corporations. Typically, higher-end and larger hotels subscribe to franchise agreements that impose rigidity, efficiency, quality control, and standardization in the tourist product. Of Cancún hotels surveyed, 50 percent, representing 71 percent of all study-sample hotel rooms, subscribe to a franchise agreement—and 50 percent of those franchises are foreign. Study data confirm that higher-end hotels tend to be part of franchises, with 93 percent of all GT and 72 percent of all five-star Cancún hotels surveyed subscribing to a franchise relationship. Similarly, according to study data, the level of foreign franchise participation is greatest among higher-class hotels. Of all GT hotels and five-star hotels surveyed, 50 percent and 22 percent respectively were foreign franchises. Overall, however, only 25 percent (151) of all hotels surveyed were foreign franchises. Given the American flavor of the resort, the reflex assumption one makes when visiting Cancún is that it is completely dominated by American chains. This is not the case. Cancún's hotel industry, surprisingly, is dominated by Mexican chains with 25 percent (15) of all hotels surveyed being Mexican franchises representing 50 percent of all franchise hotels surveyed. There is, however, a strong American influence in the tourism industry exerted through the relatively high presence of American franchise chains (30 percent of all franchise hotels surveyed), American managers, the tourists themselves, and American expatriate settlers hired to work in upper-management positions and in the local recreation industry.

3. The data for this chapter were collected in the context of a broader study examining tourism and agriculture relationships in Quintana Roo. During sixteen months (1996–1997) of fieldwork conducted in the Yucatán Peninsula, this study employed an integrated approach utilizing both quantitative and qualitative methods. The quantitative component included extensive surveys of sixty Cancún hotels and 615 Yucatán Peninsula tourists. The qualitative component of the research included in-depth interviews with tourists, Cancún tourism industry food suppliers, *ejido comisariados*, and farmers, as well as a one-year case study of a Cancún

milpero (shifting-cultivation subsistence farmer) and his family. While all elements of this research inform the analysis in this article, the majority of the data presented is from the hotel survey, and to a lesser extent, the tourist survey.

4. Transnational perspectives are useful in understanding the production of Cancún as a distinct transnational hybrid-space, with complex linkages spanning international, urban, and rural spheres. Lury (1997) suggests the creation of a new "in-between" tourist space of "artefacts and flows" in which the lines are blurred between traveling and dwelling. Cancún, which from its inception was planned as a consumption space for international tourists, constitutes this "in-between" transnational tourism space. Torres Maldonado (1997) sees Cancún as a "post-industrial tourist place" that has succeeded in reinserting the peripheral "empty quarter" into global capitalist space.

5. Edensor (2001) conceptualizes tourist space as "stages" upon which tourists exhibit different modes of "performance." In particular, Cancún fits with Edensor's notion of "enclavic" space which is typical of a carefully planned, managed, and segregated tourist bubble.

6. Postmodern concepts of transnational social space, such as "hyper-space" (Jameson 1984), "ethnoscapes" (Appadurai 1990, 1996), and "imagined communities" (Appadurai 1996), are also useful in conceptualizing Cancún as a globalized, reconstructed, hybrid social and cultural space. Appadurai's notion of "imagined worlds," constituting the collective imaginations of people stretching across the globe, is also useful (1996).

PART II

Cultural Adventures

CHAPTER FOUR

"The Beat Trail to Mexico,"
from *American and British Writers*
in Mexico, 1556–1973

Drewey Wayne Gunn

"Behind us lay the whole of America and everything Dean and I had previously known about life, and life on the road. We had finally found the magic land at the end of the road and we never dreamed the extent of the magic."[1] Thus, Jack Kerouac described Mexico as it appeared to many of his generation. This was in his book *On the Road* (1957), which introduced to most Americans a new breed of bohemians, the beatniks. Kerouac and his friends, particularly Allen Ginsberg and William Burroughs (to be joined later by others, like Gregory Corso and Lawrence Ferlinghetti), formed an inner circle of the Beat literary scene, sensitive to the new directions American youths were exploring. They held ambivalent feelings toward the United States, brought on by such circumstances as the threat of the atomic bomb, the destruction of the old Left in an increasingly conservative atmosphere (climaxing in McCarthyism), and the general uncertainty of the cold war. Rejecting almost all the values of the middle class, which seemed somehow responsible for these things, they were drawn variously to the criminal, the primitive, the exotic, and the hallucinatory—anything on the far edge of society.

Consequently Mexico, the nearest alien culture to America's, provided magic. Since apparently none of them, contrary to what they thought, actually entered into the life of that country, they easily imagined existing there whatever conditions satisfied their needs. Mexico was primitive. It seemed free, presenting, as Kerouac later explained in an essay (echoing undoubtedly Spengler's use of the word *fellaheen*), a "fellaheen feeling about life, that timeless gayety of people not involved in great cultural and civilization issues."[2]

And drugs were easily available. Because drugs so often provided an escape, these five writers seem superficially to have followed the paths that Hart Crane and Malcolm Lowry had mapped. Perhaps Burroughs and Corso, and later Kerouac experienced a disquieting sensation in Mexico; but Ginsberg and Kerouac at first plunged into the foreignness of the place with a kind of joyful abandon, devoid of fear, even at their worst radiating a saintly innocence. Ferlinghetti alone of their number held B. Traven's political interests, the others having only a very generalized belief in anarchy; but Traven (as Kenneth Rexroth, a sort of elder statesman for the Beats, observed) was their real antecedent in Mexico.[3] Dean in *On the Road* summed up:

> There's no *suspicion* here, nothing like that. Everybody's cool, everybody looks at you with such straight brown eyes and they don't say anything, just *look*, and in that look all of the human qualities are soft and subdued and still there. Dig all the foolish stories you read about Mexico and the sleeping gringo and all that crap—and crap about greasers and so on—and all it is, people here are straight and kind and don't put down any bull.[4]

Kerouac (1922–1969) first entered the country in the summer of 1950 in company with Neal Cassady—the Dean Moriaty of *On the Road* and perhaps the archetypal Beat—and another youth. Since the novel (written in 1951), like all of Kerouac's, provides a Wolfe-like transcription of actual events, it is fairly easy to follow the thread of Kerouac's Mexican life.[5] For two years he, Cassady, and others had whizzed back and forth across the United States. Kerouac was attracted by the apparently simple life of the Mexican Americans, and he lived with them in California for a while. Then he and Cassady turned south, crossing the Mexican border at Nuevo Laredo, and "bearded, bedraggled" drove along the Inter-American highway almost nonstop to Mexico City. One respite did come in Ciudad Victoria. There they discovered a Mexican youth who provided them with marijuana and directions to the red-light district, where they spent a wild afternoon. Everywhere the police amazed them: the courteous officials at the border, the quiet ones outside the whorehouses, the sheriff at the little town below Victoria where they pulled the car over and slept the night. Of this man Kerouac wrote: "Such lovely policemen God hath never wrought in America. No suspicions, no fuss, no bother: he was the guardian of the sleeping town, period."[6]

Undisturbed by filth and poverty, they felt at one with the Indian earth and its people, excited equally by the gaunt landscape around Monterrey and Mexico City and the lush jungles in between. Yet ironically, although Kerouac wanted to identify with the natives, he was slightly depressed by their naïveté concerning the direction the world seemed to be taking since Hiroshima. He wrote about one group they met on the highway:

> They had come down from the back mountains and higher places to hold forth their hands for something they thought civilization could offer, and they never dreamed the madness and the poor broken delusion of it. They didn't know that a bomb had come that could crack all our bridges and roads and reduce them to jumbles, and we would be as poor as they someday, and stretching out our hands in the same, same way.

Still his general exhilaration continued all the way to the capital, "the great and final wild uninhibited Fellahin-childlike city that we knew we would find at the end of the road."[7] In Mexico City, Kerouac stayed with the Burroughses, who had just arrived. The Mexicans seemed to them all completely free in contrast with the people in the tight American cities. Kerouac's happiness lasted even through his becoming ill and Cassady's simply leaving him to make his way back to the States as best he could.

Kerouac's next visit began in May 1952.[8] By now, he had published one rather conventional novel, but no publisher liked the direction Kerouac had then taken, as he turned out almost automatically a stream of rambling, picaresque works. He felt at loose ends. Entering Mexico at Nogales, he made his way down the west coast on a second-class bus in company with two Mexican youths whom he had met at a rest stop. Together they sought out marijuana, opium, and other stimuli. By the time he arrived in Mexico City, he was completely broke and depended for the rest of his visit on the generosity of Burroughs. This trip Kerouac described in the essay "Mexico Fellaheen," published in *Lonesome Traveler* (1960). He glimpsed this time something of Mexico's somber side. A bullfight, the bloody image of Christ in all the churches, reminders of the Aztec rites—all suggested to him the grimness of mortality. In June he worked on a novel, *Doctor Sax: Faust Part Three* (1959), while sitting on Burroughs's toilet in order to escape all the junkies coming in and out of the house. This rather impressive novel concerns the nightmarish fantasies that come to a boy growing up in Massachusetts. Intertwined in them is Doctor Sax, a character considerably influenced in its delineation by the figure of Burroughs. By using symbolically the picture of the great Mexican eagle destroying the serpent, Kerouac ended his novel hopefully. Earlier he had said that "Doctor Sax made a special trip to Teotehuacan [*sic*] Mexico, to do his special research on the culture of the eagle and the snake—Azteca; he came back laden with information about the snake, none about the bird."[9] But the doctor too sees clearly the meaning of the final vision and thereafter "deals in glee" (here Kerouac was creating fiction, not a portrait of Burroughs). Throughout the novel are scattered other references to the country, and it is permeated with the ambivalent feeling Kerouac held toward Mexico at this time.

William Seward Burroughs (1914–1997), Kerouac's and Ginsberg's mentor, had come with his wife to Mexico in order to escape legal conviction as an addict.[10] Although he agreed, as he wrote in *Naked Lunch*, that "something falls off you when you cross the border into Mexico," he lacked the childlike wonder that Kerouac generally managed to maintain.[11] To Burroughs the land was "a sinister place." These were the years of Miguel Alemán's presidency, when spectacular gains were being achieved, including the building of the new University City, but when corruption was rampant. Many people went around armed. Burroughs too bought a gun; shortly afterward, while he was cleaning it, it went off and killed his wife. His drug-induced paranoia also distorted the scene. He tried several times to find a cure, but cocaine, heroin, marijuana, peyote, and others drugs came to hand too readily. There were even dangers provided by tequila, as he discovered when he almost died of uremic poisoning. Nevertheless, he felt "safe in Mexico" to make his contacts and watch "refugee hipsters," including William Garver, fleeing from the growing conservatism of the United States. Yet Burroughs was bored. For a while he attended Mexico City College. Then about 1950 he began to write a number of letters to Ginsberg in which he tried to describe, as he has said in an interview, "in a more-or-less straightforward journalistic style something about my experiences with addiction and addicts."[12] From these grew his first book, *Junkie*, published in 1953 under the pseudonym William Lee.

This book, like all his works, moves uneasily among fragmented memories, extended scenes, and expository digressions. Had he not gone on to make his later stylistic and structural experiments, beginning with *Naked Lunch*, we would ignore *Junkie*. But since it depicts objectively the experiences of an addict rather than attempting to re-create subjectively those experiences as his later books do, it provides a useful introduction both to Burroughs's world and to that of the hard-drug scene. Here we find none of De Quincey's ornate descriptions; instead we possess simple and generally ugly insights into the routine life of a man totally committed to "junkie sickness." The fictionalized autobiography begins with Burroughs's first acquaintance with morphine near the end of World War II and continues through several brushes with the law in New York and New Orleans. In these scenes he is in familiar surroundings, however, and the world does not seem particularly scary. But after his flight to Mexico, the pattern expands, spinning off increasingly abhorrent visions: "A series of faces, hieroglyphics, distorted and leading to the final place where the human road ends, where the human form can no longer contain the crustacean horror that has grown inside it."[13] The book finishes with his decision to move on to South America in July 1952 in order to look for "the final fix" in yage (an experience recounted in *The Yage Letters*, 1963, coauthored with Ginsberg, who likewise traveled to South America in 1960). By 1952, Burroughs seemed possessed.

After this journey, he moved to Algiers. There he began creating the vignettes that he would eventually combine into *Naked Lunch* (1959). His paranoia had convinced him that an intricate system, though it was slowly falling apart, controlled the world. Even before he went to Mexico, he had been fascinated by the undeciphered Mayan codices and saw in the Mayan calendar an earlier system whereby the priests could control even the most minute activities of the people. Drugs were another total control system: "Junk takes everything and gives nothing but insurance against junk sickness," he had written in his first book.[14] Thus, if he examined his life as an addict, especially the horrible visions that had matured in those years in Mexico, he could explore these systems, past and present. Moreover, he thought that drugs provided a heightened sense of reality and an escape from the limitations of space and time. These thoughts in part inform the rationale behind *Naked Lunch*—and later *The Soft Machine* (1961), especially in a chapter called "The Mayan Caper," and *The Wild Boys* (1971). What we get in these novels is homosexual science fiction, sometimes frightening in its continual emphasis on death and pain, sometimes humorous, almost always nauseating. Totally devoid of plot and at times even sense, except perhaps to another addict, these books can be read by cutting into them anywhere one pleases. None of Burroughs's experimental novels satisfy, but none can be easily forgotten.[15]

Allen Ginsberg (1926–1997) had planned to visit Burroughs while Burroughs was in Mexico, but the poet was unable to come until 1954.[16] Then he arrived by way of Cuba to explore the Maya country. He visited Chichen Itza, Tulum, Uxmal, Kabah, Palenque, Piedras Negras, and Yaxchilan, camping out at several of the sites. It was his first encounter with an ancient civilization. Later he recalled, "Like Shelley in Italy, I was busy poking around big history-less Mayan ruins and wandering all over alone, absorbing that kind of antiquity and sense of transience and thinking up big long poems about native grounds." The only one he has published is "Siesta in Xbalba," published in *Evergreen Review* in 1957 and collected in *Reality Sandwiches* in 1963. He wrote it, according to his note appended to the poem, in an area believed by the Maya to be inhabited by the Xibalba (as the word is usually spelled), or "people of the underworld," at the foot of a large tree to which "ancient craftsmen came to complete work left unfinished at their death."

Musing upon the "alien hieroglyphs of Eternity," he used the moment to take stock of the present:

> above the abandoned
> labyrinth of Palenque
>   measuring my fate,
> wandering solitary in the wild
>   —blinking singleminded
> at a bleak idea—
>   until exhausted with
> its action and contemplation
>   my soul might shatter
> at one primal moment's
>   sensation of the vast
> movement of divinity.

All the associations of his past, framed as by a camera in his mind, juxtapose themselves against the incredible ruins he had explored, "sunken under the flood of years" and

> leaving many mysteries
> of deathly volition
> to be divined.

But the future also intersected both his desire to visit the other classic places of the world (India and Greece later influenced him) and his pilgrimage toward the final "future, unimaginable God." The poem, grounded firmly in the realities of the area—his catalogue of the sites is unmatchable—remains one of his finest achievements.

Ginsberg must have met Karena Shields, to whom the poem is dedicated, at Palenque. A retired movie actress and later author of a memoir about her childhood on a rubber plantation in Mexico, *The Changing Wind* (1959), she invited Ginsberg to her *finca* near the Guatemala border. Several months later, he headed north to California to visit Cassady. This journey became the basis for a companion poem, "Return to the States." Though working with some of the same themes, especially in his contemplation of the mummies of Guanajuato, the poem fails to equal "Siesta." Bits of local color—a view of Lake Catemaco, a scene from San Miguel de Allende, the slums of Mexicali—and the frightening view of the United States with which the poem closes do not cohere, and the whole work seems anticlimactic after the perfection of "Siesta."[17] But he was preparing for "Howl" and its condemnation of America; from the introspective moment in Mexico he was "Returning / armed with

New Testament." Ginsberg also alluded to the country in a number of his other poems, including a touching tribute to Burroughs's wife and her unvisited grave, "Dream Record, June 8, 1955," likewise included in *Reality Sandwiches*.

In the summer of 1955, Kerouac returned to Mexico City, living in the servant's room above William Garver's house, where the Burroughses had lived. Kerouac met Esperanza Villanueva, an Indian girl, and began the affair with her described in his novel *Tristessa* (1960).[18] In three weeks he improvised the 242 choruses of *Mexico City Blues* (1956), which had a strong influence on Ginsberg's poetry. The poems are wild chants, composed—some while under the influence of drugs—more for sound than sense, but they seem appropriate to the depressed mood in which Mexico then left Kerouac. Later that summer he left for Berkeley to join Ginsberg and the large number of other poets who would effect the San Francisco poetry renaissance. That winter Kerouac returned home briefly to North Carolina, catching glimpses on the way there and back of Mexicali and Juarez (described in *The Dharma Bums*, 1958).[19] But both times nothing seemed right; he got a "vomity feeling." He was supposed to return to Esperanza Villanueva in the spring, but he had run out of money. They exchanged letters in which he eventually confessed that he loved her. Some of the fantasies assembled in *Book of Dreams* (1961), which often recall Mexico, may come from this same period.

In the fall of 1956 Kerouac returned to Mexico City.[20] He wrote in *Desolation Angels* (1965), the record of this visit, that he always remembered Mexico at a distance as "gay, exciting," but when he returned he would find that he had "forgotten a certain drear, even sad, darkness."[21] The relationship with Esperanza Villanueva soon failed. As Kerouac remembered in the second half of *Tristessa*, finished almost as soon as the episode itself, she was now sick and looked at him with hatred, and her friends robbed him. At a party she fell over, spitting blood; thinking that she was dying, Kerouac tried to get help. "My poems stolen, my money stolen, my Tristessa dying, Mexican buses trying to run me down, grit in the sky, agh, I never dreamed it could be this bad," he wrote. Their later reunion was tender, but obviously the affair would not work, and so they separated.

In October Kerouac learned that Ginsberg was coming down for a visit. Ginsberg dashed off a poem, "Ready to Roll," in San Francisco in anticipation of the journey; it too is collected in *Reality Sandwiches*. Ginsberg traveled down the west coast with his companion, Peter Orlovsky, Orlovsky's brother, and Gregory Corso. The four men stopped briefly in Guadalajara to see Denise Levertov and Mitchell Goodman, and then walked casually into the Garver household. Ginsberg was perfectly content and rushed around to all the sights of the capital: University City, Teotihuacan, Xochimilco. But Corso (1930–2001) felt less assured, finding the same frightening conditions that he had observed in the United States. Kerouac in *Desolation Angels* remembered Corso's saying, "There's *death* in Mexico—I saw a windmill turning death this way—I don't *like* it here." This attitude permeated *Gasoline* (1958), a collection of poems Corso was writing during the trip. In one of them he summed up his disappointment less flamboyantly by pointing out:

> In the Mexican Zoo
> they have ordinary
> American cows.[22]

At Corso's urging, the five men decided to return to the States, since at least there Corso could be comfortable if not content. Garver had become gravely ill (he died soon thereafter) and begged them not to leave him. But late that November they slipped out and made their way north to Nuevo Laredo. For the others it was apparently their last trip to Mexico, but Kerouac crossed at Juarez in 1957 to show his mother something of the country and returned to Mexico City in 1961 to finish the second half of *Desolation Angels*.[23]

These writers represented the East Coast in the Beat world; Lawrence Ferlinghetti (1919–) was a chief figure of the West Coast. He too went to Mexico, having visited the country first before World War II and then a few times in the 1950s. But most of the notes, poems (both in English and Spanish), and drawings collected in *The Mexican Night: Travel Journal by Ferlinghetti* (1970) date from the 1960s.[24] Though entertaining and oftentimes perceptive, Ferlinghetti's early comments offer no really new insight; "the new Mexico still the Old Beat Mexico," he jotted down. Narcotics and the stupidities of artificial borders remain a theme. In 1961 he reexplored Baja California, the towns of which he found hopelessly depressing. In 1962 he traveled over the new railroad opened between Chihuahua and Topolobampo through some of the most spectacular scenery in North America, but it was for him a "wild junkie landscape."

In his attack on borders, Ferlinghetti had echoed the revolutionary note that sounds in much of his writing. When he returned in the fall of 1968 to visit Oaxaca and Mexico City and again in the spring of 1969 to Guadalajara, this theme strongly focused his observations. In fall 1968, Mexican students were actively criticizing the government for spending too much money on the Olympics soon to open in Mexico City while so many of its people were going hungry. In one angry confrontation that October, an unknown number of students were killed and more arrested. Thus Ferlinghetti had forced upon him the fact that life in Mexico is fully as complicated as that in the United States. He commented bitterly—and sometimes not very lucidly—on this state of affairs, the only notable American writer so far to have done so. He felt personally involved. Two of his friends, Margaret Randall and Robert Cohen, had lost the backing they previously enjoyed from the government when their little magazine, *El Corno Emplumado*, supported the students, and they finally felt that they must flee the country. Ferlinghetti reproduced a letter setting forth their version of this troubled period in *The Mexican Night* immediately following his poem commemorating the spirit of Che Guevara. But by mid-March 1969, when he settled in San Miguel de Allende to start working over Cassady's manuscripts, his notes seem like excerpts from Kerouac's apolitical vision. Obviously Ferlinghetti was fascinated by Mexico (he also visited South America in 1960) or he would not have returned so often, but it seems ultimately to have influenced his life much less than it did earlier Beats. *The Mexican Night*, however, is quite pleasant, often capturing some scene perfectly.

Other writers came during the 1960s, but they in general found little to incorporate into their writing. Thomas Pynchon (1937–) finished *V.* there early in the decade,[25] and the heroine of his second novel, *The Crying of Lot 49* (1966), remembers a trip to Mazatlan. Terry Southern (1926–) may have visited about the same time; his Burroughs-like story "The Road Out of Axotle" appeared in *Esquire* in 1962 (it was collected in *Red-Dirt Marijuana*, 1967). Michael McClure (1932–) composed a number of his *Ghost Tantras* (1967) in Mexico City.[26] Richard Brautigan (1935–) took the main characters of *The Abortion: An Historical Romance 1966* (1971) to Tijuana. The most dramatic episode, however, was left for Ken Kesey (1935–), who arrived in 1966.[27] He had jumped bail, arranged for his second arrest on charges of possessing marijuana, faked a suicide, and then fled to Puerto Vallarta and later Manzanillo. For several months, in company with Cassady and others, he played an elaborate game of cops and robbers, described in a fragmented way in a series of fifteen letters to Larry McMurtry, published in 1967 in a limited edition, and in a screen play, "Over the Border," published in *Kesey's Garage Sale* (1973). Mexico scarcely presents itself in these works except as a fearful setting in which his pursuers could hide away: we return to the paranoia of Burroughs.

By now most of the hippies were demanding in the United States the same freedom to do as they pleased that the beatniks had sought in Mexico. Flight south would no longer suffice, as Kesey discovered—he soon slipped back into the States—and as perhaps Cassady foresaw before he fell dead on the railroad tracks outside San Miguel de Allende in February 1968. The Mexican government, as the new youth movement became worldwide, also began to look upon the beatnik type in an unfriendly fashion, and officials no longer greeted bearded and bedraggled visitors with the same warmth Kerouac and Cassady had received twenty years earlier. A number of communes managed to spring up, especially in areas where peyote and the magic mush-room grow, but these groups tend to be completely anti-intellectual and do not express themselves in writing.

In fact, one of the surprising aspects of the Beat movement was its extreme literacy. Though the writers (except Ferlinghetti) were less knowledgeable about Mexico than other writers had generally been, their reading ranged widely from European existentialists to Eastern sages. Their ultimate worth as a group remains to be seen. Kerouac, Ginsberg, and Burroughs, and to a lesser extent Corso and Ferlinghetti, have all been extravagantly praised and equally damned at various points in their careers, but remarkably little attempt has been made to examine their work critically.[28] Perhaps they were a fad. As Imamu Amiri Baraka (LeRoi Jones) remarked in one of his poems in the early sixties:

> Beatniks, like Bohemians, go calmly out of style. And boys
> are dying in Mexico, who did not get the word.[29]

Nevertheless, their influence at the moment was considerable, even on Latin American writers, and their writing in a period of flaccidity was among the best.

They also point up most clearly the American writer's repeated need—not just the beatnik's—to escape from his own culture for perspective, and they emphasize Mexico again as a possible direction to go. In the oftentimes wild-ness of their flight, the Beats represent an extreme, as they did in other aspects of their lives, but it was in a direction perceived by almost every other visitor to Mexico from the United States. They are set apart, however, by their gregariousness; they formed the only noteworthy group to have worked together in Mexico. And they differ from most other writers in their reactions to primitivism. Whereas Lawrence, Huxley, and others before the war rejected this way of life, the Beats (except Corso) left Mexico for the more alien worlds of South America, Algeria, and India, moving deeper and deeper into such cultures, before returning to America.

Notes

1. Jack Kerouac, *On the Road* (New York: Viking Press, 1957), 276.
2. Jack Kerouac, *Lonesome Traveler* (New York: McGraw-Hill, 1960), 27.
3. Thomas Parkinson, ed., *A Casebook on the Beat* (New York: Crowell, 1961), 186.
4. Kerouac, *On the Road*, 278.
5. Kerouac, *On the Road*, 274–306. Also, Ann Charters, *Kerouac: A Biography* (London: Deutsch, 1974), 124–25. Charters also prepared a bibliography.
6. Kerouac, *On the Road*, 295.
7. Kerouac, *On the Road*, 299.
8. Kerouac, *Lonesome Traveler*, 21–36; see also, Charters, *Kerouac*, 158–69.

9. Jack Kerouac, *Doctor Sax* (New York: Grove, 1959), 149; Ted Berigan, interview with Jack Kerouac, *Paris Review* 43 (Summer 1968): 84.

10. William S. Burroughs, *Junkie*, introd. by Carl Solomon 5–6, 98–126; George Plimpton, ed., *Writers at Work: The Paris Review Interviews*, third series, introd. by Alfred Kazin (New York: Penguin, 1977), 145, 163, 167; William S. Burroughs Jr., "Life with Father," *Esquire* 76 (September 1971): 113.

11. William S. Burroughs, *Naked Lunch* (New York: Grove, 1962), 14.

12. Plimpton, *Writers at Work*, 145.

13. Burroughs, *Junkie*, 112.

14. Burroughs, *Junkie*, 106.

15. Daniel Odier, *The Job: Interviews with William S. Burroughs* (New York: Grove, 1974), 28–36, 171; Kerouac, *On the Road*, 144. See also, Burroughs, *Naked Lunch*, 233; William S. Burroughs, *The Soft Machine* (New York: Grove, 1966), 12–29, 85–97; and William S. Burroughs, *The Wild Boys* (New York: Grove, 1971), first section.

16. Jane Kramer, *Allen Ginsberg in America* (New York: Random House, 1969), 40, 120, 137–38, 161; Charters, *Kerouac*, 201–202.

17. Allen Ginsberg, *Reality Sandwiches, 1953–1960* (San Francisco: City Lights Books, 1963), 21–39. Edward Z. Menkin prepared a bibliography.

18. Jack Kerouac, *Tristessa* (New York: Avon Book, 1960); Berigan, interview, 91–92, 101; Charters, *Kerouac*, 217–29.

19. Jack Kerouac, *The Dharma Bums* (New York: Viking Press, 1958), 124–26, 155–56.

20. Jack Kerouac, *Desolation Angels*, introd. by Seymour Krim (New York: Coward-McCann, 1965), ix-xxviii, 221–57; Charters, *Kerouac*, 272–77.

21. Kerouac, *Desolation Angels*, 222.

22. Gregory Corso, "Mexican Impressions," in *Gasoline*, introd. by Allen Ginsberg (San Francisco: City Lights Books, 1958), 7, 23–26. Robert A. Wilson prepared a bibliography. Kerouac, *Desolation Angels*, 234. The possible Corso character is called Raphael Urso, while the possible Ginsberg character is called Irwin Garden.

23. Kerouac, *Desolation Angels*, 342–46; Charters, *Kerouac*, 340–41.

24. See Lawrence Ferlinghetti, *The Mexican Night: Travel Journal by Ferlinghetti* (New York: New Directions, 1970).

25. *Contemporary Authors* (Detroit, Mich.: Gale Research), vols. 19–20, pp. 352–53.

26. Michael McClure, *Ghost Tantras* (San Francisco: City Lights Books, 1964), 26–27.

27. Tom Wolfe, *The Electric Kool-Aid Acid Test* (New York: Farrar, Straus and Giroux, 1968), 301–62; Jerome Charyn, ed., *The Single Voice: An Anthology of Contemporary Fiction* (New York: Collier Books, 1969), 414–26.

28. Harry Russell Huebel, professor of history at Texas A&I University, who helpfully criticized this chapter, finished a dissertation on the subject at Washington State University, 1970; Bruce Cook, *The Beat Generation* (New York: Scribner, 1971).

29. LeRoi Jones, "The New World," in *Black Magic*, 22.

CHAPTER FIVE

"Dangerous Journeys: Mexico City College Students and the Mexican Landscape, 1954–1962"

Richard W. Wilkie

Driving over the crest of a low rolling hill as the first sunlight of the morning began to break across the highest points of the landscape, I could see a valley ahead at a lower elevation that was filled with early morning fog. Only a far distant church steeple and the tops of a few other rolling hills with scattered trees stood out above the mist. As the car dipped down into the fog, reminiscent of an airplane diving into a cloud, everything turned dark again. After a few kilometers, dark shadows of what turned out to be men, women, children, and an occasional horseman appeared as gray ghosts along the roadside, all heading in the same direction that I was driving. I could now see that the sun was beginning to burn its way through the ground fog that was slowly beginning to rise as it was warmed by the sun. The number of walking figures began to increase and then to merge with two other streams of people and animals moving toward an intersection, where a cobbled road turned left and disappeared back into the mist. My traveling companions were still asleep, as I instinctively turned left to join the slow stream of people with loads on their backs, horseback riders, and a few heavily loaded horse- and cattle-drawn carts. Our open car—idling along at the speed of the walkers—was the only nontraditional means of transportation in this expanding flow of travelers, and it seemed as though we were invisible to everyone else, since no one looked at us or made any attempt to move over to let us pass. Not that I wanted to pass. It was exhilarating being part of this extraordinary procession in the mist.

Within minutes I also began to hear a church bell ringing in the distance. With the sun rising in the direction we were headed, the fog began to break up rapidly with rays of sunlight penetrating through and falling onto the travelers and the still damp roadway. The rounded shapes of the cobblestones glistened as the light rays bounced off them and into my vision. Looking directly toward the sun through the mist created a perspective of penetrating light rays that was very powerful. This scene with rural *Tarascan* Indians wearing broad-brimmed sombreros, ponchos of muted natural colors over white outfits, and huaraches on their feet as they slowly walked toward those rays of light, accompanied by the sounds of a distant bell and the clatter of horseshoes and metal cart wheels on that cobbled roadway, is a picture that will be etched forever into my memory. As I glided almost silently through this scene, I felt the magnetic pull on my soul of the Mexican landscape, its people, and its history, and that pull has never left. I vividly remember to this day my feelings of awe and appreciation of the scene I was witnessing.

Five of us were driving from northern California on our way to Mexico City College in September 1956, and this was my first real encounter with a Mexican village. We had entered Mexico at Nogales in a yellow 1940s convertible pulling a small trailer. It had taken three days to drive the west coast highway to Guadalajara, where my brother and I and three companions had an evening of celebratory carousing in a mariachi-filled nightspot. I had decided not to drink and to watch over our group. Since we were behind schedule, we set out in the middle of the night after closing time on old Route 15 heading toward Morelia and Mexico City. Somewhere in the state of Jalisco, south of Lake Chapala near Tuxcuenca, or perhaps across the border in the state of Michoacán, I first experienced "Village Mexico."

Village Mexico was still a strong reality in the 1950s. At that time there were very few cars and trucks on the roads, and nearly three out of every five of all Mexicans lived either in rural villages with populations under 2,500 inhabitants (51 percent) or dispersed across the rural landscape in isolated homesteads (7 percent). Throughout most of southern "Mesoamerican" Mexico, close to 80 percent of the people lived rural lives in the 1950s—not greatly changed from the 90 percent who were rural in the entire country when the revolution began in 1910.

Time and Place in Mexico in the 1950s

I have thought about that initial event many times over the past half century, wondering if I could return and find that place. But I never traveled that particular road again, and I never returned to that village. I do not even know its name. Thus one of my earliest and most powerful memories of Mexico is also one of my most elusive, in that I was never to repeat that first dream-like experience with Village Mexico in the same way.

But of course, that village scene at present is exceedingly rare in Mexico, although I still know a few remote places that represent an earlier landscape and time. Today, villages that had two thousand people in the 1950s are mostly urban centers of twenty thousand or more. The population of Mexico rose fourfold between 1950 and 2000 to nearly 100 million, with nearly half the population of the country living in the twenty-six largest metropolitan areas. Mexico City's current extended metropolitan population of nearly 25 million equals that of all of Mexico in 1950, while the proportion of those dwelling in rural villages has dropped to only 15 percent—fewer than one person out of every six.

The appreciation of a "sense of time and place" in Mexico has both personal and intellectual aspects. My brother and I had an apartment in Mexico City on the Paseo de la Reforma near the corner of Río Neva from 1956 to 1957. That first fall term I spent a lot of time in the afternoon studying outside on the old stone benches along the Reforma. Traffic along the Reforma in September 1956 was virtually nonexistent compared to the present, and the greenery and trees on the broad islands along either side of that great boulevard were ideal places to read, study, and people-watch at the same time. In those days well-dressed horsemen wearing large Mexican sombreros would still pass by occasionally on the hard-packed earth pathways that today are tilled and covered. When I had time to break from my studies, I read books about the historical events that occurred in Mexico City, many of which turned out to have taken place along the Reforma. While reading Prescott's book on the conquest of Mexico, I envisioned how Cortez and his men fought their way out of Tenochtitlán, the island Aztec capital on what is now called Lake Texcoco, along the southern causeway very close to where I sat reading. I also read books on the U.S. invasion of Mexico under General Scott in 1848—only a century before—and how his men fought up the Reforma to capture Chapultepec Castle from the *Niños Heroes*. I remember how extraordinary it felt to be reading at the precise place where history had been made in the sixteenth and nineteenth centuries. Little did I know then that two blocks away from where I sat thinking about those earlier events, Che Guevara was living with his Peruvian-born wife, Hilda Gadea Acosta. Their apartment was at 40 Calle Nápoles, Apt. 5, near the corner of the block with Calle Hamburgo in the Pink Zone. Between September and late November, Fidel Castro and his lieutenants came to Guevara's apartment from time to time to plan the invasion of Cuba. On many occasions during that fall, I played pool with my friend Murray in a second-story pool hall on the corner of that block, not knowing what was happening in the building next door in Che Guevara's apartment.

History seems to remember those events of the past that involve conquest, invasion, revolution, death, and destruction. Clearly those are turning points in history when societies are going through dynamic periods of upheaval and change. In my case, I do not think that I was drawn to the violence of those events, but more to the drama in the clashing worlds of ideas, ideologies, and often completely different worldviews of the combatants. My point in telling the previous story is that I was caught up with being at the place where two major turning points in Mexican history had occurred—the conquest of the Aztec by Cortez and his men and the U.S. invasion and conquest of Mexico City and Chapultepec Castle that I could see just down the Reforma from where I sat reading. But I was completely oblivious to the history that was going on figuratively under my feet with regard to the Cuban Revolution.

The juxtaposition of those events helps to point out what I feel is one major element of life in Mexico: that one is surrounded at all times by a sense that the unexpected can occur at any moment, that often there is a sharp contrast between the surface appearance and the reality, and that sometimes very different events happen in the same place at the same time—each unrelated to the other. This concept might be called the "unexpected juxtaposition of events"—historically, as in the above case, but also when viewing life in the city. Some of these daily events would be considered once-in-a-lifetime occurrences in the United States. Surviving the volatility of unexpected events was a skill that Mexico City College students were forced to hone and bring into play, if not daily, then quite frequently. Even though danger and the possibility of death were in the air at all times, I do not remember my friends worrying about it. It was just a fact of life, as were the reality of the potential for natural disasters such as earthquakes and volcanic eruptions.

Regarding the latter, I always felt that the title of Malcolm Lowry's book *Under the Volcano* (1947) best captured the feeling for me of my time in Mexico. In the late 1950s it was still possible to see clearly Popocatepetl and Ixtacihuatl virtually every day, and we even climbed them along with other mountains and volcanoes. But the concept of the "volcano" was also a metaphor for life in Mexico City and the countryside, where the most peaceful scene could suddenly explode into fast and furious action and sometimes violence and death. A number of my friends and acquaintances died or nearly died in Mexico at that time. There was a saying then that "half of the students will probably go on to get PhD degrees and something bad will probably happen to the other half."

A Brief History of Mexico City College

The life of American students at Mexico City College (MCC) in the mid-1950s to the early 1960s was one of constant excitement in a multidimensional world of cultural diversity, an ambience of sights, sounds, color, and most of all, opportunities for adventure. The orderly, linear expectations of one's family, friends, and community that often directed one's life path at home—school, girlfriend, marriage, children, car, home, job for life, grandchildren—were dramatically altered in a number of ways once one entered Mexico. One of those ways was that in Mexico people were most often respected and honored for what made them different and unique—in contrast with life in the States during the 1950s when people were most often respected and judged by how much they conformed to a common ideal and how well they fit in as a member of the group.

Another important factor in the lives of MCC students was the fact that nearly half the students were military veterans of World War II, the Korean War, or of occupation duty in Japan or Europe. These ex-GIs were sophisticated and somewhat jaded, and they desperately wanted to avoid the bland college experience in the States, which was often dominated by the fraternities and sororities that were so appealing to younger students directly out of high school. Most ex-GIs were between the ages of twenty-five and thirty-five, and most had experienced the world in times of turmoil. These veterans thrived in the diversity and excitement of the Mexican cultural environment that they found at MCC, and in the international lifestyle of one of the world's oldest and grandest cities. Some of these veteran GI expatriates were developing skills as writers, artists, and critics, and since Paris of the 1920s no longer existed, they were searching for that kind of ambience and lifestyle. In many ways Mexico in the 1950s felt frozen somewhere in time between the two world wars. The Mexican Revolution (1910–1925), with sporadic conflicts up to 1940 or so, had put modernization into a holding pattern throughout the country. Parts of Mexico City located between Chapultepec Castle and the Central Zocalo had recognizable elements of Paris in the 1920s—more so than any other Latin America city except Buenos Aires. For many of the intellectually oriented veterans and students at MCC, this was potentially the new Paris where ideas, art, literature, and revolution could be discussed in cafes, taverns, and at numerous and risqué parties where inexpensive liquor and "Acapulco gold" could be found.

Though GI veterans made up between 40 and 50 percent of the student body at MCC, they were far from a homogeneous group. Aside from being mostly male and ten to fifteen years older than the other students, they were as diverse in their aspirations and lifestyles as the rest of the student body. In attempting to assess the different subcultural groups at the college, I want first to define the group in which my brother Jim and I fit most closely. We were among a group of students who came to explore new worlds, to discover new ways of seeing and thinking, to help open new roads to remote places, to climb snow-capped volcanoes and explore all of southern Mexico, to feel the historical and artistic heartbeat of Mexico, and to do it with companions who thrived in the extraordinary milieu that existed there at that time (see fig. 5.1). Having the chance to live and study in Mexico City was adventure enough, but when all the natural and human landscapes of southern and central Mexico became part of the experiential classroom, the education that each of us received went far beyond anything most of us had anticipated.

Mexico City College was unique because it was the only American liberal arts college south of the Rio Grande, and one of only several in the world in the 1950s. Students at MCC frequently discussed the only other options, Sofia University in Tokyo, Japan, and the American University in Beirut, Lebanon, but because of distance and cost, those academic institutions were

Figure 5.1. Four Mexico City College students and future professors at a roadside cantina, March 1958. From left: James Wilkie, Colin MacLachlan, James Hamon, and Richard Wilkie. Photo courtesy of Richard W. Wilkie.

something for most of us to only fantasize about. MCC had it all: proximity to the United States, moderate costs, membership in the Association of Southern Universities (so that credits transferred easily to the States), and most of all, location in a country that was a fascinating and inspiring place to be. Mexico added a dangerous and volatile element to our daily lives, but there was also a sense of "power of place" in a landscape and people that could not be matched anywhere else at that time.

Mexico City College was quite young, even younger than I was as an eighteen-year-old freshmen in fall quarter 1956. Henry L. Cain and Paul V. Murray had founded the college in 1940 in downtown Mexico City with a nucleus of five teachers, six students, and no books. The college grew beyond its earlier scattered buildings in downtown Mexico City, and in 1954 it moved to a new campus with room to expand on the site of an old country club located west of downtown Mexico City on the road to Toluca at km 16 on Highway 15. By the late 1950s its most well-known departments were anthropology, archeological field studies, art, creative writing, international relations, business administration, and Latin American Studies. Alumni records for the eleven years from 1947 through 1957 show that MCC conferred 1,113 bachelor's degrees, 273 master's degrees, and had a yearly average of 126 degrees—101 BAs and 25 MAs (*Journal of Collegiate Registrars* 33, no. 3, Spring 1958). It should also be noted that in 1957 the college opened a branch campus student center for field studies in Oaxaca City in the state of Oaxaca, which was called the *Centro de Estudios Regionales*.

For those of us who look back on our MCC experiences, the mid- to late-1950s and early 1960s were a "golden age" for American students. The decline of MCC began in early 1961, when it was discovered that the business manager had absconded with large sums of money from the college, throwing the future of MCC into sudden disarray. At that time MCC had more than a hundred faculty members, a regular student body of nearly six hundred (it used to reach nearly one thousand as a result of college exchange programs during the winter and summer quarters, with students arriving from such academic institutions in the United States as Ohio State University, Michigan State University, and the University of Washington), and a library with nearly thirty thousand volumes. But with the loss of its operating funds, MCC never really recovered from this major financial crisis that threw the administration, faculty, and students into turmoil.

In 1963, as part of the resolution of MCC's unstable financial situation, the name of the college was changed to the University of the Americas, and later, in 1970, the campus made a third move, this time east of Mexico City to Cholula in the state of Puebla. But students of the old MCC had had the good fortune to be there at a time in the 1950s when an international student body from more than twenty countries, nearly all the U.S. states (California was frequently represented by more than one hundred students), and from throughout Mexico could get a full four-year undergraduate or graduate education in the humanities, social sciences, or fine arts. That dream faded and then virtually disappeared after *La Universidad de las Americas* (UDLA) moved to Puebla. Only a decade and a half after the glory years of MCC in the 1950s, the new president of the UDLA, Macías Rendón, moved quickly to transform the university into a technocratic institution designed more to provide job training for future engineers than a true liberal arts education. During Rendón's first year (1975–1976), the new president openly indicated that the new policy of UDLA would be to replace its former faculty, who held PhDs and did research, with holders of BA degrees who would only teach. In mid-March 1976, Rendón fired 24 of the 110 member faculty without due process, including distinguished Professor of Biology Dr. Paulino Rojas, who was replaced by a young man who had failed to earn his BS degree at the university. At the same time, Rendón announced the elimination of or deep cuts in many of the undergraduate and graduate studies programs in the arts, humanities, anthropology, and Mexican history portions of the academic curriculum so that the institution could focus on a more technocratic approach to higher education. The final death of the ideas behind the old MCC, and the academic battles that went on over the next decade or more in an attempt to resurrect those ideas, will not be covered in this study. What will be noted is that the old MCC—as it existed between 1954 and 1963 as a liberal arts college at km 16 on the Toluca highway—had completely disappeared by the end of 1976.

Impressions of Mexico City College

Most students living downtown in Mexico City caught the MCC school bus behind the fountain of Diana, the Huntress, that was located in the center of the circular *glorieta* where the broad avenue Paseo de la Reforma angles west and Chapultepec Park begins. The bus was parked between two enormous black-colored lions on pedestals, each lion the size of a Volkswagen. These lions sat on either side of the road that continued up a short distance to Chapultepec Castle and had a commanding view looking straight back down the Reforma toward the center of the city. The MCC bus departed every half hour from the *liones*, passing through a corner of the park, past a massive monument to the 1938 nationalization of foreign oil companies by President Lázaro Cárdenas, and then through the palatial Lomas de Chapultepec district. Following a curving and slowly rising roadway with trees and greenery in the median and on both sides of the road, the bus rode the highway up a ridgeline, flanked by *barrancas* on both sides, and ultimately to the college at km 16. Those ten-mile trips every school day gave the students time to shake the late-night cobwebs from their minds and to make the transition to an entirely different world up above the teeming city.

From the college there were magnificent views of the city to the east, the wooded *barranca* below the college, and on most days, the volcanoes Popocatepetl and Ixtacihuatl to the far south, both of which stood out against the horizon at elevations just under eighteen thousand feet. The campus had taken over a former country club, so a number of buildings were already in place, including the two-story building housing the cafeteria, theater, and art department (see fig. 5.2). The cafeteria opened onto a large, open patio that projected out into the upper branches of old spreading eucalyptus trees growing from the slope below, with a lovely view south. On campus, the tiled mosaic murals on the walls of many of the open-air classrooms, along with the green, finely-groomed grounds with open patios and clusters of stone seating for outdoor seminars, gave the campus a strong aesthetic sense of belonging in that location. It fit with everything else around it along a beautiful wooded ridgeline rising to the west toward Desierto de los Liones (Desert of the Lions National Park). Beyond the campus was the pass to Toluca and its glorious Friday market. Everything about the place felt right (see fig. 5.3).

Figure 5.2.   Mexico City College campus at km 16 on the Toluca highway; walkway to Spanish and economics, postcard circa 1955. Photo courtesy of Richard W. Wilkie.

Figure 5.3. Mexico City College students on the terrace outside the cafeteria; campus at km 16 on the Toluca highway, postcard circa 1955. Photo courtesy of Richard W. Wilkie.

Some Classroom Experiences at
Mexico City College: 1956–1958

What stands out when I think about the courses offered at MCC is the range of unusual, and sometimes bizarre, professors who taught there. Most of them were extraordinary individuals whose life experiences went far beyond that of the faculty one might find in institutions of higher learning in the States. I later had excellent professors at the University of Washington, Seattle, but they generally did not add that layer of worldly-wise experience to their courses in the ways that the MCC faculty did. Teaching in Mexico was chosen for the lifestyle it offered, for love of the country, and for the research possibilities available rather than for financial gain. A number of MCC faculty members had other jobs in the city and taught almost for the joy of doing it; some were ambassadors from other countries who liked the idea of teaching. One faculty member who stood out for me was Dr. Pablo Martinez del Río, from the Mexican National Institute of Anthropology and History, a famous anthropologist in his seventies with sweeping gray hair who typically wore a baggy black suit with tie, a black felt hat, and white spats over his shoes. I still keep and cherish my lecture notes from his course on the Indian tribes of Mexico. He must have known more about the topic than anyone alive.

One of the first classes I attended was an economic geography course taught by a Mexican army officer—Colonel Carlos Berzunza—who seemed to think he was Napoleon. He was very short, barely over five feet, and smoked a big cigar during his lectures. Sitting next to me on the left was a bearded, long-haired American student wearing a colorful Mexican poncho along with open-toed huaraches on his feet. He had a gold-colored ring in his earlobe, and a parrot was sitting on his right shoulder. I doubt whether anyone attending college at home in the States at that time looked anything like him, but a decade later by the mid-1960s, this student would have fit into many U.S. academic institutions. The classroom we were sitting in had open windows on opposite sides, and its door opened onto a big patio with the backdrop of Mexico City beyond. This setting was vastly different from my high-school classrooms in Boise, Idaho.

Colonel Berzunza paced back and forth with big fast steps in front of the class as he lectured without notes while munching his cigar. After every half dozen trips back and forth across the room, he would continue right through the door a dozen paces or more and stand lecturing to the class from the patio, while looking out over the city. All we could see was his back and his wildly gesturing arms, while the cigar was shifted from hand to mouth to hand with an occasional pause followed by a cloud of smoke. We were never certain whether he was lecturing to our class or to the populace of Mexico City. It was hard enough following his lectures in English with his accent and the cigar, but it became very difficult to follow what he was saying at such a distance. No matter—the class loved his showmanship. We all just strained a little harder to hear him as we leaned forward on the edges of our chairs.

Professor Willis Austin was my English Literature professor whom, along with his wife and young son, my brother had gotten to know the previous year. My course with Austin had only eight or nine students and was taught in a room of a house where one door opened to a kitchen. Austin had a strong fondness for drink, often taking a short break to disappear into the kitchen for a slug of scotch or rum (the popping of the cork was the giveaway), and wiping his wet beard with the back of his hand as he returned. Austin held his liquor well, and it even seemed to spice up his quotes from English writers, especially one of his favorite poets, A. E. Housman. We often met Austin and other friends for afternoon drinks downtown where everyone talked of literature, art, and current world events. One of his friends—a Mexican writer who grew up in Paris and spoke French, Spanish, and English equally well—was seriously involved in bullfighting and tried to convince me to join his bullfighting friends for their weekly training sessions. After noticing nasty scars on his arm and neck, I prudently decided that I already had too many activities during my first term of studies.

My second English Literature course that first year was with Professor Claire Bowen, who oversaw production of the college newspaper—the *Mexico City Collegian*. The class was small—only seven students—and it was a wonderful course. We had a major problem, however, and it was not anything Professor Bowen could control: three of the seven students in the course died violently during that short ten-week quarter. The first to go was a young man in his mid-20s from Wyoming who drove a fancy red convertible sports car. It was said that earlier that year his father had died and left him a million dollars, so he set off to Mexico for college. One afternoon he backed out of the narrow parking lot in front of the entrance to the college and into the path of a runaway bus—an infamous "Toluca Rocket," overloaded with people, purchases, and livestock—and with nonexistent brake pads screeching and grinding against metal the bus slammed into his low-slung car and he was beheaded. The second student to die was a handsome young man from New York City who was one of the editors of the *Mexico City Collegian*. According to his friends, while in Acapulco during a long weekend break and somewhat despondent from losing his girl friend, he decided to swim to China after an evening of drugs. Needless to say, he did not make it.

The final classmate to die failed to return from a Thanksgiving-week trip to Acapulco. He had gone with friends to a famous bar in the tough red-light district of town, Río Rita's. Sometime around 2 a.m., being totally drunk, he left to sleep in the back seat of their parked car outside the nightclub. When his friends finally left Río Rita's a few hours later, the car was gone. The stranded students had to return to Mexico City the next day on a bus. A week later the car was found about fifty miles from Acapulco on a side road above a cliff and burned to a shell, with the charred body of our classmate inside. The police said it was an accident, but his friends said that it had to be murder. They never found his wallet or any of the things that were in the car. During the last class in that course the four of us who were still alive looked at each other with relieved eyes—we had survived.

In spring quarter 1958 I was in a sociology course taught by Morton Sloane, when he took us to visit the Distrito Federal Penitentiary at Lecumberri—*El palacio negro* (The Black Palace). My strongest memory from the visit was the thirty minutes that our small group spent talking with and interviewing Ramón Mercados (Mercader) del Rio—the Spanish communist who killed Russian revolutionary Leon Trotsky (age sixty) at his home in Coyoacán, a southern suburb of Mexico City. Mercados, acting as the friend of Trotsky's personal secretary, struck Trotsky in the back of the head with an alpine climbing axe, and Trotsky died the next day, August 21, 1940. Mercados was thought for a time to be a Canadian named Frank Jacson Mornard, but his true identity ultimately came out. Mercados had been in prison for nearly eighteen years at the time we talked with him. The longest sentence in Mexico for murder is twenty-five years, and with only a few years to go in his term, Mercados was cheerful and friendly. He had a corner cell by himself during the daytime, barred on two sides, and he seemed to be friends with a number of the passing guards, prisoners, and visitors. At night he had a more private cell.

Our group of about ten stood next to his cell and talked with him as he stood on the other side of the bars, holding them with both hands. He seemed to enjoy this interaction and the discussion in Spanish that was led by Professor Sloane. I later read that he was released two years later in 1960 and was seen boarding a flight to Prague from Paris. Mercados lived in Moscow for a number of years, where he received the Order of Lenin. Many years later in the 1980s he was living in Havana, Cuba, where he died of cancer.

The Mexico City College Student Body

Of the nearly one thousand or so students enrolled at MCC in the 1956–1957 academic year, about four hundred were U.S. military veterans studying on the GI Bill. On the fifteenth day of each month, Salvador López Tello from the Visa Department at the U.S. Embassy arrived at the college to give out checks of $115 to the ex-GIs—what they referred to as "life blood." Three major groups stood out among the ex-GIs, the largest group being that of the adventurers and drinkers who after a number of years in Europe or Asia could not face the stifling uniformity of life back in the States. The second largest contingent of veterans was made up of the more serious business-school-bound veterans who, after learning Spanish and graduating from MCC, often went on for graduate degrees at Thunderbird Business School in Phoenix, Arizona, and then dispersed into Latin America with companies like Pan American Airlines, Coca-Cola, and United Fruit. A third but smaller group encompassed those veterans who were later to become teachers or college professors, thus building on their international experiences in several regions of the world.

The exchange students who came for the winter or summer quarter constituted another important group. Spanish teachers and students also studied at MCC for a year or more to improve their Spanish communications skills. Another large cluster of students, and one that was career and creative arts oriented, included the artists (people called them "the painters and the potters"), archeologists, creative writers, journalists, historians, and social scientists, and there were also those students who were training for business or foreign service careers in Latin America.

Finally, there were many American and some European students at MCC who were there primarily for the outside activities that were available to them within a rich and varied array of natural settings and for the cultural diversity that existed in Mexico City and its hinterland. It seemed that we all felt the power of place in Mexico's landscape and its people, and at the time it was a place where physical and human landscapes blended harmoniously together.

The largest subgroup among these students who came to Mexico for opportunities outside the classroom centered on the Mexico City College Explorer's Club, but included many independent adventurers as well. Oriol Pi-Sunyer, a Spanish Civil War refugee via France, England, and Venezuela, captured a number of the elements that this group shared:

> It is possible that I learned as much outside academic contexts as in the classroom. Travel in Mexico was cheap, particularly for those ready to patronize country buses and third class carriages. Few of my friends owned cars, but we were certainly mobile, making numerous trips through much of central Mexico and beyond. We trekked mountain trails and went on indigenous pilgrimages, often following routes dating back to Aztec times. A good deal of this activity would now be classified as "adventure tourism," but it formed part of a venerable travel tradition premised on the assumption that knowledge of people and places was gained through personal experience. ("El mosaic de la memòria," *Revista d'etnologia de Catalunya* 25 [November 2004]: 117–18)

Also within this subgroup of students who came primarily for the available outside activities were students who came to MCC to become the "new American expatriates" by creating or finding a 1920s Hemingway-like Paris or Pamplona; to play team sports; to use the campus as a base for commuting back and forth to Acapulco as surfers and beach bums; and to thrive in the active bar culture.

The latter group, who came to enjoy the bar culture, included students who can be classified as "big city drinkers, brawlers, and thinkers." These students were often older, experienced urbanites from Manhattan, Brooklyn, the Bronx, Chicago, and other major cities where drinking was considered a major activity. Occasionally these students ended up in jail for a time, after getting into fights and conflicts. Pete Hamill (MCC, 1956–1957) wrote about this drinking subculture at the college in his book *A Drinking Life*:

> There was drinking everywhere, and Tim and I were part of it. We went drinking in the small hut across the highway from the school, in the *cantinas* near

where we lived, at weekend student parties all over the city. Those parties bound us together. In some ways, it was like the navy. Everyone was far from home, far from Ohio and Illinois, for states with age limits on drinking, far from inspection by friends or family, all using drink to deal with strangeness and shyness and a variety of fears. At MCC there were two American men for every American woman, and the sense of male contest gave the parties a tension that occasionally resembled hysteria. The rule was BYOB, bring your own bottle, and in the doors came cases of beer, bottles of tequila, mexcal, pulque, rum. These were 1950s parties, young men and women packing the chosen apartment, dancing, as said, teeth to teeth, to the music of Benny More and Los Panchos, drinking with little care about food, faces swirling, ashtrays overflowing with butts, hot eyes falling upon asses and tits, tits and asses, until the midnight hour had long passed, and finally the last of the women were gone, and the remnants of the bleary male squadron kept drinking on until the beer ran out and you could see the worm in the bottom of the mescal bottle and it was time to face the gray dawn. I was happier than I'd ever been. (*A Drinking Life: A Memoir* [Boston: Little Brown, 1994], 194)

Obviously, Hamill and his friends found instant satisfaction. A number of other younger students took a little longer to adjust. Many of them started out by not liking the college, the city, or the people. Perhaps it was culture shock or just an old-fashioned national chauvinism that played out along the lines of "everything at home was better." The "old timers"—anyone who had been there at least two quarters—knew what the litany of comments would be every quarter when a new wave of students arrived, especially the "Winter Quarter in Mexico" students from Ohio State and Michigan State universities. The old timers also knew that the new students' negative feelings would evaporate within a short period of time, and that within a short ten-week quarter they generally would become quite emotional over their pronouncements of affection for everything about Mexico, its culture, and its people. Before leaving, the vast majority of students started working out a strategy for staying permanently in Mexico, although only a small number of them were able to accomplish it. Nearly every student left Mexico reluctantly and with thoughts or plans of returning as soon as possible. In my own case, I left for the University of Washington in January 1959, but returned to MCC while working on my master's degree in the 1960–1961 school year.

Another interesting group centered on the expatriate hangers-on. This smaller group of students, often in their forties or sixties, included the "premature antifascists" who fought in the Lincoln Brigade in the Spanish Civil War, or they were armchair philosophers who lived up the hill from the college in the small village of Cuajimalpa. Many were beyond taking courses, but they frequented the library and liked talking in the cafeteria to each other, to ex-GIs, and to other students. Another group lived up the hill in Cuajimalpa because there they could dress like Mexicans and have an authentic experience living in a Mexican village. A number of them thrived on drinking pulque, a fermented alcoholic drink from the maguay plant, which tended to keep you at a low level of inebriation all day. These students attended some classes, and others spent time around the campus.

And it is important to mention the small group of cold-war agents at MCC who were pretending to be students. They enrolled as students at the college, but their actual purpose was quickly revealed by the kinds of questions they asked as they investigated the social and political lives of the other students and international refugees. We were not concerned that the agents were on campus, since every other type of student was there as well, and these "Keystone Cops" added something to the unique *ambiente* at the college.

Student Economics

The question of expenses accompanied us at all times, and it was a major reason why many American students came to Mexico. It was a simple fact that the American dollar went a very long way in Mexico—much farther than back home. A student in the States had to live very modestly, while American students in Mexico, under most circumstances, could have a far grander standard of living. Not only did the United States rank first in the world in 1957 in per capita income at $2,343 (Norton Sydney Ginsburg, *Atlas of Economic Development* [Chicago: University of Chicago Press, 1961], 18–19), it was 40 percent higher than second-ranked Canada at $1,667 per person. Switzerland, the highest-ranking European country, was in fourth place with a per capita income of $1,229—about half that of the United States, while the per capita averages for the other major European countries included France at $1,046 (ninth place), the United Kingdom at $998 (eleventh place), West Germany at $762 (fifteenth place), and Italy at $442 (twenty-sixth place). Mexico, in fifty-seventh place, was even lower on the world economic scale, with an average income in U.S. dollars of only $187 per person. That fact that the average Mexican earned only 8 percent of what the average American earned at that time meant that American students could live at a far higher level than back in the States. Life in Mexico City clearly was more expensive than it was in the countryside, but it was still an overwhelming bargain. Tuition at MCC in the 1955–1956 school year was $105 per quarter, plus a medical fee of $10.

Two years later (1957–1958), tuition with medical included was up to only $130 per quarter. Since the ex-GIs were receiving $115 a month on the GI Bill during that period, they could easily afford an education at MCC.

Even so, surviving economically was a topic that MCC students talked about much of the time. Veterans had to wait for the fifteenth of the month for their GI Bill checks to arrive, and others of us had to constantly check the mail from home to know whether we would have to borrow money from friends or whether we would be the ones who could be tapped for a loan. There was an unwritten code about borrowing, repaying, borrowing again, and asking, "Who has the money this week?" There was a vast network of connections, the major requirement of which being that records needed to be maintained. The overwhelming majority of loans among MCC students were repaid, but there were a few students who thought it was okay to ask others for loans, though if others, when they themselves were then broke, asked them to repay those loans, the response was, "Stop dunning me, I pay my bills!" Since these deadbeats never volunteered to repay the money they owed, and then objected when the situation was reversed, they were soon cut out of the large "friendly aid" network that had been constructed among students who sometimes felt stranded and with nowhere else to turn.

Working in Mexico on student visas or tourist visas was illegal, but there was an accepted gray area within which everybody operated. Students at the college often needed to supplement their finances. Several of us were paid between fifty and sixty dollars a game to play American football for two Mexican universities. The league officials were seeking to expand the top league from four teams to six, so they hired a handful of imported players from Texas, as well as a few MCC students, to strengthen the two new teams and to improve the quality of play in the league in general. Officially this was illegal, but it appeared to be out in the open. I played for the Mexican Military Academy (*Academia Militarizada Mexico*) with three other MCC students. The league also brought in an American coach from El Paso, Texas, with eight west Texas players to add to our team, so considerable tension developed between the Mexican players and the Texans on the issue of who would start the games. The solution was to rotate the starting teams from week to week. The four MCC players, however, were in the strange position of being wanted desperately by both teams, so in the first game, and before eighty thousand fans, I found myself starting at tackle after only five days of practice with the Mexican team, and then staying in to play for the American team when they entered the game. By the end of the game I could barely crawl off the field.

Other students found odd jobs when they could. One of my friends was hired by a hotel chain to test their security systems by entering the premises and stealing things. Several times he was nearly killed when caught, since the guards did not know ahead of time that the hotel had hired him. It finally became too dangerous, so he quit. In that case, personal survival took precedence over economic survival.

The following excerpts from a letter written in March 1960 by an unnamed graduate of MCC (1959) best illustrate how some jobs (and sometimes life after MCC) played out:

I left Mexico in September. Last year there I really had a good time. While finishing at the college, I lived with Freddie W. for awhile and then the police kicked me out of the apartment because of a wild party. I then moved in with some girl who left me (the bitch) in June with $8 in my pocket, and I wasn't getting any money from my folks. So—I went to Acapulco and the "Snake Pit" and the old lady owner, who always kind of liked me informally, adopted me and gave me free room and board all summer. . . . I was of course broke, so I got a job managing the nightclub in the Aloha Hotel, which was a ball. It was really going for a while, but then the tourist season ended and I went broke trying to keep the place going. When it was really strong, though, I had a seven-piece cha-cha band and floor show.

I went [back] to Mexico City then and ran into the girl who was entitled "Miss Universal Beatnik" and was in *Life* magazine because of it. She was down there with a bunch of beatnik friends and since none of them had a place to stay, I got a room in the Hotel Rey with her and her girl friends. This sounds like a good deal, but you ought to try and live with a bunch of beatniks. Man, in a little while they would have driven me crazy. Besides they were always taking dope and I was afraid the cops would raid us, so I moved out and came up to the states and here I am at present . . .

[After realizing that his economic situation was in shambles, he joined the Army.]

When I got to Massachusetts I went down to New York City and Greenwich Village and ran into the same beatniks again, so I'm sharing an apartment with four girls now on weekends, including "Miss Universal Beatnik."

Well I sure wish I was back in Mexico. I hate this cold weather up here. I'm in the Army Security Agency, which is a pretty good deal as far as the Army goes. They are sending me to school for 6 months and then overseas to the Orient or Europe, which will be all right with me.

Other Special Places for Americans in Southern Mexico

Americans in Mexico in the 1950s were attracted to a number of places in the greater hinterland around Mexico City and the southern part of Mexico. Greater Mexico City, with fewer than three million people in 1950, was the most important place for Americans in the country, and the U.S. students at MCC added significantly to the numbers of Americans living in the city. While on weekends certain smaller villages and towns near Mexico City drew some Americans who worked or lived in Mexico, most of the country-side was almost exclusively Mexican. Other favorite places for Americans were Cuernavaca, Taxco, and Acapulco to the south, Puebla and Oaxaca to the east and southeast, and to the west in the state of Mexico beyond Toluca, the newly developing resort area at Valle de Bravo, as well as the mineral baths at Ixtapan de la Sal. Other mineral baths at San José Purua in the state of Michoacán, where the Spanish film director Luis Buñuel lived throughout the 1940s and 1950s, also attracted Americans, as did the old colonial city of Morelia and the villages around Lake Patzcuaro. Farther to the west, favorite places for Americans were found in San Miguel de Allende, Guanajuato, and Guadalajara, as well as on the north side of Lake Chapala in Jalisco state. The beach resort centers of Puerto Vallarta and Mazatlán were still in their infancy, but they represented the beach resort options in that part of Mexico. Beach options on the Caribbean side of Mexico centered on the city of Veracruz, but because of the arduous trip from Mexico City, many travelers often stopped over at the spas of Fortín de las Flores under the eastern flank of Mexico's highest volcano, Orizaba, and close to Córdoba, Veracruz.

At that time, no highway existed along the Pacific Ocean between the state of Colima and the Isthmus of Tehuantepec in eastern Oaxaca, and no major highway directly connected Mexico and Guatemala. The Yucatán Peninsula was virtually an island, linked to Mexico only by one rail line via the state of Tabasco and boat traffic, mostly from Veracruz. The first major road connecting the Yucatán with the rest of the nation was not opened until late in 1960, and even then more than a half dozen ferry crossings had to be used, including those connecting along the Caribbean coast via Isla del Carmen. Thus, options for Americans for comfortable leisure time in favorite places were far more limited in the 1950s than at present.

The Drive to Acapulco

Driving on the rural highways and back roads of Mexico was something like playing Russian roulette—especially at night. Most of our drives back and forth to Acapulco were on a Friday night after classes, or while returning on Sunday night after taking advantage of the beaches all day. The drive each way was at least six hours and sometimes more, depending on what tragic event we would come upon. On those trips the driver had to constantly scan the road ahead with total intensity, often aided by a "lookout" in the passenger's seat. Things popped up in the headlights out of nowhere very quickly—usually cattle or other animals—but sometimes a bad wreck or a dead person in the road—and then suddenly the car had passed and it was difficult to look back. The advice was always never to stop, or else you would assume responsibility for what had happened. As the night progressed, especially on weekends or moonless nights, it was very difficult to spot the men who had passed out from overdrinking and were crumpled along the side of the highway or sometimes in it. We never hit anyone, but we came close a few times, and we seldom made the trip at night without seeing a dead man on the road.

Several memories are etched in my mind. One evening as we were on our way to Acapulco at about 11 p.m., a much faster car tore past us on a straight section of the highway at a speed that must have been over 80 mph. As the car went beyond the reach of our headlights, its red taillights all of a sudden shot straight into the air for ten or fifteen feet before falling back to the highway just as our headlights illuminated the shattered car bouncing around on its tires. We slowed and pulled up to a smoking, steaming late-model car with one passenger partially through the windshield, and with bits of metal, glass, and animal parts all over the highway. It turned out that the car had hit the back end of a nearly one-thousand-pound bull dead center, directly between the car's headlights. The sizzling engine had been pushed into the open seat space between the driver and the passenger, and somehow both of them were still alive. The only thing that saved them was that they hit the bull directly in the center of the car rather than with a glancing blow that would have thrown the car rolling and flipping down the highway.

That same evening and south of Chilpancingo, about two hours later, we arrived where a second-class bus with passengers had gone off the highway and down a hillside of thorn trees into the canyon bordering Río Omitlán. Here we ignored the usual advice not to get involved, and we worked well into the night helping several dozen volunteers form a human chain down the hill by which the badly injured survivors of the accident were lifted and passed back up to the roadside.

Breaks in Acapulco

Acapulco at that time was the favorite Mexican coastal vacation spot for nearly everyone at MCC, especially during the breaks between quarters. It was a more relaxed break from classes, and from long weekend explorations to more remote places in the interior of the country, and it was so decidedly Mexican that it now stands in sharp contrast to the new Mexican super-resorts that are carbon copies of one another. These resorts are often set in unique and interesting places, but they would have held little appeal for most MCC students. Better a place like Acapulco, set in a Mexican city, where Mexican tourists and families had vacationed since before the 1920s. Acapulco in the 1950s was an ideal place for our vagabond group of poor students. On the main beaches of the harbor there were no grand hotels, and hardly any hotels of any size. Across the palm-lined boulevard, Avenida Costanera Miguel Alemán, that was named after Mexico's president from 1946 to 1952 and that bordered the long harbor, there were some low-rise hotels, but for the most part, views from the Avenida of the main beaches remained sweeping and unhindered. Locals and visiting Mexicans used the beaches for soccer games, sunning, swimming, and fishing. In the late afternoon, chefs and housewives waited while crews of eight or ten oarsmen rowed their boats up to the beach. Behind the boats trailed long nets teeming with live red snappers and other fish. Once the boats reached the beach, the rowers jumped into the surf to begin pulling in the nets full of fish. After some heated bargaining, the chefs carried their newly purchased fish directly to their open-air restaurants throughout the downtown and along the *costanera*, while the housewives shuffled toward home carrying straw baskets with the fish half hanging out.

The peninsula and areas around Caleta Beach and Caletilla Beach had one grand hotel, the Hotel Caleta, that perched on the point above the beach. A little farther up the hill to the west was the famous Hotel Flamingo that John Wayne had owned since 1950 and where he hosted his Hollywood friends, including actor Johnnie Weismuller (Tarzan) who lived there until he died in the 1980s. Our band of poor college students and ex-GIs, however, never frequented either of those places but hung out around the other low-rise and small hotels and their pools or beaches that were easily accessible. Our favorite place to stay was the Hotel del Pacifico at the far end of Caleta Beach. The hotel was shaped something like a battleship but with a large, covered, open-air restaurant on the second floor. We stayed there for only a few dollars a day.

Most of the hotel managers seemed to like the presence of gringo students, so we had the run of virtually every place in Acapulco. They seemed pleased when our group arrived to use their swimming pools, bars, restaurants, bathrooms, or lobbies. It was especially true when members of our group brought guitars for impromptu parties after the *cuba libres*, or local beers, as the sun set and the hotel guests returned from the beaches. All the small places wanted to create a certain *ambiente* for their clients, and for some reason a rough and tumble group of relatively benign gringos seemed to please nearly everyone. If the party got too lively for the hosts, as it sometimes did, we just moved to the next hotel, or perhaps back to the Bum-Bum Club on Caleta Beach, or even to someone's suite for a jam session of raunchy and rowdy songs.

During spring break of my freshman year, late March 1957, six of us drove to Acapulco for a ten-day break from our studies: my brother Jim, Ted Turner (a GI veteran from Nashville), Murray Pilkington (a southern Californian), Elvis look-alike Mike Johnson (a northern Californian), and a friend with a car—an ex-GI named Gil from New York City. The second night in town, we ran into a weird and wonderful social group that drew us into their parties and scene for the rest of our stay. One of the leaders of the group was Lady Sanchez, an older woman who had spent so much time in the sun her skin had the texture of a brown leather mummy. She claimed to be the daughter of the Duke of Buckinghamshire, and that her first husband had been the actor Rex Harrison. Another leader of the group was Tony Clark, who wrote *The Hucksters*, which later became a movie. Tony, who was also English, was in Mexico writing an article for a magazine. Since he was on an expense account, he kept our glasses full of rum, and our plates filled with grilled *huachinango* (red snapper), *cerviche* (raw fish in lime juice), and fresh shrimp at every restaurant and nightclub where we spent time. As poor, struggling students, we were certain that we had arrived in paradise. (At the end of the week, Tony Clark asked six of our MCC group to accompany him as "armed guards" on a ten-day pack trip into the mountains of Guerrero in search of material for his article. Reluctantly we had to return to classes, and we never heard whether he took the trip on not, or whether his article was ever published.)

Members of the Lady Sanchez/Tony Clark group included Lucy, a lovely ballet dancer from New York City who kept Tony company; Pearl, a music teacher from St. Louis; a secretary from Oakland named Marge (one of the most beautiful women in Acapulco); and Peter, a book publisher from New York. Other college friends joined us from time to time, including the ex-GIs Sherm (from California) who disappeared frequently for an affair with a married woman; "Phantom" (an Alaskan fisherman) who was staying with his pregnant Mexican girlfriend; and Bill (from Houston) who managed to get in a fight with some prostitutes at one of the sidewalk restaurants on the Central Zocalo where we were spending the evening, with the police being called in to end the fracas. Others individuals were involved as well during this stay, but this group made up the core of the revolving whirlwind of our letting off steam from our studies back at MCC.

Driving to Zihuatanejo

Most of our school breaks were not spent leisurely in Acapulco, however, but instead were spent hiking or traveling to out-of-the-way places. During spring break in March 1958, after reading that a new "all weather"

road had finally been opened to Zihuatanejo, six of us made that our primary destination. We did spend a few nights in Acapulco coming and going each way, since the 140-mile road up the coast departed from and returned there. The news article alerting us to the trip said that "depending
on the season, the trip could be made in 10 hours to two days." During the
rainy season from May to November the rivers were extremely high and
difficult to ford, especially the Río Coyuquilla, Río Petatlán, and Río de
las Cuevas, and you could "count on spending at least a day stuck in at
least one river." Fortunately we were still in the so-called dry season when
passage was not easy but possible if a driver had help to ford the rivers (see
fig. 5.4).

On our trip we discovered that this "new road" petered out into narrow,
dusty trails after crossing the Coyuquilla River and still about fifty miles
short of its destination. Those final miles involved fording another four
rivers with water well up into the car and all hands pushing. Between those
crossings, we struggled not to lose our way among the jungle cattle-trails and
footpaths leading out of small villages along the way. One thing was evident—the people were the friendliest we had seen in Mexico. They waved,
shouted, and helped us on our way, marveling at the 1950 Ford we were
driving as a *coche nuevo*.

**Figure 5.4. Mexico City College students fording Río Coyuquilla (the fourth of seven
rivers to be crossed) on a journey to Zihuatanejo: Richard Wilkie (driving), Tom Held,
and Bill Jagoda (ready to push), April 1958. Photo courtesy of James Wilkie.**

In an article my brother Jim wrote for the *Mexico City College Collegian*, "Intrepid Gringos Discover Poor Man's Acapulco" (May 15, 1958), he noted:

> Zihuatanejo may be the place Zane Grey emphatically declared more like the South Seas than the South Seas themselves, and again it may be the "coming" tourist resort on the Pacific coast, but both statements may stretch their points. Zihuatanejo is typical of Mexico's West coast, according to Mike Johnson, and not so typical of the South Seas. It will be several long years before Zihuatanejo reaches the level of even Mazatlán's cleanliness and modernness, let alone Acapulco's fame.

The first place we encountered in town was a police checkpoint, and they were so surprised at our arrival that we had to wait nearly a half hour while they found the chief of police. He was very welcoming, but said that he was concerned for our safety and that he was assigning an armed policeman to accompany us. "Remember, this is Saturday night, and all the machete swinging men come into town to get drunk and rowdy. Why pick a fight with a man who also has a machete, when you can fight with foreign *gringos?*" he said.

Having a guard with us was not a bad idea, we thought, especially after seeing the characters drinking at the main bar in town. Even the building housing the bar was disreputable, with a dirt floor, tree branches for walls, and wooden beams holding up a flimsy roof. This was like the wild west of the American cowboy picture shows of the 1920s.

But we had one thing strongly in our favor while we were in this bar: John Freeman played his rock and roll guitar for the crowd, while several of us sang off-color blues and rock songs. None of the crowd understood our Spanish, and we were not sure which of the many Indian dialects they were speaking. One man among the rural woodcutters stood out well above the others in his size and ferocious appearance. He appeared to be over six feet, six, and in facial features had a Boris Karloff look about him. I was so awestruck that I don't remember taking my eyes off him the entire evening. To make matters potentially more ominous, it appeared that he did not speak a word of Spanish, or perhaps any language, but used instead strong guttural sounds when attempting to communicate. The other woodcutters seemed to defer to him and keep out of his way, so it turned out that most of the evening he spent with us at our table. He clearly liked our music, as he laughed frequently and showed his approval by heartily downing the Carta Blanca beers we kept pouring for him. I remember that his hands were so big that when he clutched the beer glass, he appeared to be drinking from his giant fist. In all my time in Mexico I never saw a more colorful or fascinating fellow.

The beach near this two-street village was not a good place for swimming, so we hired a boat to go to the other side of the bay to perhaps the most beautiful beach we had seen in Mexico—*Las gatas* (She-Cats). It was there that lush jungle foliage swept down to meet white sands, which bordered the softly tinted green waters of a sheltered nook on the bay side of the palm-tree covered shoal that arched out from the shore. Ocean waves crashed one hundred yards off the point over a coral reef that protected this magic location. Not all of our adventures ended on such a high note, or in such a dramatic setting, but hopefully my companions then, Jim Wilkie, Mike Johnson, Tom Held, Bill Jagoda, and John Freeman, still remember the feeling of discovery that we all felt at the time.

Unfortunately, even paradise has problems, and before leaving the beach that afternoon, while looking for colored blowfish, John Freeman stepped on an underwater spine plant. A half dozen quills pierced the skin in the soft bottom of one of his feet, and their toxic poison caused a fever for a day and real discomfort for a week or more. Removing the quills took the expertise of an old Indian couple living near the beach on a site that is now probably occupied by a giant beach hotel. But having never returned to Zihuatanejo, I have the luxury of dreaming that dramatic changes have not taken place there and that the beach at *Las gatas* remains as it was in 1958.

Mexico: Learning to See the Details

Experiencing the Mexican landscape in those years helped me to see more clearly the everyday world, something that life back home with its tranquility and blandness would not have provided. Vistas in Mexico in their natural and built environments were so full of rich details of color, pattern, and variety that I realized even more strongly the importance of seeing things on three different levels: the overview level or wide-angle perspective, the medium-level for observation of one's immediate surroundings, and the more focused low-level for examination of up-close details in what could be called "still-life scenes." This helped me to gain a taste for wanting to understand the complexity and diversity of my surroundings—something that helped me begin to understand life in Mexico more completely—so that what might seem chaotic to some became commonplace to me and other MCC students.

Reading the landscape and grasping what I was seeing was something I had learned to do instinctively through a wilderness upbringing in the Salmon River country of central Idaho. I learned, as did my brother Jim, that survival could depend on remembering details in the landscape and how they varied at different times of the day. We had to construct very accurate mental maps if we were to find our way back home or find the safest and best route up or down a mountain face. My high-school art classes in Idaho also had been an important setting for learning to focus on details. Now in Mexico, it was possible to hone those skills as the landscapes and the human activity that filled them came together in a honeycomb of action and excitement.

Take, for example, a periodic Mexican market, where a multitude of visually exciting elements is jammed into a handful of street blocks. The density of the mix would be the same if these people and their activities had been thrown into a bowl and stirred with a giant wooden spoon. Add the sounds, smells, and tastes of the market, and for some it can be a nearly overwhelming experience.

The Toluca Market on Fridays, for example, was so rich in actions, sights, sounds, and smells, and all of it flooding one's senses, that most non-Mexicans reacted in one of two ways. Either they jumped into the scene and reveled in it, or they looked around for a bit before fleeing to a bar or café where it was possible for them to focus their senses on a less dizzying scene. I often had another strategy that helped me give structure to the apparent chaos and disorder. I first looked for a high place from which to get an overview of the basic layout of the market, and where I could best gain a perspective on the activities that were clustered in each part of the market below. Getting a feeling for the whole gave me a solid understanding of the parts and even of those places that it might be best to visit early and of the others that were just beginning to evolve. Every market has a rhythm, and it is imperative to feel that ebb and flow of events and activities. Arriving at dawn along with the market vendors is the best time to get in sync with that rhythm, but that is not always possible. From above one can feel the pulse of a market in the myriad of sights below, and one can discern which areas of the market are building toward some kind of a crescendo. Some people shy away from climactic events, but I am drawn toward them. Thus, the overview-level or wide-angle perspective is a time to get in touch with these feelings and to form a flexible plan of action.

After coming down from our overview perch, it is time to explore the intermediate-level perspectives within the market area. This is a phase of observation and exploration in which it is important to screen out the chaos and look much more closely at clusters of activities: the actions of one or two vendors surrounded by their array of colorful produce or handicraft; the people who bargain or talk with them; the young child pulling on its mother's dress or father's pant leg to get their attention as the parent is handing change to a customer; the dogs under foot that are searching for and finding scraps—all of these events and more are taking place in micro-settings, of which there are thousands of versions, each occurring simultaneously in the big weekly Mexican markets. Exploring them, framing them in the mind's eye—even sketching them or photographing them—is all part of experiencing the intermediate level of observation. During this phase I generally spend time in every section of the market, pausing at times near central points—perhaps near a fountain or a smaller mini-plaza, where I can sit for a while and people-watch. The endlessly passing array of human characters of all ages and backgrounds, as well as animals, can keep an observer entertained for long periods of time. Where else other than in periodic markets do the worlds of rural peasants and urban dwellers come together so completely?

Finally, there is the level that is often overlooked by market goers and travelers: the focused, low-level perspective used for close-up details. For a final trip through the market, walk slowly as you try screening out the jumble of organized chaos, just thinking and framing your vision into small detailed spaces. Perhaps it is noticing the wrinkles on the back of an old vendor's hand; spotting a military medal on the lapel of someone's jacket; appreciating aesthetically the light angles and shadows on a small pile of yellow lemons or on the rounded shapes of small bread rolls; catching visually the meeting of two hands as money is exchanged between vendor and buyer; or spotting such things as the sparkling gold tooth of the flower lady or the textured look of a well-used sombrero. Details in the built environment are just as important, such as an old manhole cover in a cobblestone street or the grillwork over a window that opens to the market. These visual treats are like a dessert at the end of the day.

These markets touched my soul in ways that make them live on. Clearly they were vital elements in my search to capture a "sense or spirit of place" in Mexico, a spirit and a place that included natural and built environments and the spaces of human activity, and that involved people of all ages, socioeconomic levels, and rural or urban backgrounds. It was understanding something about that combination that helped me appreciate the complexity of Mexican diversity.

Conclusion

Mexico City College was an important institution of learning for American students who wanted to experience life outside the United States during an important period in the 1950s and early 1960s, a time when those kinds of educational experiences were not freely available elsewhere. On a personal level, where else but Mexico could I, a college student directly out of high school in the States, have had the range of experiences that I had at that time? During only my first year and a half in Mexico, I climbed peaks higher than anything in the forty-eight contiguous states (18,887 and 14,969 feet); played an American Olympic diver in a Mexican movie; played football games before crowds of 80,000 to 100,000; explored much of southern Mexico and Central America—often pushing a car through rivers or riding with it on the flatcar of a train; listened to countless stories of the adventures of ex-GIs who had fought in Europe and Asia in World War II and the Korean War; and experienced the everyday life and intrigues of Mexico City.

On a broader level, Mexico City College provided me and its other students with a dynamic setting for intellectual and personal growth, and it was a place that offered unimaginable opportunities for exploration, discovery, adventure, and creativity. The intellectual, artistic, and emotional pull of Mexico was strongly felt, and the years each of us spent there changed us for the better. Following the McCarthy era at home during the early 1950s, the image of a colder, sterner Uncle Sam contrasted sharply with the image of a warm and nurturing Mother Mexico. And for those of us who gave Mexico a little time, the pull of Mother Mexico would be with us for a lifetime.

My experiences in Mexico helped expose me—and I think others—to new ways of viewing our own countries. Life in Mexico helped all of us to develop a feeling for diversity and a belief that because of it life can be richer and more meaningful. Living in a place where everyone has to think and act the same way generally becomes stifling, and creativity then suffers. In every direction I looked in Mexico at that time, I was stimulated and inspired by art, the grandeur of the landscape, and the warmth of the average Mexican. From this visual excitement came the realization that in Mexico during those years the physical and human landscapes were in harmony and balance. There are many advantages to living in the modern world, but a major cost is that the kind of balance and harmony I found in Mexico is often thrown out of sync by the modernization process. Urbanization, suburbanization, and the resulting sameness of place can change a landscape and its people in ways that tear the life out of the spirit of place that existed there previously. Many different regions and places in Mexico still maintain a strong self-identity and sense of place, but unfortunately, many other places in Mexico have lost it completely.

CHAPTER SIX

"American Merchants and Mexican Folk Art: The Buying and Selling of Oaxacan Wood Carvings"
Michael Chibnik

The sale of crafts in the global marketplace is an increasingly important source of income in many Mexican communities. Bark paintings from Guerrero, weavings from Chiapas, and pottery from Chihuahua change hands in complex commodity chains that link artisans from rural areas to consumers from the upper and middle classes of the United States, Canada, and Europe. The trade in such "ethnic and tourist arts" (Graburn 1976) provides an economic niche for Americans who make a living by buying crafts at relatively low prices in Mexico and selling them at higher prices in the United States.[1] These peripatetic wholesalers and store owners are only partly motivated by the love of money; few get rich in this complicated and unpredictable business. Most of these traders enjoy traveling to Mexico, meeting artisans, and escaping their lives in the United States. Many are colorful characters with strong personalities who are somewhat alienated from mainstream Western culture.

I became aware of the economic importance of American merchants in the folk art trade while carrying out a long-term ethnographic study of the making and marketing of Oaxacan wood carvings (Chibnik 2003). Since the mid-1980s these whimsical, brightly painted pieces have adorned the shelves of gift stores throughout the United States, and they have been the subject of countless magazine and newspaper articles, museum exhibits, and television programs. Many men and women in the principal carving communities of Mexico who once eked out a living through farming and wage labor are now able to build concrete houses and purchase automobiles, satellite dishes, cell phones, and compact disk players as a result of the popularity of these wood carvings. When I first learned of the wood-carving trade in the late 1980s, I assumed that most pieces were sold to either tourists or shops in the city of Oaxaca. I soon found out, however, that the only way carvers could earn significant amounts of money was by selling pieces to folk art dealers from the United States. The traders' ideas about what pieces were likely to sell and why consumers bought wood carvings were the driving force behind the production and marketing of this new craft.

Observers of the folk art scene in Mexico often assume that these traders are exploiting the artisans by buying pieces for much less than their market value in the United States. Yet the wood carvers eagerly seek out dealers and often speak about American wholesalers and store owners with affection and respect. Some might regard these artisans as having a "false consciousness" in which they are unaware of how traders take advantage of them. These same carvers and painters, however, have shown themselves to be quite willing to protest the unfairness of local merchants, political leaders, and government bureaucrats. I found that the relationship between wood carvers and American traders is for the most part mutually beneficial, and that the intermediaries do not make unreasonable amounts of profit. Although many of the wholesalers and store owners are tolerant and well-intentioned, it would be naive to attribute the relative lack of exploitation in the wood-carving trade to the dealers' good hearts. Instead, the practical difficulties associated with the trade in Oaxacan wood carving (and perhaps Mexican folk art in general) make the returns on labor for dealers rather low.

Craft Sales in Mexico

Postrevolutionary governments in Mexico have consistently encouraged craft sales in rural communities. The state has sponsored contests for artisans and established government-run stores that buy and sell crafts from all over the country. In parts of Mexico with large Indian populations, the government promotes an ethnic identity based on craft sales in national museum outlets and bazaars sponsored by regional artisan institutes.[2] State tourism agencies prominently display the products of local artisans in their brochures.

The postrevolutionary state's interest in popular arts and crafts was initially ideological. The leaders of Mexico in the 1920s and 1930s were seeking to unite a country divided along ethnic, linguistic, and political lines (Atl 1922; Kaplan 1993). In particular, they attempted to draw the indigenous population into the state by creating national symbols of identity that reflected the country's pre-Columbian past. By the mid-twentieth century, the state's promotion of tourist art was also motivated by economic concerns. An increase in tourism spurred by transportation improvements brought many visitors who were willing to buy Mexican crafts. At the same time, most rural residents were finding it harder to support their families through agriculture because of small plots, low crop prices, and poor soils. The economic situation of many peasant farmers had worsened as land became scarcer as a result of population growth and government policies that favored large-scale, capital-intensive agriculture. The state therefore encouraged craft production in order to foster rural development, reduce the pace of rural to urban migration, and attract tourists to regions with large indigenous populations.

Even the most casual tourist in the city of Oaxaca can see that craft production is an integral part of the local economy. Visitors in the city's historic center pass shop after shop featuring the region's artisans. Tours feature potters, weavers, and wood carvers. Vendors in squares and marketplaces hawk handmade rugs, earthenware, tin ornaments, cloth and leather belts, and wall hangings. Few tourists realize that their purchases are only a small part of the international trade in arts and crafts. The livelihoods of most Oaxacan potters, weavers, and wood carvers depend primarily on sales to intermediaries based in the United States.

The History of Oaxacan Wood Carving

Oaxacan wood carvings are an extraordinarily apt illustration of how the global demand for exotic indigenous crafts can lead to an "invented tradition" (Hobsbawm 1983). The origins of Oaxacan wood carvings differ from those of most other ethnic and tourist arts. Accounts of craft commercialization ordinarily describe how objects that were at one time integral parts of indigenous cultures become transformed as a result of a global marketplace. The hybrid nature of such crafts leads to heated debates about artistic merit and authenticity. Oaxacan wood carvings, however, are late-twentieth-century creations made mostly by monolingual Spanish speakers. The pieces nonetheless are stylistically similar in some respects to other local crafts with longer histories and are often promoted as a symbol of Zapotec Indian identity by merchants dealing in ethnic arts (see fig. 6.1).

The wood-carving boom originated in the activities of Oaxaca-based shop owners and two particular carvers—Manuel Jiménez of Arrazola and Isidoro Cruz of San Martín Tilcajete. Jiménez, born in 1919, began to carve wooden figures as a boy to pass the time while tending animals. In the late 1950s and early 1960s, owners of crafts shops in Oaxaca began buying Jiménez's carvings

Figure 6.1.   An example of the Oaxacan woodcarver's skill. Photo courtesy of Michael Chibnik.

and selling them to folk art collectors such as Nelson Rockefeller. By the late 1960s, Jiménez was giving exhibitions in museums in Mexico City and the United States. His carvings were later featured in books and films about Mexican art. Tourists started to visit Jiménez's workshop in Arrazola during the 1970s. The master kept his techniques secret, however, and for a long time the only carvers in Arrazola were Jiménez, his sons, and a son-in-law. In the early 1980s, other carvers in Arrazola began offering pieces for sale to tourists visiting Jiménez. Still, there were only about six carving families in town as late as 1985.

Isidoro Cruz learned to carve when he was thirteen years old, during a long illness in the late 1940s. While Cruz was working as an oxcart maker in the city of Oaxaca in 1968, his carvings were noticed by Tonatiúh Gutiérrez, director of expositions for the Mexican National Tourist Council. Gutiérrez, who knew of Jiménez's work, urged Cruz to make masks for sale. Gutiérrez later became head of a national government agency aimed at increasing craft sales. He appointed Cruz the director of the agency's buying center in Oaxaca. During the four years Cruz held this job, he was able to place his neighbors in offices of the agency throughout Mexico. Cruz was open about his carving methods, and about ten men in San Martín began carving in the early 1970s.

Carvers in Arrazola and San Martín in the 1970s and early 1980s sold their pieces mostly to store owners in Oaxaca. Only Jiménez supported his family primarily by making wood figures; other carvers spent more time in farming and wage labor. Wood carving during this period was a part-time occupation for a few adult males; women and children occasionally helped with painting and sanding. Many carvings were of human figures, ox teams, devils, angels, and skeletons.

In the mid-1980s, wholesalers and store owners from the United States began visiting Arrazola and San Martín to buy carvings. These communities became the principal centers for the craft. A change in the dollar–peso exchange rate also made dealing in Mexican folk art more lucrative for dealers from the United States. Traders could earn significant sums of money by selling carvings in the United States at three to six times their cost in Mexico. As more dealers visited the carving communities, artisans developed new styles in their efforts to attract clients. Animal carvings sold the best and came to dominate the trade. Water-based aniline paints gave way to house paints that did not run as much and were less likely to fade in the sun. Carvings became more complicated and paint jobs more ornate as families competed to show their skills.

By 1990, most households in Arrazola and San Martín earned part of their income from the sale of carvings. Interest in the wood figures was further stimulated when Shepard Barbash published an article about the carvings in *Smithsonian* (Barbash 1991) and a popular art book (Barbash 1993). The book and article have striking photographs by Vicki Ragan. Although Barbash feared that the wood-carving boom would soon fade as dealers moved on to other crafts, sales increased throughout the rest of the decade.

When the demand for wood figures increased in the 1980s, male carvers needed their wives and children to help with painting and sanding. Carving quickly became a family activity carried out in workshops in which men contributed considerably less than half the total labor. By 1990 the ordinary—but far from universal—division of labor saw men carving and doing some painting, women painting, and children sanding and doing simple painting (see fig. 6.2). Families sometimes found that they could not fill large orders by using only household labor, and they hired one or two workers to help with the carving, painting, and sanding. In addition, several carving workshops employing ten to twenty workers were established in Arrazola in the 1990s. While the owners of these businesses—often women—sold some pieces to wholesalers, they concentrated on producing cheap carvings for tourists seeking souvenirs.

Traders and Artisans

Although many different dealers occasionally bought pieces in the late 1980s, there was a limited number of wholesalers and store owners who bought in quantity and regularly returned to Arrazola and San Martín. Because these important traders exchanged information, artisan families who succeeded in establishing connections with one or two dealers were ordinarily later able to sell to others. Economic stratification among artisans rapidly developed. The most successful carvers sold mostly to dealers from the United States; the less successful carvers sold mostly to tourists and store owners in Oaxaca. Relationships with American traders therefore became tremendously important for artisans. The experiences of two successful carving families from San Martín show the complex and often happenstance ways in which ties between dealers and artisans were formed and maintained.

When artisans from San Martín discuss the origins of wood carving in their community, they usually mention the activities of Coindo Melchor, who began carving around 1970. Coindo, a close friend of Isidoro Cruz, is a versatile carver willing and able to make a variety of pieces. He is particularly known for making imaginary beings such as pegasuses, mermaids, and bird-women (*ilusiones*). When Isidoro ran the government buying center in Oaxaca in the early 1970s, Coindo regularly sold pieces through this outlet.

Figure 6.2.   Oaxacan artisans at work. Photo courtesy of Michael Chibnik.

Nonetheless, his main occupations remained farming and masonry. After Isidoro left the buying agency in 1975, Coindo had trouble selling pieces for almost a decade. Although Coindo and his wife Eva García were not especially well-off economically, they somehow managed to provide exceptionally good educations for their two sons, Jesús and Inocente. Both sons almost finished engineering degrees in the 1980s.

Because Coindo was already a well-established artisan, he was one of the first carvers sought out by dealers visiting San Martín in the mid-1980s. Coindo's most important customer at this time was Patrick Charles, a wholesaler from Emeryville, California. Charles regularly featured Coindo's pieces in his catalogs. He commissioned Coindo to make three hundred wooden dinosaurs every two months. Because Coindo continued to farm, he could not possibly fill such a large order working alone, and he enlisted Eva and his sons to help. Charles told the family that he anticipated making orders of this size for at least ten years. Around 1988, however, Charles suffered business reverses and his orders stopped. By this time the Melchor family had a number of other customers, however, and the loss of Charles's orders was not disastrous. Jesús and Inocente became full-time carvers; Eva did much of the painting.

María Jiménez, arguably the best-known painter of Oaxacan wood carvings, has a distinct style that is immediately recognizable. She paints pieces (carved by her brothers) with tiny, repeated decorations involving geometric, religious, and animal motifs. The family is particularly known for their meticulously painted virgins, angels, and saints that sell for hundreds of dollars apiece. They have so much business now that clients often are told that a requested piece will not be ready for six to nine months.

Despite their current fame and prosperity, the pious, close-knit Jiménez family had a hard time gaining the patronage of wholesalers in the late 1980s. The five sons and three daughters of Agapito Jiménez and Celia Ojeda ranged in age from eight to twenty-three in 1985. The family sewed embroidered dresses and farmed about seven hectares of corn, beans, and squash. In 1986 the Jiménezes started trying to sell pieces carved by two teenaged sons and painted by twenty-one-year-old María. At the beginning the family had little luck in their attempts to sell their crudely carved, simply painted pieces. Then María developed her intricate painting style around 1987. The family's first clients were twin sisters who ran a shop near the Artisans' Market in the city of Oaxaca. The unsigned Jiménez carvings sold well, and the sisters put in frequent orders.

Clive Kincaid from Arizona was the first wholesaler to buy Maria's pieces. In 1989, Clive saw several wonderfully-painted pieces in the store of the twin sisters. Clive asked who made the carvings, but the sisters would not give out this information. Not long afterwards, Clive was in San Martín at the end of a difficult day when Maria's eleven-year-old brother, Aron, asked Clive if he wanted to see "the best carvings in town." Clive reluctantly accompanied Aron to a modest adobe house and discovered the origin of the pieces he had seen in Oaxaca. He stayed until ten at night talking with the family. Clive thought that the pieces were carved stiffly and made suggestions about how to indicate motion by showing examples of other artisans' work. The family's carvings improved, and by the early 1990s, the Jiménezes were selling to a number of dealers. Although Clive remained friends with the family, he eventually found himself unable to afford their better pieces.

Nowadays the most successful carving families sell almost exclusively to dealers and may have only a few pieces available for the drop-in visitor. Wholesalers place orders for a number of pieces of a certain type at an agreed-upon price. No one expects carving families to produce standardized pieces. While orders are usually placed in person, they have been increasingly requested by telephone, fax, and e-mail.

Many dealers specialize in expensive, individualized pieces made by well-known artisan families. These carvings are sold in ethnic crafts stores in urban areas, university towns, and upscale resorts. A number of traders sell pieces over the Internet, where there are several hundred sites from which carvings can be bought. Carvings are also regularly sold on eBay. Some wholesalers also buy large numbers of cheap pieces. These carvings, usually sold in trade shows, often end up in gift shops. One low-end dealer told me that his target customer was "a married woman between twenty-eight and fifty-five looking for a present."

Anthropologists writing about Mexican crafts (e.g., Cook and Binford 1990; Novelo 1976) have pointed out how artisans are embedded in capitalist relations of production. These writers place particular emphasis on the power that intermediaries have to dictate the productive activities of artisans. They note that seemingly independent artisan households in rural communities are often actually pieceworkers in urban-based enterprises. These observations seem pertinent to some aspects of the wood-carving trade. Certainly a carving family has little autonomy when asked by a dealer to make "one hundred turtles at twenty pesos apiece." The employees of the Arrazola workshops in the 1990s were involved in prototypical capitalist enterprises. Nevertheless, many carving families have considerable control over what they make. These skilled workers with individual styles are producing an item for which there is considerable demand. Although most are willing to make whatever a dealer requests, they are not at the mercy of intermediaries. They can demand prices that provide locally good returns for labor (and are better than any alternative other than migration to the United States). A very successful carving family might earn US$15,000 per year. Earnings of US$4,000–$5,000 per year from carving are common, and this is ordinarily supplemented by other sources of income. The carvers know that they are much better-off than most rural Oaxacans, and they appreciate the patronage of the traders.

Portraits of the Traders

Barbash (1993, 109) has aptly described the intermediaries in the wood-carving trade as an independent-minded, colorful group of individuals who lead hectic, bilateral lives. Most traders appreciate the intercultural exchanges their work requires. They usually begin selling wood carvings after visiting Oaxaca as tourists. Although their knowledge of Spanish varies, all know enough to conduct their business transactions. Many have long-term friendships with wood-carving families; some have brought artisans to the United States for exhibitions.

The wholesalers differ considerably in the methods they use to buy and sell pieces. A few sell only wood carvings; most also buy Mexican textiles and pottery. Many deal in diverse ethnic crafts from around the world. There are several large-scale dealers who have warehouses filled with wood carvings and spend thousands of dollars hawking their pieces in enormous gift shows in major cities. The large, regular purchases of two such dealers—Jerre Boyd and Clive Kincaid—were so important to the livelihood of many wood-carving families in Arrazola and San Martín in the 1990s that there were serious repercussions in these communities when both dealers cut down on orders. While other folk art dealers buying Oaxacan crafts had bigger businesses, none bought as many wood carvings as Boyd and Kincaid. Most folk art dealers visiting Oaxaca operate on a much smaller scale. They may make one or two trips to Mexico a year in which they buy carvings and other crafts. These small-scale dealers usually sell crafts directly to shop owners. Their profits sometimes barely cover the costs of their trips.

The descriptions that follow of four wood-carving wholesalers and their businesses in the late 1990s illustrate some of the varied niches for intermediaries in the wood-carving trade. Clive Kincaid ran a successful, large-scale wholesale operation specializing in inexpensive wood carvings. Carol Cross and Steven Custer sold high-quality pieces during the summer and fall that had been purchased during the winter and spring in Mexico. Fran Betteridge was a retired lawyer whose small-scale dealing in wood carvings paid for her travels in Mexico. Rick (a pseudonym) was a dealer with very little working capital who eked out a living buying and selling wood carvings from Arrazola.

A Large-Scale Operation

I had wanted to meet Clive Kincaid long before I first talked to him. He seemed to be the second most important buyer of Oaxacan wood carvings (behind Jerre Boyd from California), and he employed my friends Antonio and Saúl Aragón from Arrazola as his representatives in Oaxaca. Clive was known in Mexico as "Andres," which is a Hispanicization of Andrew, his middle name. Although Clive and I were occasionally in Oaxaca at the same time, he was too busy working with Antonio, Saúl, and the carvers to meet with me. I eventually interviewed Clive in May 1998 in his warehouse in Wickenburg, Arizona.

Clive, who was about forty-five at the time, had dealt in folk art for more than a decade. After graduating from the University of California, Los Angeles, in the 1970s with a major in anthropology, Clive received a master's degree in wilderness management and then founded an environmental organization in the mountain states where his wife, Chris, was employed as an archaeologist for the National Park Service. Clive's work was busy and tense, involving testimony before Congress and conflicts with logging and ranching interests. In 1989 Clive became exhausted, quit his job, and had what he describes as a "life crisis." After sitting around his house for several months, Clive drove a van into Mexico, where he traveled for three months. On this trip Clive first met the Aragón family in Arrazola, where he had gone to look at wood carvings. Chris joined Clive for his last two weeks in Mexico.

During the 1989 trip, Clive bought a variety of crafts, which he and Chris packed into eight large baskets. After some confusion concerning customs forms at Douglas, Arizona, the couple crossed the border and took their purchases to a department store (Bullock's) in Los Angeles. When the store was willing to pay nine thousand dollars for the crafts, Clive decided to go into the import-export business, and he later bought Designer Imports, a company that sold mostly rugs from the weaving town of Teotitlán in Oaxaca. Between 1990 and 1993, Clive continued to specialize in rugs, working with an intermediary from Teotitlán. He also sold carvings, pottery, and other Mexican crafts, and he continued to visit the Aragón family. In 1994, Clive decided to try to sell more carvings and hired Antonio Aragón to be his representative. Clive wired money and orders for wood carvings to Antonio, who then bought the pieces and sent them via airfreight to Clive's warehouse in Page, Arizona. Antonio received 10 percent of what the carvers were paid for the orders. In 1998, Saúl Aragón replaced his brother Antonio as Clive's representative.

The wood-carving business started out small-scale, but by 1995 Clive was spending sixty thousand to seventy thousand dollars a year on wood carvings. The couple's son was born about then. Chris left the Park Service and began working full time for Designer Imports. Clive later moved Designer Imports to Wickenburg, a small town about fifty miles northwest of Phoenix. In 1998, wood carvings comprised about 60 percent of the business of Designer Imports, which also sold Mexican pottery and Panamanian baskets. Clive employed about eight people at the Wickenburg warehouse. Two employees in Wickenburg spent most of their time painting and gluing pieces that had been broken. Clive estimated that about 3 percent of the pieces that arrived by airfreight needed repairs. Although Designer Imports sent pieces to its customers in zip-closure bags, some additional breakage also occurred at this stage of the commodity chain. When this happened, Designer Imports would repair the broken pieces without charge. Most of the relatively few returns to Designer Imports were of irrevocably damaged pieces. While the shops that bought from Clive sometimes had the option of returning unsold pieces, this rarely happened.

In 1998 Clive had five to six hundred clients for wood carvings, and he said that the market seemed to be holding firm. Although he sold mostly to gift shops, his clients included about one hundred museum stores. Most of his sales took place during seven gifts shows that Clive attended each year, paying on average eight thousand dollars each time for his exhibition space. Some of these shows (e.g., Los Angeles, San Francisco, and Phoenix) were at the same time and place each year; others (for example, museum shows held in conjunction with meetings) changed their times or places from year to year. Clive's exhibitions at the shows included examples of his artisans' work, a catalog, and a price list. Clive had customers in about thirty states in 1998, and he thought that the regional concentration of his clients in California and Arizona had more to do with his location than any particularly southwestern appeal of the carvings. But the very features that make wood carvings appealing to buyers from the United States created certain problems for Clive. Many people from industrial countries are attracted to Oaxacan wood carvings because they are handmade and no two pieces look exactly alike. However, this meant that buyers could not be guaranteed that they would receive pieces exactly like those exhibited by Clive or shown in the Designer Imports catalogs.

Clive's airfreight bill for a typical shipment of wood carvings was about two thousand dollars. Even though most handicrafts are duty-free (the major exception is textiles), Clive had significant expenses associated with import regulations. In 1998, anyone who imported more than $1,200 in wood carvings (or other handicrafts) needed to employ a customs broker. Clive ordinarily spent about three hundred dollars on a customs broker and on other minor government-imposed fees when importing carvings by airfreight. The size of his shipment was largely irrelevant to this cost.

Between 1995 and 1998, Clive bought pieces from 119 different carving families. While Designer Imports bought some expensive pieces, the company specialized in the medium to low end of the market. Clive bought a carving only if he thought that a retailer would be able to sell the piece for five times its original cost in Arrazola or San Martín. He estimated that if he paid ten dollars for a piece in a village, there would be another five dollars of expenses (airfreight charges, customs fees, and Saúl's commissions) associated with getting the carving to Arizona. In the United States, Clive had overhead costs such as his employees' salaries, gift show costs, and rent (one thousand dollars monthly for the Wickenburg warehouse). Clive's wholesale price for a carving was typically three times what Saúl or Antonio paid in Oaxaca. This markup enabled him to make a net profit of 15–18 percent of the wholesale price. According to Clive, retailers sold the pieces for 1.7 to 4 times the wholesale price, with 2.2 times being the average.

I was able to obtain records of all of Clive's wood-carving purchases in 1995, 1996, 1997, and 1998. During this time the average price he paid for a piece in Oaxaca was about five dollars. Clive's estimates of costs and profits along the commodity chain can perhaps be most easily understood by examining the economics of the sales associated with a five-dollar carving. Designer Imports might sell this carving for fifteen dollars at a gift show. The retailer buying the piece would sell it in a shop to a customer for perhaps thirty-five dollars. While I cannot estimate the retailer's net profit on the carving, I know enough about the overhead costs of other people involved in the commodity chain to estimate what they clear. The carvers would earn about $4.50, Saúl or Antonio $0.50, and Clive $1.60.

The figures I obtained also allow estimates of annual incomes that Clive and his Arrazola representatives earned from wood-carving sales. Clive spent on the average about $60,000 on wood carvings annually between 1995 and 1998. This meant that commissions for Antonio (1995–1997) or Saúl (1998) averaged about $6,000, and that Clive grossed about $180,000 annually from his sales to retailers. Assuming that Clive cleared 17 percent on such sales, his annual net profit from wood carvings was about $31,000. Even if my estimates of profits are off a bit (I suspect that they are low), Clive clearly did not get rich trading Oaxacan wood carvings.

Clive's purchases provide some hard-to-get quantitative evidence about what kinds of Oaxacan carvings are being sold in the United States. Obviously, his purchases were to a certain extent unrepresentative since Clive specialized for the most part in medium-priced and inexpensive pieces bought from selected carvers and villages, and he had his own particular preferences. Nonetheless, he bought from a wide variety of carvers and sold to stores and museum shops all over the United States. His purchases therefore reflected consumer demand in the United States fairly well.

My data on Designer Import purchases come from notebooks in which Saúl recorded purchases that he or Antonio made at Clive's request. Saúl listed 170 different types of carvings bought between 1995 and 1998. The diversity of niches in the wood-carving trade is shown by the lack of dominance of any particular carving type. Designer Imports spent the most money on carved cats, which comprised 7 percent of total expenditures. The company spent only 39 percent of its total expenditures on the most popular ten items combined and 58 percent on the top twenty types of carvings.

The fifteen types of carvings that Designer Imports spent the most money on were (in descending order) cats, armadillos, frogs, dogs, *alebrijes* (fantastic figures that would fit on the cover of a science-fiction magazine of the 1940s), iguanas, lizards, dragons, porcupines, gazelles, burros, cactuses, giraffes, crabs, and coyotes. The relative ranking of these items for the most part did not vary dramatically from year to year. There are diverse reasons for the popularity of these particular items, which include animals found in Oaxaca, nonindigenous animals, fantastic creatures, and a plant. Cats and dogs are beloved pets of many potential customers. Armadillos, coyotes, and cactuses are semi-iconic in parts of the Southwest of the United States; burros and lizards are emblematic of Oaxaca. The shapes of iguanas, dragons, gazelles, and porcupines enable artisans to demonstrate their carving skills; *alebrijes* and dragons are fantastic creatures that may have an appeal similar to that of characters in Disney cartoons. Frogs, first popularized by Manuel Jiménez, are perhaps the most traditional Oaxacan animal wood carving. The reason for the popularity of the remaining item, the crab, is not obvious to me.

Clive's purchases reflected the dominance of animals in the wood-carving trade. I divided the types of carvings recorded by Saúl into six categories: (1) animals, (2) folkloric and religious beings (e.g., saints, angels, devils, *alebrijes*, and unicorns), (3) humans, (4) plants, (5) inanimate objects (e.g. frames, jewelry boxes), and (6) others (including hard-to-classify items). Designer Imports spent 72 percent of its wood-carving expenditures between 1995 and

1998 on animals, 13 percent on folkloric and religious beings, 7 percent on inanimate objects, and 8 percent on other kinds of items (including human beings and plants). These proportions were about the same in Arrazola and San Martín and did not vary much from year to year.

Upscale Wholesaling

Carol Cross and Steven Custer began selling high-quality Mexican crafts to collectors and store owners in the late 1980s. Although most of their business took place in seven summer and fall art fairs and gift shows in different parts of the United States, they also sold directly to clients they had known for many years. Wood carvings were only part of the couple's business, Fish Out of Water, which they ran out of their home in Chicago and a rented apartment in Oaxaca. Carol was much more active than Steven in buying and selling wood carvings because she liked them more. Steven was more interested in antiques. However, Carol spoke only rudimentary Spanish and relied heavily on Steven's knowledge of the language when communicating with the artisans.

Carol and Steven were in late middle age when I met them in March 1998. Their personalities contrasted notably. Carol, who once worked as a news editor at a Chicago television station, was enthusiastic, chatty, and opinionated. Steven, who had studied many years ago in Mexico and knew a lot about its local cultures, was low-key and quiet. Fish Out of Water supported their travels and provided some useful income, but obviously was not nearly as profitable (or time-consuming) as Designer Imports.

The couple drove a van from Chicago to their apartment in Oaxaca every winter. The couple's buying took place at leisurely pace during their annual stay in Mexico from early January to late April. Carol and Steven bought pieces from all the high-end carvers and were willing to pay several hundred dollars for something they liked. Most of the pieces they bought, however, cost between twenty-five and seventy-five dollars.

Carol and Steven became close friends with several artisan families. Carol and Steven regularly brought used clothes to Mexico. Of all the dealers I met, they were perhaps the most involved in the personal lives of the wood carvers.

Fish Out of Water typically sold pieces for two or three times their original price in Oaxaca. Carol and Steven could afford to do this because their overhead was less than that of a store owner or even a large-scale wholesaler such as Clive Kincaid. They had no employees and avoided airfreight fees and breakage by transporting crafts by van across the border. The low markup on their pieces might also have been related to their relatively high prices. Retailers do not seem to have problems selling pieces that cost eight dollars in Oaxaca for forty dollars in the United States. It may not be so easy to sell a piece that costs sixty dollars in Oaxaca for three hundred dollars in the United States.

Small-Scale Wholesaling

Frances Betteridge is a retired lawyer from Tucson, Arizona, who likes to travel. She has paid for some of her trips to Mexico by buying wood carvings, which she sells to shops in Arizona. Small-scale dealers such as Fran earn insignificant incomes by U.S. standards. While there are artisans whose livelihoods depend on sales to Designer Imports and Fish Out of Water, no wood-carving family would suffer if Fran stopped buying. Nonetheless, purchases by small-scale dealers are an important part of the wood-carving trade. Fran buys much more than even the most enthusiastic collectors and tourists.

After Fran graduated from college (Mount Holyoke), she married, raised four children, divorced, and received a law degree. Fran worked as a lawyer for the city of Greenwich, Connecticut, for a number of years, but eventually decided to move to Tucson, where her anthropologist daughter lives. Anne Betteridge, a University of Chicago PhD who works with a Middle East association at the University of Arizona, is married to an Iranian architect. Fran worked primarily as an immigration lawyer in Tucson. Her clients were mostly Iranians and other people from the Middle East whom she met through her daughter and son-in-law.

In the mid-1980s Fran went to a Thanksgiving dinner in Tucson at which Jane and Thornton Robison, who later became owners of a guesthouse in Oaxaca, were present. Fran decided to go on a tour to Oaxaca that Jane was about to lead. The group stayed at the guesthouse, which at that time was owned by a cousin of Jane's. Fran liked Oaxaca and bought some carvings. She was planning to leave her law practice when she reached seventy in 1992 and was looking for something to do during her retirement. Fran is a lively and energetic woman who likes to keep busy.

When I met her, Fran was coming to Oaxaca four times a year. On two trips she co-ran Elderhostels (an organization that provides educational travel programs aimed at older people) based at one of the better hotels in Oaxaca. Fran bought carvings either before or after the Elderhostel trips. The other two trips to Oaxaca, which lasted as long as a month each, were devoted strictly to wood-carving purchases. Since Fran ordinarily stayed at the

Robisons' guesthouse, which cost forty-five dollars a day (including some meals) in the late 1990s, wood-carving sales may not have entirely covered her expenses on these trips.

Fran sells carvings out of her house in Tucson. She has found customers in several ways. Fran volunteers as a docent at the Tucson Museum of Art, where she meets people and tells them about the carvings. She has a home page on AOL with information about the carvings, and she also sells some pieces in Oaxaca to Elderhostel participants and to guests at the Robisons' guesthouse. Many of Fran's sales in Tucson are to the organizers of shows run by nonprofit organizations such as national parks and museums.

Getting Fran's purchases from Oaxaca to Arizona was somewhat complicated. She typically flew home with four baskets filled with carvings. The airlines sometimes, but not always, charged her excess luggage fees. Fran, who listed her reasons for travel as both "business" and "tourism" on her tourist card, tried to keep the official value of her merchandise below $1,200 in order to avoid paying for a customs broker. With the help of a friend in Oaxaca, she filled out a form called a pro forma invoice that described her merchandise and listed its cost. In theory, this had to be done for every carving purchased, but in practice customs officials had no objection when similar pieces were lumped together. Fran worried that if she came through the same airport too many times a year she would be required to use a customs broker even if the value of pieces on any one trip was less than $1,200. Although this had not happened when I interviewed Fran, the customs officials in Phoenix knew her well.

Fran sold her pieces on average at about twice what she paid for them. Her relatively few big, expensive carvings sold for less than double the buying price; small, cheap pieces often sold for more than twice what Fran paid. Fran sold mostly to the medium end of the market, with typical pieces costing her ten to thirty dollars in Oaxaca. Because of her dislike of most cheap carvings, she preferred not to sell them. Fran's shipping methods prevented her from taking back many big, expensive pieces; in any case, she could not afford to deal in high-end carvings. Her reluctance to buy pricey carvings was exacerbated by the wood-carving market around Tucson. According to Fran, there were few customers for expensive pieces there. Fran contrasted Tucson with Phoenix, where she thought there were more wealthy aficionados of folk art.

When Fran was in Oaxaca, she made buying trips to Arrazola and San Martín. Because Fran speaks only basic Spanish (better than Carol Cross but not nearly as good as Clive Kincaid and Steven Custer), Fran usually went on these trips with her friend Toni Sobel, a New Yorker married to a Oaxacan doctor. Fran especially liked to buy pieces made by female carvers, and she has written a short, unpublished paper about these women. On trips to carving communities, Fran bought about half the pieces she would sell. She bought the rest of her pieces from Victor Vásquez, the owner of an excellent shop in Oaxaca (Teresita) specializing in wood carvings.

A Novice Wholesaler

One day in March 1998 I went to the Abastos market in Oaxaca to catch a collective taxi to Arrazola. (This trip costs about five pesos and is the ordinary mode of transportation between Arrazola and the city of Oaxaca.) One of the other passengers was a fellow in his mid-thirties with long blond hair who was carrying a Guatemalan bag. In another generation, Rick would have been a stereotypical hippie. In the late 1990s, he was a minor entrepreneur attempting to support himself and a Mexican wife by importing crafts to the United States.

Although Rick is originally from Minnesota, he had been living for a number of years in Missoula, Montana. He had worked for an architectural firm and also supported himself as a carpenter and flute maker. Rick had recently married a rural Oaxacan woman who ran a vegetable stand near the hotel where he had been staying. Conversations between Rick and his bride must have been limited in scope since his Spanish was not good and she spoke no English. Rick complained to me about having had to buy four sheep for the wedding, and he said that he was having trouble obtaining papers for his wife that would enable her to enter the United States. He was not in a particularly good mood the day I talked with him.

Rick bought wood carvings and Teotitlán rugs, which he sold to stores in the mountain states and in an outdoor market in Missoula. He paid only thirty dollars a summer to rent a stand in the Missoula market. Rick sold pieces for double or triple what he paid for them. The wood carvings that Rick sold were an eclectic mix that varied considerably in price. He took them across the border as a tourist, paying custom fees if he declared that he was bringing in more than four hundred dollars of merchandise. (Presumably, he never brought in more than $1,200 since he said nothing about using a customs broker.)

All the pieces that Rick bought were from Arrazola. He obviously had not been dealing in wood carvings very long when I met him, since he knew almost nothing about the artisans and the places where pieces are made. He was unsure of Manuel Jiménez's name, for example, and had never heard of San Martín Tilcajete. Rick's ignorance may have hurt his business, given his obviously limited funds. He could have found cheaper pieces in other carving communities.

I thought that the most intriguing aspect of Rick's forays into the crafts trade was his attempt to barter for wood carvings. He had brought with him two wooden flutes modeled on North American Indian instruments. Using machines, Rick had taken five hours apiece to make the flutes. On our visits to carving families, Rick played haunting Native American melodies that are popular in western parts of the United States. The wood carvers were intrigued by both the music and the artisanship of the flutes and seemed tempted by Rick's offer of an exchange for wood carvings. Rick told me that he had already traded one flute for wood carvings worth three hundred pesos (about forty dollars at the time). Since Rick said that he had sold similar flutes in Montana for the equivalent of 1,200 pesos, this struck me as a reasonable exchange. If wood carvings in the United States sell for three to five times their price in Mexico, a fair price for a flute in Mexico might well be one quarter its price in the United States. Although I was surprised by Rick's attempt to barter flutes for wood carvings, what he was doing was really not all that unusual. Dealers from the United States sometimes exchange televisions and other electronic items for wood carvings.

Rick had brought little money with him the day I accompanied him in Arrazola. He ended up buying a number of small, inexpensive pieces. I knew, however, that he was occasionally willing to buy more expensive carvings. Rick's favorite artisan, Damian Morales (who specializes in deer and moose), makes pieces that cost twenty-five to fifty dollars. Furthermore, the Teotitlán rugs that Rick buys often cost fifty to one hundred dollars. Nonetheless, he obviously had much less capital than any of the other wholesalers I have profiled here. Given Rick's ignorance of the wood-carving trade, I had my doubts that he would be dealing in Mexican wood-carving crafts for long.

The Romanticization of Indigenous Crafts

Most Oaxacan wood carvers are straightforward and matter-of-fact when asked about their craft and ethnicity. They readily say that wood carving is a new art form, that their primary motivation for making pieces is monetary, and that they would abandon the craft with little regret if the market collapsed. Many like making pieces and appreciate the artistic talent of their neighbors. But they know what it is like to be poor and cannot afford to be sentimental about their work. Although carvers in Arrazola and San Martín acknowledge indigenous ancestry, they talk about themselves as residents of a particular community, the state of Oaxaca, and the country of Mexico. I have never heard artisans in these places identify themselves as Indians or Zapotecs. Very few speak an indigenous language.

The portraits of the wood carvers and their craft that appear in many of the advertisements written by the traders differ greatly from what the artisans tell anyone willing to listen. The artisans are depicted as Zapotec Indians working in a craft tradition hundreds of years old. Men and women (never children) work together when they can spare time from farming. The inspiration for their pieces, it is said, comes in dreams and often has a spiritual component. The discourse of the marketers of wood carvings says nothing about the makers' color televisions, Michael Jordan t-shirts, and relatives in California.

Why is it necessary to portray the wood carvers as noble Indians practicing an ancient craft? Is not a realistic story of ingenious men and women inventing an imaginative, appealing art form more interesting? The answer is obvious. The traders know that crafts sell well when they fit into a romantic narrative that places the maximum cultural distance between artisans and their customers. Many marketers of folk art are not being consciously untruthful, because they honestly believe that the carvers are Zapotec Indians who have been making these pieces for many years. More knowledgeable dealers may be willing to mislead their customers by simply noting that the Indians of Oaxaca have been making crafts for many years. Customers are then allowed to infer that the carvings they purchase are part of this indigenous tradition.

Although Oaxacan wood carvings are an invented tradition, the artisans are not the primary creators of this tradition and are often surprised to learn how their craft has been depicted. The invented tradition results from cultural assumptions that romanticize indigenous crafts and are shared by the marketers and buyers of folk art. The artisans' lack of control over how they are represented is a consequence of their peripheral position in a global commodity chain. But would the carvers change the advertisements if they could? The romantic misrepresentations, after all, help the artisans sell their pieces. The wood-carving trade depends in part on intercultural miscommunication.

A Trader Stops Buying

In May of 2002 I had an unsettling telephone conversation with Clive Kincaid. Although I knew that Clive's company, Designer Imports, was having some problems, I was surprised when Clive told me about a dramatic business decision that he had recently made. Designer Imports would no longer sell Oaxacan wood carvings.

Throughout the 1990s, potential customers had crowded around Designer Imports's displays at gift shows. But at the beginning of the new millennium, store owners and museum representatives were walking right past

Clive's booth. Oaxacan wood carvings had become old news; the retailers of folk art, as always, were searching for something different. Clive's response was to reduce Designer Imports's purchases of wood carvings and to rely more on sales of baskets from Panama and pottery from the Mexican state of Chihuahua. Despite this new business strategy, Clive lost thousands of dollars during fall 2001. He was forced to give up his warehouse in Arizona and to lay off his eight employees. In spring 2002, Clive and his wife Chris were running the business from their home and exploring alternative employment possibilities.

When I talked to Clive, he and Chris had just turned down job offers from the U.S. Park Service and were attempting to keep Designer Imports operating a while longer. They had reached the conclusion that dealing in wood carvings was a dead end. For the next year, the business would focus exclusively on Panamanian baskets and Chihuahuan pots. The decision to stop buying wood carvings was only partly related to dropping sales. The transaction cost for selling a wood carving was much greater than that for baskets and pots. Designer Imports received on average $9.50 for a wood carving; sales of baskets and pots averaged $40 to $50 apiece. Moreover, wood carvings usually consisted of multiple parts that were sometimes lost or broken in transit from Mexico to Arizona.

Clive dreaded the phone call that he was going to make later in the day. The time had come to tell Saúl that there would be no further wood-carving orders. Because Saúl is educated, resourceful, and capable, I thought that he would eventually find another good job. I was more worried about the many wood-carving families who relied on Designer Imports as their most important customer.

Although Clive's decision reflected a weakening of the market for inexpensive Oaxacan wood carvings, there is no reason to assume that the trade will disappear. At the beginning of the twenty-first century, there was still a strong demand for high-end wood carvings. Furthermore, one cannot make inferences about the fate of a craft from the actions of one company. Designer Imports, for example, had stopped buying weavings from Teotitlán after rug sales dipped in the early 1990s. Nonetheless, Teotitlán rugs were selling well in 2002, if perhaps not at the level of previous years.

Despite a genuine desire to help the wood carvers of Oaxaca, Clive Kincaid ultimately reached the bottom-line conclusion that Designer Imports would do better by selling different products made elsewhere. This decision will affect the livelihoods of hundreds of people in Oaxaca, Chihuahua, and Panama. Critics of globalization might suggest that Clive's actions illustrate how Mexican artisans have lost autonomy as they have become more integrated into the world economy. Proponents of globalization might then point out that the purchases of Designer Imports enabled many families from Oaxaca and Chihuaua to improve their standard of living over the past two decades. Both the critics and the proponents would be right. I cannot think of a better example of the double-edged impact of globalization. When I told this story to my friends, many asked if they could do something to help the wood carvers. In the long run, individual actions can have only a limited effect on the inexorable changes in demand for particular types of folk art. But there is a small way in which everyone can help right now. Just buy a Oaxacan wood carving.

Notes

This chapter is based on research in Mexico and the United States that was carried out for a total of seventeen months between July 1994 and May 2002. Much of the chapter consists of modified excerpts from my book about the trade in Oaxacan wood carvings (Chibnik 2003).

1. I use the term *Americans* here to refer to people from the United States. I recognize that this term often refers as well to all the inhabitants of North, Central, and South America.

2. There is considerable controversy over which residents of Mexico should be considered indigenous (Cook and Joo 1995). Within Mexico and the rest of Latin America, the preferred term for *Indians* (however defined) is *indígenas*.

References

Atl, Dr. Gerardo Murillo. 1922. *Las artes populares de México*. Mexico City: Secretaría de Industria y Comercio.

Barbash, Shepard. 1991. "These magicians carve dreams with their own machetes," *Smithsonian*, May, 119–29.

———. 1993. *Oaxacan Wood Carving: The Magic in the Trees*. Photographs by Vicki Ragan. San Francisco: Chronicle Press.

Chibnik, Michael. 2003. *Crafting Tradition: The Making and Marketing of Oaxacan Wood Carvings*. Austin: University of Texas Press.

Cook, Scott, and Leigh Binford. 1990. *Obliging Need: Rural Petty Industry in Mexican Capitalism*. Austin: University of Texas Press.

Cook, Scott, and Jong-Taick Joo. 1995. "Ethnicity and economy in rural Mexico: A critique of the Indigenista approach." *Latin American Research Review* 30 (2): 33–59.

Graburn, Nelson, ed. 1976. *Ethnic and Tourist Arts: Cultural Expressions from the Fourth World*. Berkeley: University of California Press.

Hobsbawm, Eric. 1983. "Inventing traditions." In *The Invention of Tradition*. Edited by Eric Hobsbawm and Terence Rangers. Cambridge: Cambridge University Press, 1–14.

Kaplan, Flora. 1993. "Mexican museums in the creation of a national image in world tourism." In *Crafts in the World Market: The Impact of Global Exchange on Middle American Artisans.* Edited by June Nash. Albany: State University of New York Press, 103–25.

Novelo, Victoria. 1976. *Artesanías y capitalismo en México.* Mexico City: SEP-INAH.

Young, Biloine. 1998. *Mexican Odyssey: Our Search for the People's Art.* St. Paul, Minnesota: Pogo Press.

PART III

Colonies

CHAPTER SEVEN

"Bridging the Cultural Gap," from *A Gathering of Fugitives*
Diana Anhalt

Editorial note: This chapter provides an intimate portrait of life among American left-wing expatriates in 1950s Mexico City. Anhalt and her family, like many others, fled the United States for political reasons.

"When somebody asks why we've moved to Mexico, you tell them we're here on business," my mother instructed. No other explanation was forthcoming. My parents never discussed their real reasons for moving to Mexico—certainly not with me—and, as I later learned, not with their friends either. But they weren't the only ones to keep a low profile. Many of the others did too: They varied daily routines, avoided discussing sensitive subjects over the phone, and, if they did, used Yiddish or some personalized version of pig Latin. Controversial books were rarely left out in the open. My parents kept theirs in a cardboard box on the upper shelf of their closet. Berthe Small told me that, at one point, the situation in Miami had grown so alarming she drove across the Everglades and dumped hers into the canal alongside the Tamiami Trail. In short, they were always on their guard.

Discretion was essential: The same FBI that had placed us under surveillance in the States would continue to do so in Mexico. In addition, the American business community could not help but be aware of our presence. Ironically, many of these expatriates shared the same sense of dislocation we felt at having to adapt to life in a foreign country. But, generally speaking, this would not draw us together. On the contrary, in time, we would discover we had run straight into the arms of the very people we were running away from: white, middle-class, conservative Republicans. Although they lived in

Mexico, they continued to inhabit their own little America—an America far less diversified than the ones we had fled, bringing with them their gift for turning everything they touched into Everywhere, USA. No matter that we shared a common language and a national identity. Our politics set us apart.

Because of our politics, our whereabouts were routinely recorded, our passports withdrawn without notice, and subpoenas delivered to our doorsteps. The local and foreign press publicized our names and political histories, and some of us lost jobs when pressure was placed upon our employers. Deportations, though less common, also occurred along with the occasional detention. Such dangers were real and deprived us of the security of planning for what the future might bring. Indeed, we had little sense of the future, forced as we were to live from one day to the next.

At the beginning, those were the things we shared, and sharing gave us the security of belonging. It drew us together by defreakifying the *I* and making us part of a *we*, an extended family. What we had in common kept us from standing alone. We could be a part of something, and that masked the pain and isolation. Freaks stand alone, but we didn't. Ergo, we weren't freaks.

With time, we glanced less at our watches and idled a little longer over a heavily spiced meal, learned to roll our tortillas around their fillings and our *R*s around words like *ferrocarril and carretera*, to gesture with our hands, to kiss casual acquaintances on the cheek, and to revel in the warmth of Mexico's people and its climate. We learned to adapt. Time numbed the gnawing sense of unease and diminished—though never completely—our sense of alienation.

Mexico City during the 1950s had a decidedly rural flavor, despite its more than a million and a half inhabitants, who referred to it as a *pueblote*, a huge town. Cows grazed, chickens pecked, and corn grew in vacant lots just blocks away from the city center; the surrounding mountains and snow-capped volcanoes—Ixtacihuatl and Popocatépetl—were visible most of the year, and on Sunday mornings, *charros*, Mexico's elegantly clad horsemen, cantered down the Paseo de la Reforma, the wide, tree-lined avenue said to resemble the Champs Elysees.

Minor drawbacks, of course, were to be expected: American movies took over a year to arrive; a good malted and shoes in extra-large sizes were unavailable; drinking the tap water or eating fruits and vegetables like strawberries, lettuce, grapes, and plums was ill-advised; medical and dental care could be careless; and a cloudburst brought the city to a standstill. Such things we took in stride. But reconciling ourselves to widespread poverty, institutionalized corruption, and the casual disregard for punctuality was more difficult.

In an attempt to understand, my father read exhaustively, took notes, and practiced his Spanish on bemused waiters and cab drivers. After a short time, he reconciled himself to the country's shortcomings and summed up Mexico as delightfully *meshugge*—crazy—and consequently, incapable of understanding. Thus, he distanced himself from the place and reduced it to something manageable. (My mother never did. An indefatigable crusader, she would, thirty years after her arrival in Mexico City, cast aspersions on anyone who tried to bribe an official, run a red light, or cut in front of her in line.)

Adaptation was easier for the children. My sister Judy and I didn't have to understand the country, just live in it. We could approach it gleefully, which was probably the only sensible way to go about it. I had no trouble with Mexico. My problem was with my parents and the holes in my life. Most likely I would have harbored similar resentments had I remained in the States. Perhaps, if I had been able to keep my old friends and acquire new parents, I would have been happy.

If leaving our homes and coming to terms with life in exile was hard enough for us and others like us, for some, surmounting the initial obstacles—finding a place to live, earning a living, learning the language, helping the children adjust, and making friends—was impossible. A few returned to the United States or went elsewhere after brief stays. While cultural gaps narrowed in time, they were rarely bridged. But there were enormous compensations: A small group shared the "one big happy family" security provided by a tightly-knit inner circle.[1] Many made new friends, expanded their interests, developed a growing appreciation for a new culture and language, and, sometimes, improved their standard of living.

Although this last would eventually prove true in our case, you would never have guessed it to judge from our first apartment in Mexico City, a decided step down from Parkchester in New York. Located in Polanco, a peaceful residential area in the north of the city, the two-bedroom, second-story walkup was chilly and damp and reeked of gas. My mother described it in her journal:

> It was brand new when we arrived but the rate of deterioration was alarming. Immediately adjacent, another building was going up, and water was constantly poured onto the cement wall to keep it moist. Their walls were moist but ours was soaking wet. What could we do? We tolerated the inconvenience. It reached the breaking point when we heard the noise of a drill making its way through the wall. We stared as the hole grew larger and larger, and finally a startled face appeared. "Pardon me, *senores*. There must be some mistake."

Unlike my parents, many others, George and Mary Oppen for example, settled in the south of the city following their arrival in 1950. A former Communist Party (CP) activist, George had attended a Party school and been closely associated with the Workers' Alliance, the King's County Party, and the Farmers Union Milk Strike during the 1930s. After serving in France during the Second World War, he settled in California and gave up full-time Party work but continued to head the Redondo Beach Party Chapter. As a functionary, he was vulnerable to prosecution under the Smith Act, but after he and his family moved to Mexico, the Party expelled him for desertion. Upon their arrival in Mexico, the Oppens installed themselves in the picturesque San Angel area. Subsequently, many later arrivals—particularly those from the west coast—would follow them. During his time in Mexico, George worked as a contractor and built custom-made furniture, but shortly before returning to the United States in 1959, he returned to the calling he had abandoned twenty-four years earlier. In 1969 he won a Pulitzer Prize for poetry.[2]

But that was much later. Upon their arrival, finding a place to live was the Oppens' primary concern. In her autobiography, Mary wrote that casual acquaintances helped her locate an apartment. "[It] had been built from an old wine storage room in the Monastery of Carmen in San Angel. The plumbing was faulty, so we bathed in the garden in the fountain where water flowed more freely. The garden was the chief reason for living [there]." Believing they should "be prepared to receive other political refugees," Mary later found a thirteen-room colonial house with a patio, a ballroom, and a chapel that shared the premises with the San Angel post office and a bank.[3]

Years later, screenwriter Jean Butler recalled, "People kind of got crushes on the Oppens. That crazy life style of theirs and whacky houses, and the way they did everything with such a flair made their impecuniousness seem so fascinating and wonderful."[4]

The Butlers also rented in San Angel, next door to Mexican artist Diego Rivera's studio. The boxy lines of the two-story glass and concrete structure were softened by a dusty coat of pinkish paint, and the house was skirted by a stand of cactus on one side, an overgrown garden on the other. A Juan O'Gorman mural covered their dining room wall.

Blacklisted writer Dalton Trumbo, on the other hand, lived briefly in the posh Lomas district in an imposing marble palazzo, a stark contrast to his former quarters in the Ashland federal prison.

Others were taken in by friends: Hollywood writers Bernie and Jean Gordon arrived with their toddler and moved in with the Oppens; artist Philip Stein, forced to leave the San Miguel de Allende Art Institute when his wife, Gertrude, contracted a mysterious ailment, lived for a short time with Mexican art expert José Gutierrez and his wife, Ruth.[5] When Spanish Civil War veteran Bart van der Schelling and his wife ran out of money, composer Conlon Nancarrow offered them the gatehouse on his property.[6]

Eventually both the Steins and the van der Schellings found living quarters on Insurgentes, or Insurgent Street, a location favored by many refugees. Two buildings, in particular, housed close to a dozen families. (Those interviewed assured me, however, that convenience dictated their choice of address; the street's name had nothing to do with it.)

When Berthe and Charles Small arrived from Miami in 1954, Albert Maltz, one of the Hollywood Ten, who also lived in San Angel, arranged for them to take over literary agent Maxim Lieber's Insurgentes apartment. After approximately three years, the Liebers had given up on Mexico and taken off for Poland. Berthe Small told me:

> We simply took over, furniture and all. I remember they gave us a price for the complete apartment, which was some ridiculous thing like three hundred dollars, but [we didn't have the money] so we paid it out . . . to Albert Maltz [who] had a checking account—we didn't—and could send the money to Poland.[7]

Unlike members of the American community who arrived in Mexico with positions in large American companies or the U.S. Embassy whose stays were limited to a few years and who were provided with a reliable support system, most political expatriates did not know how they were going to earn a living. Because this was a prime consideration, some chose to settle in towns like Guadalajara, Oaxaca, Cuernavaca, and San Miguel de Allende where they could live even more cheaply than in the city and, perhaps, get by on their savings. Furthermore, those few fearing deportation believed living in the provinces made it easier to keep a healthy distance between themselves, the FBI, the press, and the American community. Yet, for those who worried about supporting themselves, Mexico City was the most logical place to settle. Some opened small stores and businesses, invested in construction, raised chickens, produced films, wrote, taught at the American School or Mexico City College, or practiced a profession.

Among these were a few who entered Mexico as tourists, exiting every six months. Others, seeking to legitimize their status, had to enter either as "capital investors"—an irony not lost on present or former Communists—or as immigrants. This second option entitled them to work legally in Mexico and was generally preferred by those who, like my parents, intended to find a job or set up a business.

Belle and Mike, my parents, arrived with their life savings, one thousand dollars. I don't know why they mentioned this to me, but I do remember thinking it a hefty sum and resenting that such imported luxuries as Heinz baked beans (over a dollar a can) were not mine for the asking. (My parents had one thousand dollars, and they were denying me the pleasure of beans?) Within a few weeks my mother found a job—illegally, since she still lacked the proper documents—as a legal secretary in the American law firm of Goodrich, Dalton & Little, where no Spanish was required. Her salary, a pittance compared to what she would have earned in a similar capacity in the United States, allowed her to pay for a maid to take care of us after school and still keep a bit extra.

On weekends, we traveled by second-class bus to nearby villages where Mike, previously a salesman for a New York printing company, first saw and fell in love with the hand-crafted pottery, colonial figurines, and occasional pre-Columbian artifacts, not readily available in Mexico City. "A salesman can sell anything," he claimed, and so he rented space in a small flower shop on the Avenida Juarez where he sold lamps made out of curios purchased in the outlying markets. He also stocked ex-votos, or *milagros* (miracles): crudely painted pieces of tin salvaged from flattened-out cans that were meant as thank-you notes to God. They hung in churches, manifesting gratitude for the making of such miracles as saving crops, wreaking revenge on one's enemies, and impregnating the sterile. (If my father had been able to make a living at it, it would have been an even greater *milagro* but, alas, the talismans did not work for us.) When the futility of this venture became apparent, my mother's younger brother, Ben, came up with a solution. He suggested my parents set up a sales representation firm to import and distribute electronic components, which he manufactured in the States, in order to capitalize on Mexico's rapidly expanding television industry.

In addition to Ben's assistance, we had something else going for us: the low cost of living. Theatrical technician Asa Zatz, one of the earlier arrivals, summed it up this way:

> If you were a drinking man, you could get cirrhosis of the liver for practically nothing. . . . [Fortunately] I had enough foresight to bring papers along for the GI Bill. . . . I went to school, and that gave me about a hundred and eighteen dollars a month. . . . and I had a U.S. income of maybe one hundred or one hundred and twenty-five dollars, so I had somewhere around two hundred and fifty dollars a month. With two hundred and fifty dollars, I lived regally.

Some, unlike Asa who could depend on a stateside income, often chose to invest in Mexico since money was scarce and interest rates high. A few, Vanderbilt heir Fred Field, for example, would live to regret it. Fred wrote in his autobiography:

> Looking back, it almost seems as if I had an obsession to lose money. I went into three business ventures and came out with three total losses. Not twenty-five or ten cents on the dollar. No, in two of them it was a zero on the dollar, and on

the third, less than zero because I assumed responsibility for paying off the losses of a number of people whom I had persuaded to join in the investment.[8]

Others had similar experiences: When a member of the left-wing community purchased a fleet of ice-cream trucks, a number of political expatriates enthusiastically raised money to invest with him. Screenwriter Gordon Kahn, one of the Hollywood Nineteen, was so impressed by the venture that he insisted on recovering part of his own capital, tied up with a local businessman, only to discover that his savings had completely vanished, along with the businessman. Similarly, those who invested in the ice-cream business also lost their shirts. Victims later claimed to have been taken in by a Ponzi scheme whereby investors initially receive an impressive return on their money because the interest is being financed by new money coming into the venture. (Once that new money is no longer available, the schemer leaves town with the principal.) Screenwriter Hugo Butler put it this way, "We were fleeced by one of our own." However, artist Philip Stein, also an investor, told me, "People weren't ripped off, it's just that the business floundered . . . he did the best he could, and it didn't work out."

Investors also learned the meaning of the word *devaluation*. Since the Mexican peso had been stable for many years, few had considered that possibility. But in the spring of 1954, the dollar rose in value against the peso. Previously worth Mex$8.65 to the dollar, the peso shot up overnight to Mex$12.50, leaving those who had invested U.S. currency in the Mexican peso 30 percent poorer in dollars.

Many, regardless of whether they had savings or investments, struggled to get by. Former Spanish Civil War nurse Lini Fuhr deVries, for example, had been identified by Elizabeth Bentley as the person who had recruited her for the Communist Party. When Constancia de la Mora, a Spanish refugee who had promised to assist Lini upon her arrival in Mexico, died suddenly, Lini was left homeless and unemployed. She gave English lessons and nursed a few private patients. Eventually, she was able to rent a large property, sublet it, and move into the gardener's cottage. But, convinced that her life in Cuernavaca alienated her from a genuinely Mexican experience, she moved to Oaxaca. While teaching English and—despite her broken Spanish—public health and ethnology at the local university, she learned about Mexico's Papaloapan Commission. Engaged in a monumental project to build a dam in southeastern Mexico, which would require the relocation of approximately 200,000 Indians, the commission hired Lini. Working closely with local school teachers, she developed a program capable of reaching out into the native communities, teaching basic health and nutrition, and helping the inhabitants adapt to change.[9]

Like Lini, many of the expatriates turned to teaching upon arrival: Economist John Menz and Enos Wicher—described as a former Communist Party organizer in the state of Wisconsin, physicist, or political scientist, depending on whom you spoke to—taught at Mexico City College; Alan Lane Lewis, a director and producer, worked in the Drama Department of the University of Mexico; and Bart van der Schelling gave a course in German *lied* at the National Conservatory of Music.[10]

For the U.S.-accredited American School, always on the lookout for qualified U.S.-trained personnel willing to work for peso wages, the influx of teachers proved a blessing. They hired former literary agent Maxim Lieber's wife, Minna; Sonia Strand, American poet Mark Strand's mother; Edna van der Schelling; Edith Halperin, Boston University professor Maurice Halperin's wife; and several others. Some, like Gertrude Stein, who with two young children and no household help was unable to work full time, gave private English lessons.

At the beginning, few had it easy. When I asked Miami refugee Berthe Small how they supported themselves, she replied: "We didn't . . . It took one year to get our sea-legs, to figure out [what to do], to make contact with people, to get the whole thing set up. Charles's brother, Jerry, supported us. . . . The early years were really tough [but] Charles opened a silver shop."[11]

But building up a business, particularly for those unaccustomed to working outside the United States, was no easy matter. Spanish Civil War veteran Eddy Lending, my parents' friend from New York, arranged to represent American manufacturers in Mexico. However, a recently enacted law taxed all but essential imports, and his products hardly qualified. High import duties, which fluctuated with each order, dissuaded potential clients, and Ed, fearing his business was about to collapse, requested an appointment with the Mexican general in charge of processing all merchandise sent through the Mexico City airport.

> "No problem," the general told me. "Simply do the importing yourself. All your goods will come in labeled as non-lucrative samples." The tariff would be about one half of 1 percent of the actual value. He would get a spiff for his trouble. My customers would all get their merchandise. They'd make more. I'd make more. Everybody would be happy. I was back in business.[12]

For business people like my parents, Eddy Lending, or the Smalls, starting up was difficult but by no means impossible. However, for professionals like Miami dentist David Prensky, establishing a practice in Mexico was far more challenging. In accordance with Mexican law, David could work as an employee during his first five years in the country but could not command a salary. Once he had completed the five year requirement and attained professional certification by revalidating his U.S. studies, he could open his own office. However, the Mexican statutes governing professionals required he be a Mexican citizen. He, therefore, had to file a suit demonstrating that, in spite of his American citizenship, he was, in keeping with the Mexican Constitution, entitled to earn a living in a manner consistent with the training he had received. Although he won the case, the law remained unchanged, and subsequent applicants would have to repeat the same procedure.[13]

As a result of such experiences, it didn't take us long to discover that earning a living in Mexico was no picnic for newcomers. Screenwriter Dalton Trumbo wrote, "As for our condition, we are living out an old truism: 'The first time you see Mexico, you are struck by the horrible poverty: Within a year, you discover it's infectious.'"[14]

Because of the nature of their work, the screenwriters were in a class of their own: In Hollywood, they had gained a foothold in the competitive film industry. (The Butlers, for example, discovered upon arrival in Mexico that of twelve English-language films being screened in Mexico City, they had worked on four, and they were by no means the most successful of the group.) But following the establishment of the blacklist, their names were no longer theirs to use, and they were forced to take on new identities in order to peddle their work. Some were able to acquire *fronts*, individuals who, in exchange for a commission, would loan them their names and stand in for them if the need should arise. On other occasions, a pseudonym was adequate. (Writers like Dalton Trumbo, for example, had a half dozen.) Yet, inevitably, as newcomers, they were paid a fraction of what they had earned previously.

In addition, losing one's name could be a traumatic experience. Jean Butler wrote:

> That his (Hugo's) name was banished, now and for a long time to come—perhaps for our lifetimes—I had somehow gotten used to. But that my own, my maiden name, the name I'd acted under and continued to use professionally in writing jobs and story sales after my marriage, the name that was my whole identity—the idea that this too was condemned to oblivion, swept over me like a black wave. I felt as though I were losing an arm or a leg.[15]

They lost their names but not their determination to succeed outside the United States. By the beginning of 1952, most of the Hollywood crowd had settled in, placed their children in school, and started to work: Dalton Trumbo wrote an unmarketable screenplay, *The Jean Field Story*; Julian (Hallevy) Zimet wrote for *Oil World* and translated speeches into English for Mexico's oil industry manager; Jean Butler worked on a short story set in Mexico, and screenwriters Gordon Kahn, Ring Lardner Jr., and Albert Maltz began to write novels.

The former executive secretary of the Hollywood Independent Citizens Committee of Arts, Sciences and Professions (HICCASP), George Pepper, turned to production. He established contact with exiled Spanish director Luis Buñuel and convinced a group of blacklisted musicians to invest in the production of Hugo Butler's version of *Robinson Crusoe*. (Afraid he might be identified during the filming, Hugo was introduced as *Señor* Addis, a Canadian investor and wheat farmer who had struck oil. He hung around the set during the day and rewrote the script at night under the name of Hugo Mozo—*Mozo* meaning "houseboy" or "butler" in Spanish.)[16]

Writer Margaret Larkin had a unique opportunity fall from the sky—almost literally. Married to Albert Maltz, she had already established a reputation as a journalist, union activist, folk singer, and folk song collector by the time she got to Mexico. During a flight to Oaxaca a bomb, planted in the luggage compartment of the plane on which she and her daughter were traveling, exploded. Her subsequent account of the criminal investigation and trial of the man responsible for the bomb, and who had hoped to collect insurance on seven passengers he had hired to work in a gold mine, was published by Simon and Schuster under the title *Seven Shares in a Gold Mine*.[17]

Although the West Coast émigrés were starting to adapt to life in Mexico, they were barely getting by on their rapidly diminishing savings. "It's true that the first years were economically very hard . . . [but] we were living as colonizers with all the comforts entailed," Jeanette Pepper told me during an interview. Despite this, life was not easy. She explained:

> We were literally eating from each other's borrowings. . . . We would all—the Trumbos, Butlers, Hunters,[18] Lardners, and ourselves—sit around a table and say, "Who can we borrow money from now?" And somebody would say "I have a cousin," and we would hit him up. And at the end of two years, the Trumbos were . . . preparing to return to the States and . . . [they] got some money, maybe $600. The Trumbos were a couple with three kids. The Peppers were just a couple, no kids. The Trumbos took this money . . . split it in half, gave the Peppers half and with half the remaining money took off for Los Angeles. You don't forget things like that.[19]

When times really got tough, there was always the pawnshop. Dalton Trumbo wrote:

> I am by now an old customer of the *Monte de Piedad* (Mount of Pity) so called because it is the government pawnshop and charges only 36 percent interest per year. We have at the moment reposing in the vaults of this benign institution a diamond ring, two gold cigarette lighters, a gold cigarette case, my

watch, a Leica camera, as well as certain objects of the Butlers I hocked for them in a moment of need. The appraisers down there regard me as a thief, but apparently one who knows how to stay out of trouble, hence they respect me.[20]

At the beginning the political expatriates not only established homes, found jobs and, when necessary, hocked the family silver, they did it in Spanish.

For my mother, learning Spanish was a source of such great anxiety that most of her writing about Mexico, adapted years later from early journal entries, dwells on it:

Our bilingual friends assured us that in no time at all we would be speaking fluently. They were not reckoning with my language resistance. Originally, I would try to say some simple thing like, "Where is Juarez Avenue?" When the response was "Sorry, I don't speak English," it was quite a letdown.

However, there were times when I had to accept full responsibility for my lack of comprehension. On one such occasion, we were at a resort hotel. We had finished lunch, and it was time for dessert. I noticed a large plate of watermelon at the next table. I called the waiter and, much to his astonishment, asked for a plate of *zanahorias*. I was insistent and added, "Don't tell me you don't have any because I can see a large plate of *zanahorias* at the next table." The waiter smiled and diplomatically told me I was asking for carrots.

I wasn't the only American experiencing these problems. I was visiting a recently arrived acquaintance when the maid rushed in and pointed to the front of the house where the family car was on fire. My friend dashed to the phone, seized the receiver and stood still. She didn't know the word for fire. Fortunately, the neighbors were able to give the alarm. The fire engine arrived after a lengthy interval, but had to be pushed up the steep hill. When this obstacle was overcome, they discovered there was no water. The car slowly burned to cinders. At the Spanish professor's following visit, he was greeted with an account of what had transpired and a request for basic vocabulary. After all, words like fire, water, help, may be mundane but they're infinitely more useful than butterfly, briefcase, or archipelago.[21]

I wish I could report that after decades in Mexico my mother could roll her *R*s with the best of them, but the truth is, even we had difficulty understanding her. Fortunately, Agustina, my mother's cook for over twenty-five years, acquired an uncanny ability to decipher her Spanish and would diligently serve as her intermediary to the outside world for as long as my parents remained in Mexico.

Certainly, learning the language was easier for the children, and by the time they left the country, most were bilingual. Shelley, Miami builder Max Shlafrock's fourteen-year-old step-daughter, at first refused to speak Spanish. She told me: "One day my mother confronted me. She said, 'Shelley, if you want someone to iron this skirt, you're going to have to learn how to ask for it yourself.' So I learned. But, I felt that my life was again being interrupted or destroyed. I guess the word is resentment."[22]

Feelings of resentment, confusion, or alienation were not confined to the offspring of political expatriates. (When families, regardless of their motivations, leave home, they don't ask their children for permission.) So, while their parents' politics may have provided one more barrier to adaptation, it was certainly not the only one.

Crawford Kilian, who was the son of television technician Mike Kilian, one of the Hollywood refugees, wrote: "Twice an outsider, I was already a *gringuito* in Mexico, a foreigner to be tolerated but not really accepted by Mexican kids. Now America had receded psychologically as well as geographically. It was another country, hostile to me and my family for reasons I couldn't really understand."[23]

In reference to that sense of isolation experienced by expatriates, screenwriter Dalton Trumbo's son, Chris, said:

> You're separate from the actual country you live in, you're not part of the culture so you're thrown back upon whatever resources exist. . . . There was no linkage, for instance, to churches . . . educational institutions. You were absolute foreigners. You were just kind of floating there. There was no connection to the society in general. . . . I didn't find Mexico a happy place particularly. But beautiful, you know.[24]

Like Chris, Mexican playwright Carlos Prieto, a close friend to several political expatriates, also pointed to the community's insularity and its effect on the children:

> The persons who . . . really suffered from exile were the sons and daughters because they lived in a never-never world. They were in a vacuum. They [went to] the American School.[25] Their friends were . . . the children of other exiles and the whole thing was hybrid. I told Charles Small, "Charlie, the least you could have done is send them to a Mexican school. They would have had Mexican friends, they would be living in Mexico. Now they're not living anywhere. They're not living in the United States, and they're not living in Mexico. They're not Mexicans, and they're not Americans. [When they leave] they'll miss a Mexico that didn't exist."[26]

Perhaps he was right. Most expatriates, however, would have defended their choice of school: Given the uncertainty of their stays in Mexico, their children's ability to readapt were they to return to the United States was of paramount concern.

Although attending the American School further isolated us from Mexico, it brought us, and sometimes our parents, into contact with each other. In Jean Butler's words, "the kids discovered each other as if by radar,"[27] because—outside a small circle of overlapping friendships—we often had no way of knowing who was who.

Yet, despite the American School's role in making us aware of each other's presence, we were still, in Crawford Kilian's words,

> literally walled off from Mexico. . . . The American School sat on fifteen acres behind a high stone and concrete wall in Tacubaya, one of the more wretched slums on the edge of the city. . . . The homes around us were shacks of cardboard and sheet metal, sometimes built in a day, and the children who swarmed the dirt streets would never see the inside of a classroom—least of all in the American School, many of whose students arrived in chauffeured limousines from the wealthy enclaves of Lomas, San Angel and the Pedregal.[28]

Nothing I'd known in the Bronx could have prepared me for the American School. All the girls had names like Lindley, Kay Sandra, Betty Ann, and Letitia, wore crinolines to school, and ate lettuce-and-tomato sandwiches with the crusts cut off. Their mothers were Pink Ladies at the American British Cowdray Hospital or belonged to the Junior League and the Garden Club. Their fathers worked for the American Embassy, General Electric, General Motors, or the CIA. Among them were a select few descended from former plantation owners who had fled the United States—with their slaves—following the Civil War. These had inherited their ancestors' political proclivities and passed them on to the others who came, for the most part, from Texas, and who hated Mexico, and who couldn't wait until Daddy was transferred. The American Legion, the American Society, and the Republicans Abroad, in that order, were the most prestigious community organizations.

Then there were the rest of us, Americans who didn't follow the norm, the politically motivated expatriates, an occasional Jew—outcasts. We read books, visited museums, listened to classical music, traveled throughout Mexico. (Some of us even tried to learn Spanish.)

Let's face it. We children were definitely not your run-of-the-mill American School students. No doubt, our politically attuned parents, recognizing this, did what little they could to prevent unpleasant incidents. Mary Oppen wrote that, prior to registration, one of the political expatriates had visited the school and asked the principal whether the children might be discriminated against. He was assured that no prejudice would be allowed to continue if any became noted. Oppen added, a bit ingenuously, "We did not, in all the years of our child's education there, hear of any such incident in the school."[29]

Screenwriter Jean Butler's daughter, Mary, remembers her mother's warning on her first day of kindergarten: "'Don't tell anybody what your father does for a living.' Not that I knew anyway, really. But she said, 'Just say that he's a journalist.'"[30]

Emmy Drucker was twelve years old when she arrived in Mexico from New York in 1952 with her mother and her father, David Drucker, counsel for Amtorg, a Russian-owned U.S.-based trading corporation:

> I was uprooted from Sunnyside, which was a fringe microcosm of things left-wing and Jewish and intellectual. . . . So suddenly I was in this high school which was much more American than anything I would have found in America. . . .
> [It] was right off the movie screen with sororities and fraternities and football games. I was there for four years; it took me about three years to make friends, and I joined the sorority that took fat girls and people with naturally curly hair and people who weren't beautiful and Jews and Mexicans. I remember my first date was with this guy named Richard Kimrey whose father was definitely in the State Department, and he was this tall, blond, very Anglo guy. I'd never seen anybody like that before in real life. We went to the movies, and I think he liked me, but he never dated me again. I was fresh off the boat and so I didn't realize, but somebody clued him in. . . . He never asked me out again.[31]

Unlike Emmy, I attended the American School from fourth grade through graduation and assimilated more thoroughly: I adopted the crinoline, joined the Girl Scouts on Foreign Soil, recited grace before meals in the homes of my church-going friends, and marched in the Girl Scout Honor Guard at Camp Camohmila each year. Still, I never could get my mother to cut the crusts off my sandwiches and resigned myself to joining Emmy Drucker's sorority, the only one that would have me.

In spite of my desire to fit in, I still relished my ability to occasionally shake the pillars of the American community—no enormous challenge—by delivering a speech for the American Legion Oratory Contest in favor of racial integration, or by wearing too much lipstick. And, because I was my parents' child, I never lost my contrary side, the one that delighted in shocking others. Consequently, I yearned for the star status reserved for the children of the "Famous Communists." (Their parents' names sometimes appeared in the newspapers. Mine never did.) I couldn't even provide a decent excuse for being in Mexico.

But in the end, I think I shared more with the school outcasts than with its insiders because, today, my memories of the things that startled me or set me apart are much the same as theirs: Chris Trumbo recalls that "At some schools they had cowboys and Indians. Here . . . they divided up into the

Confederacy and the Union, and it was considered really chic to be part of the Confederacy."[32]

A few of us remember what Linda Oppen referred to as "a bizarre field trip conducted annually to gape at the man who killed Trotsky. Trotsky was never explained or even talked about and non-leftist kids wouldn't have known who he was."[33] (Neither would many leftist kids.)

And I still recall the 1956 Stevenson-Eisenhower mock elections when I was one of only three students in a class of twenty-six supporting Stevenson.

Finally, most of us have specific incidents that we remember: Mary Butler was harassed by classmates following her down the hall chanting, "Hi Mary, how's Nikita? How's your uncle, uncle Niki?"[34] Linda Oppen recalls "fascist-communist" book-throwing battles on the San Angel school bus and the playground taunts;[35] and Mike Butler remembered the time when "somebody threw a rock at me and called me a dirty commie pinko Red or something." But he hastened to downplay it: "It's just one of those things you nurse among your scars and drag out like your Brownie merit badges [because] . . . there wasn't any long-term pattern of intimidation or harassment."[36]

Mike is right, and in fact, the younger children who entered school some four or five years after we did were less likely to be subject to such treatment. They were more readily accepted by their peers, both Mexican and American, and they often led their classes socially and academically and participated extensively in school activities.

Linda Oppen believes that the ostracism that she and some of the older children experienced helped explain why we were such excellent students. (I was the inglorious exception.) "We had no distractions or after-school activities. And we felt a terrible burden to be successful since our parents had fallen so far in their own eyes, and were competing to prove up to the heroics of the leftists, to prove they were best."[37] (Although hers was the highest grade-point average in her graduating class, she was not allowed to give the valedictory address and was listed, instead, as salutatorian.)[38]

While Linda suggests that we and our time in Mexico were inevitably colored by our parents' reasons for being there, Chris Trumbo claims that the problems "people want to lay upon the politics, I want to lay upon the family. Whatever the marriage was like veers on how the family turned out. And it had nothing to do with all the rest of it."[39]

For me, politics in Mexico was sort of like sex, [Tony Kahn, screenwriter Gordon Kahn's son, told me]. I would hear things, but they weren't grounded in any kind of actuality where I could find out what was true and what wasn't true, and I couldn't discuss it with my parents. So I knew my father had "performed" politics at some point because there we were in Mexico. In the same way I knew they "performed" sex because there I was in the family. But I could never figure out why he didn't feel comfortable discussing what he had done. I had to conclude that it was an uncomfortable subject for him for probably a multitude of reasons— [among them] the consequences on the family of what he had done. Perhaps he would have done it differently if he had had a chance. Perhaps it so consumed him with anger and rage he didn't even want to get into it. I don't know. It remains a mystery for me.[40]

Although Gordon Kahn, author of *Hollywood on Trial*—a definitive work on the House Un-American Activities Committee (HUAC) investigation of the film industry—was by no means unknown, his son, Tony, was only five when the family moved to Cuernavaca. Because he was isolated from the bulk of political expatriates in Mexico City, the implications of residing in a foreign country were, no doubt, hidden from him more successfully than from the rest of us.

Chris Trumbo, on the other hand, experienced those years differently: His father was the best known of the Hollywood Ten.

Although the "odd name" might have something to do with it, [he told me]. Dalton Trumbo, you know, is not the same as Mike Wilson,[41] a name of anonymity, and Dalton Trumbo was just one of those catchy little things. You could make rhymes with it: Mumbo Jumbo Dalton Trumbo. Anonymity under those circumstances would have been impossible. When the Un-American Activities Committee hearings were to take place in 1947, my parents spoke with my older sister and me, told us everything that they thought we could possibly understand, which was everything . . . and then we knew [Dalton] would go to jail—probably—and that did happen.[42]

Whatever the circumstances under which we went to Mexico, the country's attractions were undeniable. Crawford Kilian summed it up when he wrote,

We could walk through the ruins of its conquered empires, learn the subtleties of bullfighting, and begin to speak the language. Mexican food had substance and flavor, and light and color were more intense. Even children like us had an odd freedom: We could prowl the Thieves' Market in Tepito, and there, for very little money, purchase a cavalry saber or ancient six-gun. Occasionally, we might have a run-in with a Mexican street gang but, for the most part, we thought nothing of long trips across the city, through its slums and parks and crowds. I look back on those years in Mexico now, and they seemed suffused with a kind of glow. The streets and markets were so beautiful, the people so vivid, the sun so bright, and the air so clear that it seems impossibly romantic.[43]

While Mexicans have no monopoly on romanticism, they are far more comfortable with it than Americans, so perhaps some of us picked it up from them during our years in the country. Whatever the case, Crawford was by no means alone in remembering the Mexican years as "suffused with a kind of glow." Although we were aware of our isolation and, with rare exceptions, never fully assimilated, we romanticized our shared experiences and our relationships with each other. They drew us together into some semblance of belonging.

Along with Jean Butler, who wrote of "a close-knit feeling, as though we and our children were part of a very large family or a very small town";[44] and her son, Michael, who felt that "We cut through a lot of bullshit in our need to stick together"; and with Chris Trumbo, who never felt a sense of community at all but believed that some people "created their own communities, their own fictions, in order to belie their realities";[45] we were thrown into each other's company frequently enough to share the same experiences. The memories, however, differed. (I sometimes received three or four versions of the same event.)

Perhaps the only thing we could agree on unanimously were the hard facts: We, along with a small group of families from the United States, [46] were drawn together because we shared similar left-wing ideologies and reasons for being in Mexico, or were so perceived.

In recalling the early years, Anita Boyer, who arrived with her husband Fred Field in 1953, referred to the group as

> the incestuous clique. [We were] seeing each other all the time and . . . I didn't mind seeing these people because they were lovely people. But they were certainly a persecuted people when they came here and that's perhaps why they cohered, no? They stuck together because they felt the [need to transplant] their own little world from the United States, and that's what they did . . . they would not assimilate, and I felt that I was in a host country, and I should learn the language, and I should certainly see people other than Americans.[47]

When Anita spoke of their "seeing each other all the time" she was thinking not only of the evenings spent together in each other's homes, or of the nights out, or of the family excursions to local sites, but of a number of programmed activities involving anywhere from four to a dozen families.

Chief among them were the Sunday-morning musicales at Kurt Odenheim's house, described by one expatriate as memorable "for good pancakes and lousy music." According to a friend, Kurt had conducted a Work Projects Administration (WPA)—sponsored symphony orchestra in New Jersey.[48] A Communist Party organizer in the late 1920s and early 1930s, he had left the

Party in 1937 but his former loyalties would mark him. Berthe Small told me he was a "man without a country."[49] That would have made him particularly vulnerable had he remained in the States.

Shortly after his arrival in Mexico he was joined by his wife and four children, and he invested in a leather business, which failed. Eventually, he established a company to supply radio and phonograph cabinets to major outlets, work similar to what he had done in the States.

According to Odenheim's daughter, "[On Sunday mornings] my father played the piano, Ralph Norman[50] played the cello, Maur Halperin was a fiddler, and my mom played the violin."[51] Other musicians included David Prensky and Fred Field on the recorder. New Yorkers Frida and Harry Schaeffer, friendly with a number of political expatriates though not themselves in Mexico for political reasons, claimed during our interview on May 17, 1991, that "The largest collection of subversives we ever managed to assemble was at those Sunday-morning musicales."

The Schaeffers, obviously, were not the only ones aware of this. The FBI collected information about the musicales and other such gatherings—the Butlers' Saturday-morning softball games, for example—throughout the 1950s:

> In February, 1954, an unnamed person reported that Hugo and Jean Butler had invited a number of their close friends to a picnic and softball game at their home on the afternoon of February 13, 1954. According to this person, the Butlers arranged the afternoon to give an opportunity for a number of American Communists to get together without arousing suspicion. This person further advised that the following individuals were in attendance at the above-described picnic. [A list of eight names follows.][52]

In a somewhat different account, included in his unpublished article "Growing up Blacklisted," Crawford Kilian, today a journalist and science fiction writer, states:

> The focus of our week was the Saturday-morning softball game in the big vacant lot next to the Butlers' house on Palmas. By 10:00 A.M. we had a gathering of kids and adults. . . . We would play for a couple of hours, then convene on the Butlers' glassed-in front porch for lunch. The kids were quite welcome in the adults' conversation, but we were just as likely to go into the living room to play records or up to Michael's room to fool around with toy soldiers, or back out into the lot to chuck spears at one another while screaming, "Dog of an Aztec! Pig of a Toltec!"[53]

While tending to cling together, particularly at the beginning, political expatriates discovered that, unlike the ordinary American residing in Mexico, they were in a position to meet Mexico's Left and its intellectual community.

Because Mexican intellectuals sympathetic to the political expatriates' politics and cognizant of the events responsible for their leaving the United States sought them out, the expatriates were able to meet such luminaries as artists Diego Rivera, David Alfaro Siqueiros, Francisco Zuniga, Miguel Covarubias, and Pablo O'Higgins, and writer Luis Cardoza y Aragon. Socialite Martha Dodd Stern, in Mexico dodging a subpoena, thought nothing of inviting many of these to her celebrated affairs along with ex-ambassador Bill O'Dwyer, a couple of second-tier Mexican politicians, and a large sprinkling of American leftists. Those parties were famous.

But one party in particular still raises eyebrows. Shortly after his arrival, Dalton Trumbo hosted an affair on the advice of his *coyote*. These well-connected con-artists with legal pretensions earned a living by promising to use their political clout to keep a story out of the press or to keep agents far from one's door. Dalton hired his coyote to steer him clear of potential pitfalls. In order to maintain his legal status in the country, it was important for Dalton to make an impression, his coyote told him, and to meet the *influyentes*, the movers and shakers, and toward that end he recommended that Dalton throw a *fieston* in his marble palazzo.[54]

The guests included a large segment of the exiled community, in particular the Hollywood contingent, along with a number of local bigwigs invited by their Mexican friend, Josefina Fierro de Bright.[55] Dalton's daughter, Nikola, remembered: "At the famous party my father threw shortly after we arrived . . . a young military officer was apparently making a pass at me—a very green just-turned-thirteen-year-old—asking me to dance a lot, so Josefina, John Bright's[56] fiery Mexican wife, cut in and danced him to his knees, much to the delight of the assembled."[57]

Frances Chaney, Ring Lardner Jr.'s wife, was there alone:

> Well, all of the women in the group were quite attractive, and we were fairly young then. . . . Cleo Trumbo was a great beauty, and Jean Butler was pretty lively and . . . There was lots of food and there were drinks and oh, the works. About an hour or two into the party I ran into Cleo Trumbo wandering around, and it turned out that we all had had very similar experiences with these guys. And then we began to catch on. This was their off night, and nobody had brought his wife.

She explained that a few had brought their *casa chica*, or, literally, their "small houses," referring to the mistresses who inhabited them. The rest were on the make.

> At the end, all of us were comparing notes and saying, "What should I do with this goddamn general?" or whatever we had, [when] suddenly, who [should] appear from the States but Herbert Biberman.[58]

"Isn't this the most wonderful, glorious thing that ever happened?" [he asked].

And I asked, "Why Herbert?"

"Well, just think, you know, all these marvelous people from Mexico, the cultural elite meeting in this great rapport. . . . "

And as he spoke of this wonderful meeting between the cream of the left culture in Mexico, I knew I would never be able to set him straight.[59]

Sometimes, such occasions provided the newly arrived political expatriates with an opportunity to witness events generally closed to outsiders. Maria Asunsolo's party, attended by the Maltzes, artist Philip Stein and his wife, and by *Daily Worker* correspondent A. B. Magil and his wife, was one of these.

On February 17, 1952, Maria Asunsolo, known for her antifascist political activism during the 1930s and 1940s, her beauty, and her intimate relationships with Mexico's intellectual community, invited close to one hundred people to commemorate the reconciliation of artists David Alfaro Siqueiros and Diego Rivera. Their antagonism dated from 1937 when Rivera had enraged local Communists and been expelled from the Mexican Communist Party (PCM) after persuading Mexican president Lázaro Cárdenas to provide a sanctuary for Leon Trotsky. Some three years later, Siqueiros and a small band of followers had attempted, unsuccessfully, to assassinate the Russian revolutionary. So their reconciliation after all these years was indeed a historic event.

Held in the garden of Maria's Pedregal home, it was attended by prominent left-wing figures including the Mexican Revolution general Heriberto Jara; former cabinet minister Marte R. Gomez; Alfonso Caso, the archeologist; composer Blas Galindo; and writer Jose Mancisidor.

Siqueiros and Rivera were seated next to each other at the middle of a long table flanked on either side by two additional tables set at right angles. A large banner extolling both men hung above them. Following the meal, after leftover food had been cleared, speeches delivered, and the guests of honor toasted, both artists leaped to their feet, whipped out their handguns, and, aiming above their heads, fired gaily into the air. All around them, the assembled guests rose from their seats and cheered them on.

All except Harriet Magil. She remembered, "[When] Siqueiros and Rivera . . . started shooting their guns into the air—I [was petrified] and wanted to scream. And that was their idea of a big joke!"[60]

As she and countless others would discover, Mexico bears as little resemblance to the United States as Alice's Wonderland does to a convenience store. Even something as basic as the countries' names conveys the difference: *The United States of America* is self-descriptive, curt, and lends itself to easy abbreviation. The name means business. *Mexico*, or—as it is pronounced in Spanish—*Meheeco*, is cadence and rhythm, a lullaby of a name that gives away nothing about itself.

Moving to Mexico required more than just packing a suitcase and changing your address. It required changing your points of reference, learning to feel out a situation rather than think it out, and conditioning yourself to living with uncertainty. This was unavoidable when one lived in a country where expectations bore little resemblance to reality, where customs, values, and mores were at odds with one's own, and where personal security could never be taken for granted. According to Berthe Small:

> Because of Charles's always precarious position in Mexico—some of it real, some of it imagined—every day was an anxiety. He refused, for his own crazy reasons, to have a telephone in the shop for twenty-five years, so I couldn't reach him. If he was ten minutes late, or what I perceived to be late, as he always was, I'd figure that either he had dropped dead on a street corner from a cardiac problem or he had been picked up and was being harassed or deported.[61]

True, personal safety could never be taken for granted by political dissidents no matter where they lived, but it appeared all the more elusive in a country bristling with unknown dangers. Equally elusive was the issue of moral integrity because security, or at the very least adaptation, could hinge on compromising one's principles. Jeanette Pepper summed it up when she said:

> The people who came down were socially conscious so they were the [ones] who would be most aware. . . . People asked me, "How can you live in a country like this that's so poor?" and I said, "Well, after awhile you learn to ignore it." That's not admirable. . . . I can answer only for myself, of course, but it wasn't only a case of becoming inured to it, although that was part of it. It also meant that, in our case, we gave money to every beggar who crossed our path, paid our help more than the going wage, and that sort of thing, but we lived as "Colonials," the way people did in "Indjah." . . . I don't think we liked being "Colonials" but it was very easy to fall into that pattern [which] . . . is corruptive both to the colonizer and the colonized, and [at the time] I didn't realize the extent to which I'd been corrupted.[62]

Even as a child, I was incapable of ignoring the contradictions between what my parents said and the way we lived. On one occasion, shortly after our arrival, my father and his employee, Calixto, were driving down the Paseo de la Reforma when my father lost control of his car, striking a pedestrian. When the police arrived, Calixto took the rap and, since he had no driver's license, spent the next few nights in jail while my father arranged for his release. My mother told me that, as a foreigner, my father would have been far more vulnerable to prosecution than a Mexican citizen. I didn't buy that. Only now does it occur to me that, as political dissidents, my parents dreaded the possibility that Mexican officialdom—or, God forbid, the American Embassy—might intervene. (Upon my mentioning this to Tony Kahn, he recalled having heard of a similar incident involving one of the Hollywood writers.)

On another occasion, my parents fired an employee for attempting to negotiate a contract with a labor union. At the time, this shocked me even more than the traffic incident, perhaps because it was contrary to their espoused political principles. (Labor unions were good, weren't they?) Years later, however, my parents' lawyer, Harry Schaeffer, assured me that the man in question had been a con-artist using the threat of a union as a way to extort money from my parents. (Although such incidents certainly occurred elsewhere, Mexico's judicial flexibility increased the likelihood of their taking place. On the other hand, negotiating a speedy solution was far easier there than elsewhere.)

In spite of cultural differences and gaps in understanding, an occasional quirky incident could jolt us into recognizing our similarities. In some ways, we political dissidents were not so unlike our Mexican hosts: When Nicky, Dalton Trumbo's daughter, confessed to her Mexican boyfriend that her father had been in prison, he responded, "So? Whose father hasn't?"[63]

For some, fear of imprisonment, unemployment, or harassment were the only reasons for remaining in Mexico. Playwright Carlos Prieto observed that the best way to recognize who was in the country involuntarily was to identify the people who openly disliked Mexico but refused to leave.[64]

Others, well-known American novelist Howard Fast, for example, liked the country and certainly had sufficient reason for maintaining some distance between themselves and their government. Following Fast's imprisonment in the United States, he considered the possibility of moving to Mexico, and he and his family spent the summer of 1954 there. He wrote: "Yet this was not life, not any kind of life for us. I couldn't write, and Bette couldn't paint. Days drifted by without meaning. We could not make a life here as other American Communists, writers, artists, film people had done. We were bored to distraction."[65]

In addition, there were a few who appeared to have settled down in Mexico and then suddenly disappeared. Robert Rossen, the talented, well-regarded writer-director of films like *All the King's Men* (1947) and *Body and Soul* (1949), and one of the Hollywood Nineteen, was one of those. At the beginning of 1953 he was living in Mexico and working on *The Brave Bulls* with Anthony Quinn. During the course of his work, he became friendly with Gabriel Figueroa, a highly respected film photographer. Figueroa remembers that Rossen visited him at his Coyoacán home during the spring of 1953. Bursting into tears, Rossen told the Mexican film photographer he had been summoned to testify in Washington, and Rossen begged for his assistance. Figueroa approached international legal expert Don Luis Cabrera, a former cabinet minister and writer, and introduced him to Rossen. Cabrera assured the American he could request political asylum for him in Mexico and volunteered his services in preparing a case against the U.S. government.

Figueroa claimed that, following the meeting with Cabrera,

> Rossen embraced me, wept for joy and kissed me. I took him home to his Colonia Roma apartment. We said good-bye, agreeing to see each other the next day at four o'clock to go to Cabrera's office. When I knocked at his door the next day, there was no answer. I asked the janitor about it, and he told me Rossen had left that morning with all his luggage and had left no message. . . . Three months later, Rossen wrote to me from Spain where he was working and later from the United States. I never wrote back.[66]

Figueroa wasn't the only person Rossen had approached. John Bright, blacklisted after 1951, had written the scripts for *The Public Enemy*, *Blonde Crazy*, and a documentary, *We Accuse*. According to Asa Zatz, after Rossen received a second subpoena from the HUAC, he often visited Bright in his Mexico City apartment:

> He would pace the floor, hashing it over with John as he tried to make up his mind what to do about testifying. Finally one night, he declared himself: He had made up his mind. He was going to face up to the Committee and tell them off. The answer was to hit back, and he was going to do it. "What we need right now is someone to [pull] a Dimitrov." [Dimitrov was the Bulgarian prime minister who heroically challenged the Nazis at the Reichstag Fire Trial.]

Following this decision, he dropped from view, and Bright finally decided to check up on him, only to discover he had precipitously fled the country. Sometime in May, John Bright opened the newspaper and read of Rossen's appearance before the HUAC—as an informer. He named fifty individuals, including many of his friends. John wired him: "Did you say Dimitrov or Dmytryk?" (Dmytryk was the Hollywood Ten writer who, after serving a prison sentence, turned informer.)[67]

So while many, like Robert Rossen, returned to the States after a couple of months, those who remained—sometimes for only a year or two—became absorbed in their new lives. The process of finding a place to live, earning a livelihood, learning the language, placing the children in school, and establishing a social life required that they extend their reach beyond the tight-knit expatriate community, and in so doing, they invariably became aware of the vast cultural opportunities offered by a country like Mexico: Berthe Small studied dance with a national ballet company and anthropology and Latin American literature at the University of Mexico, earning an honorary master's degree; Brynna, David Prensky's wife, attracted by the country's art scene would eventually open a leading art gallery in Mexico City; Cleo Trumbo, an accomplished photographer, recorded her new surroundings and turned a room in her house into a darkroom; Hollywood couple Ian and Alice Hunter traveled through Mexico, following up a newly acquired interest in Mexican folk art; my father and Bart van der Schelling began to paint; George Oppen studied art and took up wood carving; Asa Zatz worked on a doctorate in anthropology; the Trumbos, the Smalls, the Hunters, the Peppers, and my parents began collecting pre-Hispanic artifacts; Fred Field turned his interest in that field into a serious pursuit, studying archeology and becoming an authority in pre-Columbian seals; Anita Boyer immersed herself in the local theater and later opened a combination bookstore-art gallery; and David Prensky and Fred Field met others who shared their enthusiasm for recorder music and formed La Sociedad de la Flauta Barroca.

Assimilation is generally regarded as an absorption process, and in time absorption did take place: Mexico never fully absorbed us, but we absorbed Mexico—gradually. We laced our hot dogs with salsa and our conversations with Spanish colloquialisms. We practiced the language on newly acquired Mexican friends, and they practiced their English. We started off by shaking hands and, as we acquired *confianza*, greeted them—and our American friends too—with a firm hug and a kiss on the cheek.

For those who stayed on, adaptation to Mexico as a foreigner and, in particular, as a political expatriate, signified transcending distances—not only geographical but spiritual ones as well. It meant taking mind leaps, traveling from a place in the brain to a place in the heart and, like the bread boy I'd spotted my first day in Mexico City, learning how to dodge danger and keep on pedaling.

Notes

1. For many American Communist Party members the Party provided more than a political reference point. Schools, social activities, literary magazines, insurance programs, legal defense organizations, and so on made it possible to function within a protective subculture. In some places, American Communists lived lives almost entirely removed from society at large, so that when they arrived in Mexico many were already accustomed to interacting within the protective, mutually dependent framework they had known back home.

2. Oppen kept his identity as a poet a secret from his Mexico City friends who learned of it only when they read about his Pulitzer Prize in the newspapers.

3. Mary Oppen, *Meaning: A Life* (Oakland, Calif.: Black Sparrow Press, 1978), 195.

4. Jean Butler, interview with the author, August 2, 1999.

5. Philip and Gertrude Stein, interview with the author, May 15, 1995.

6. Edna Moore van der Schelling, interview with the author, August 1, 1991.

7. Berthe Small, interview with the author, January 17, 1993.

8. Frederick Vanderbilt Field, *From Right to Left* (Westport, Conn.: Lawrence Hill, 1983), 275–76.

9. Lini M. DeVries, *Up from the Cellar* (Minneapolis, Minn.: Vanilla Press, 1979), 355–56.

10. Edna Moore van der Schelling, interview.

11. Berthe Small, interview with the author, January 17, 1993.

12. Edward Lending, letter to the author, August 5, 1993.

13. David Prensky, letter to the author, November 30, 1991.

14. Dalton Trumbo, *Additional Dialogue: Letters of Dalton Trumbo, 1942–1962*, ed. Helen Manfull (New York: M. Evans, 1970).

15. Jean Butler, "Those Happy Few," manuscript, 22.

16. Butler, "Those Happy Few," 3–4; Patrick McGilligan and Paul Buhle, *Tender Comrades: A Backstory of the Hollywood Blacklist* (New York: St. Martins Griffin, 1997), 168.

17. Jean Butler, "Those Happy Few," 113.

18. Blacklisted screenwriter Ian Hunter and his wife, Alice, a former screen-story analyst, who later worked for a Popular Front organization, were in Mexico briefly during the early 1950s.

19. Jeanette Pepper, interview with the author, August 2, 1991.

20. Trumbo, *Additional Dialogue*, 278.

21. Belle Zykofsky, "Elephants & Roses," in *Scenes From Our Lives*, ed. John Dennis and A. E. Biderman (San Francisco: University of San Francisco Press, 1983), 18.

22. Shelley Shlafrock, interview with the author, January 18, 1993.

23. Crawford Kilian, *Growing Up Blacklisted*, unpublished memoir, 6.

24. Chris Trumbo, interview with the author, August 1, 1991.

25. There were certainly exceptions, but the majority of the political expatriate children who resided in Mexico City did attend the American School.

26. Carlos Prieto, interview with the author, October 22, 1991.

27. Jean Butler, interview with the author, July 22, 1991.

28. Kilian, *Growing Up Blacklisted*, 7.

29. Oppen, *Meaning: A Life*, 198.

30. Mary Butler, interview with the author, July 28, 1991.

31. Emmy Drucker, interview with the author, May 20, 1991.

32. Chris Trumbo, interview.

33. In 1940, Ramon Mercader del Rio was sent to Mexico to assassinate Leon Trotsky, was convicted of the murder, and held in Mexico City's Lecumberri Prison, where he remained until his release in 1960.

34. Mary Butler, interview.

35. Linda Oppen, letter to the author, April 27, 1997.

36. Michael Butler, interview with the author, July 27, 1991.

37. Linda Oppen, letter to the author, April 22, 1995.

38. Linda Oppen, letter to the author, January 31, 1992.

39. Chris Trumbo, interview.

40. Tony Kahn, interview with the author, January 21, 1993.

41. A blacklisted screenwriter, Michael Wilson lived in France during the 1950s.

42. Chris Trumbo, interview.

43. Kilian, *Growing Up Blacklisted*, 6, 8.

44. Jean Butler, "Those Happy Few," 6, 22.

45. Chris Trumbo, telephone conversation with the author, August, 1991.

46. Although I have identified more than sixty such families, I am reluctant to give more precise numbers because it is impossible to determine unequivocally who went to Mexico for political reasons. Sometimes, the individuals themselves are uncertain; a few concealed their motivations from each other; others established no relationships with known political expatriates or lived outside Mexico City, making them more difficult to identify.

47. Anita Boyer, interview with the author, February 14, 1992.

48. Prensky.

49. Berthe Small, interview with the author, January 22, 1992.

50. The Normans were friends of the Smalls but were not in Mexico for political reasons.

51. Lynne Odenheim Kalmar, interview with the author, November 7, 1991.

52. David Drucker, FBI File, NY 100-99497.

53. Kilian, *Growing Up Blacklisted*, 10.

54. Bruce Cook, *Dalton Trumbo* (New York: Charles Scribner's Sons, 1977), 220.

55. Raised in the United States, Josefina was a glamorous left-wing figure admired for her ability to harness much-needed moral and financial support within the Hollywood community. She is remembered for her work on behalf of Mexican Americans during the 1930s and 1940s. Accused of subversion by California's Tenney Committee, she settled in Mexico in 1948.

56. John Bright was a blacklisted Hollywood screenwriter who was actively involved in the Screenwriters Guild and a founding member of the Motion Picture Democratic Committee, a Popular Front organization. (He and Josefina were subsequently divorced.)

57. Nikola Trumbo, letter to the author, November 21, 1994.

58. Director and screenwriter Herbert Biberman was one of the Hollywood Ten.

59. Ring Lardner Jr. and Frances Chaney Lardner, interview with the author, May 25, 1991.

60. Abe and Harriet Magil, interview with the author, January 20, 1993; Joel Gardner, *The Citizen Writer in Retrospect: Oral History of Albert Maltz* (Los Angeles: University of California, Oral History Program, Regents of the University of California, 1983), 835.

61. Berthe Small, interview with the author, January 17, 1993.

62. Jeanette Pepper, letter to the author, March 5, 1992. Jeanette Pepper, interview.

63. Jeanette Pepper, interview. Nikola Trumbo, letter to the author, May 5, 1997.

64. Carlos Prieto, interview with the author, September 19, 1991.

65. Howard Fast, *Being Red* (New York: Laurel, 1990), 333.

66. Margarite de Orellana, "El arte de Gabriel Figueroa, palabras sobre imagines: Una entrevista con Gabriel Figueroa," *Artes de Mexico* 2 (Invierno 1988): 90.

67. Asa Zatz, letter to the author, November 20, 1995. Victor S. Navasky, *Naming Names* (New York: Viking, 1990), 303n; Navasky reported a slightly different version: "Bright sent him a wire: 'How do you spell Dimitroff?'"

CHAPTER EIGHT

"The Lake Chapala Riviera: The Evolution of a Not So American Foreign Community"

David Truly

> Many foreigners who come to Ajijic are misfits elsewhere, and there is a tendency among them to lead unorthodox lives here. . . . Occasionally a visitor talks of purchasing a small piece of land and settling on the lake, which will one day become a Riviera of the Americas, when made accessible by highways.[1]

> It is a different wavelength, and if you can't adapt or resign yourself to it, you had better leave Mexico. If you can stand it, you will find that everything can be done here, that it is still the land of unlimited possibilities. But what you need more than knowledge or energy in order to achieve anything is plain old-fashioned patience.[2]

The first foreign residents along the banks of Mexico's Lake Chapala were an eccentric if not eclectic bunch that included a ballerina and great-granddaughter of Gideon Wells, who served as the secretary of the navy under President Abraham Lincoln; a German refugee writer and her brother who were admittedly queer; and an English author, Nigel Millet, who teamed up with Peter Lilley and, under the pseudonym of Dane Chandos, wrote *Village in the Sun*, a vivid description of the landscape and life in Ajijic during the 1940s. Another author, Neill James, a well-bred, privileged single woman from Mississippi, was an adventurous woman who settled there, became a matriarch of sorts for the indigenous people, and in 1945 established a public library for the native children of the area. Each of these new immigrants sought refuge from traditional society, although the specifics that brought them there varied. Some wanted to escape social discrimination or persecution; others sought artistic freedom in an inspired setting; and others simply sought an alternative to modern society and its rules and norms. Whatever their intentions, their decision to settle along the banks of Mexico's largest lake forever changed the nature of life in this area for the hosts and guests alike.[3]

The writings of James and Millet and Lilley depicted a romantic though difficult life—one fraught with the dangers of venomous snakes and insects, a lack of basic conveniences such as running water and toilets, and the threat of danger from bandits and drunken natives. Nonetheless, there was also a sense of honesty and tolerance among these early settlers. Their lack of political power and of any real authority in this relatively primitive area was a constant reminder that they were and would always be guests in this foreign land. Yet for many, this isolated stretch of shoreline represented the perfect opportunity to escape the pressures and realities of life in their home country. The idyllic climate and the then magnificent Lake Chapala offered them a bucolic setting in which they created a foreign outpost that was neither American or European; and for many that have visited or migrated to this area, the interconnected nature of life along the lake, that is, the relationship of immigrants with other immigrants, and the symbiotic relationship between these immigrants and the native population remain the hallmark of life here.

Although locations such as this have historically attracted small groups of adventurous migrants, the lack of modern conveniences and the difficulties inherent in negotiating the sociocultural and political differences that they present have traditionally dissuaded many North American retirees from permanently settling in areas outside their home country.[4] There are signs, however, that these issues are no longer valid. The growing size of foreign retirement communities, the increasing availability of modern services and goods due to the North American Free Trade Agreement (NAFTA), and technological advancements in transportation and communication have begun to change retirees' perceptions of Latin America and Mexico. This has prompted some long-time residents of the Lake Chapala Riviera to suggest that a new type of immigration has emerged—one more prone to "importing a lifestyle" than to adapting to their host community's established culture. This concern is shared by the residents of other similar destinations, and many of them feel this new pattern may threaten the future of their communities.

Today, the coastal communities of Ajijic and Chapala are two of the most renowned destinations among the many retirement-friendly communities located along the northwestern edge of Lake Chapala. Located just south of Guadalajara in the state of Jalisco, the Lake Chapala Riviera includes the towns, or *municipios*, of Chapala and Jocotopec, many villages or pueblos (e.g., Ajijic, San Antonio Tlayacapan, and San Juan Cosala), and a growing number of subdivisions, or *fraccionamientos*, that dot the landscape. The state of Jalisco is reportedly home to the greatest concentration of North American retirees living outside their home country, with the majority located in and around the Guadalajara and Lake Chapala region.[5] While sources often disagree on the actual numbers, government organizations and observers suggest there are between seven thousand and ten thousand full-time residents along the Riviera proper. Seasonal influxes can double that number, although some sources (e.g., the American Consulate) suggest the foreign population is as high as forty thousand residents during these times. Unquestionably, the foreign presence is most noticeable in Ajijic and Chapala, although the movement of the foreign community is increasingly towards Jocotopec, a traditional agricultural center, and even around the southwestern edge of the lake. While the villages of San Pedro Tesistan and San Luis Soyatlan have no substantial history of foreign residency, two developments, Roco Azul and Puerto Corona, are located past Jocotopec and are attracting interest from within the foreign community.[6] Thus, while this study focuses on Ajijic and Chapala, the term *Riviera*, or *Lakeside* (as the area is also referred to by many of its foreign residents), will include the entire area under discussion. These terms signify both a geographical designation and a cultural one, the latter referring to the foreign constituency that has resided there since the turn of the century.

Research suggests that many retirees are considering alternatives to the familiar retirement destinations of Florida and Arizona, and that many baby boomers are seeking out more authentic communities in the place of traditional planned-retirement communities.[7] These preferences have already had a dramatic impact on the local economies and cultures of both origin and destination communities, and have altered the existing infrastructure and service industry of each. In Europe, for example, British retirement migration to areas along the Mediterranean has attracted the attention of both government officials and researchers.[8] The growth in North American retirement migration to Mexico and other areas of Latin America suggests that the combination of economics and amenities offered by these areas appeals to a growing number of North American citizens. There is also evidence to suggest that the Mexican government may soon promote foreign retirement-migration development in much the same way that it promoted international tourism development.[9]

While Sun Belt migration has been the common retirement choice among North Americans, many international destinations located within the tropics (Costa Rica and Mexico, for example) are available to those seeking a more exotic or unique retirement lifestyle. However, only a handful of studies have examined the southerly migration to such areas that took place during the late 1970s and early 1980s.[10] Additionally, retirement researchers such as Charles

Longino[11] have cited the lack of studies examining both American retirement abroad and the role of the expatriate community in retirement-migration decisions.[12] Although previous empirical studies may have suggested that retirement abroad was inconsequential, the travel habits of today's baby boomers indicate otherwise. Many developing countries are targeting retirees in order to stimulate local and regional economic development. This increase in advertising and promotion for retirement in certain areas, both national and international, underscores the need for a better understanding of the impact of the influx of North American attitudes and ideals upon these destinations.

The Lakeside communities of Lake Chapala and Jalisco were chosen for the case-study area because of their long history of American and Canadian immigrant settlement and because of earlier doctoral research conducted in this area in the 1970s and 1980s. At that time Virgil Holder focused on the motivations, expectations, and demographic composition of U.S. retiree emigration to Guadalajara and its environs, and concluded that the idyllic environmental setting of the areas was the major attraction to migrants, but the cultural amenities and low cost of living were also significant. Eleanore Stokes, on the other hand, focused on the social dynamics of the North American enclave by examining the geographical and ideological boundaries created by U.S. immigrants and assessing their impact upon their local communities. No follow-up studies then analyzed the extent or the impact of later U.S. emigration to the area until a longitudinal study in the late 1990s, which suggested significant change in the migrant behavior and attitudes of the area's more recent visitors and residents.[13]

The quantitative results of this later study suggested that in fact a new type of immigrant had emerged—one who displayed little respect for the unique culture that characterized life in this region. Instead, these North American immigrants seemed far more interested in replicating their previous lifestyles, given all the amenities and modern conveniences that were now available after NAFTA. More importantly, however, these new immigrants showed little interest in the civic or charitable organizations in the area that had historically provided for the local population. This shift in migrant behavior also had a significant impact upon the natural and built environment along the Riviera. The relationship between the natural and built environment of an area is commonly referred to as the area's *cultural landscape*.[14] This concept, and its associated methodologies, has a long history within geography and other social sciences as a useful tool for evaluating cultural change.[15] By examining what cultural geographers often refer to as "the imprint of human activity upon the natural landscape," we are then able to comment on an area's cultural landscape and, consequently, on its culture.

This chapter examines the complex nature of international retirement migration by focusing on the more qualitative findings (i.e., the personal interviews and the cultural landscape interpretation) of the 2001 study. A brief historical summary of the evolution of the area, synthesized from Stokes's work, will be presented first, followed by highlights of the cultural landscape interpretation, in hopes of offering some insight into the nature of the North American presence in this area.

The Evolution of the Lake Chapala Riviera

The evolution of the Lakeside community began with Porfirio Diaz's vision of an international resort connected to the grand city of Guadalajara by rail. The area's transition from tourism destination to retirement community can be divided into five stages, according to Stokes, each typified by its own types and intensity of development: (1) a *discovery stage*, from the late 1800s to the turn of the twentieth century; (2) a *founder stage*, from the early 1900s to the mid-1950s; (3) an *expansion stage*, from the mid-1950s to the early 1970s; (4) an *established colony stage*, from the mid-1970s to the late 1980s; and finally, (5) a *modern stage*, which began in the early 1990s and continues to the present.

The Discovery Stage

A large portion of this stage coincides with the presidency of Mexican president Porfirio Diaz, who effectively held office from 1876 to 1911. Supportive of a number of such immigration-related projects, Diaz advocated the promotion of Lake Chapala as a popular destination for the national and international elite by encouraging both the wealthy of Guadalajara and foreigners to visit the lake and build vacation homes along its shores. Among those visitors was Albert Braniff, the American aviator, who built a home in Chapala during this time and was known for his large parties and fiestas. The establishment of rail service from Guadalajara to Ocotlan in 1889 by Governor Ramon Corona first afforded travelers the opportunity to reach Chapala either overland from Atequiza, located north of Chapala, or by water from Ocotlan.[16]

The construction on the lake in 1895 of what is now the Montecarlo Hotel, by an Englishman named Septimus Crow, signified the beginning of real-estate development in the area. Crow encouraged many of his friends to visit, initiating an influx of non-Mexican residents into the area. In 1908 a Norwegian entrepreneur named Christian Schjetnan formed a tourism-development company based in the United States and imported a prefabricated yacht club to Lake Chapala to launch the enterprise. Even with investors such as Diaz himself, however, the business was doomed by the onset of the Mexican Revolution.

Schjetnan's Norwegian development company did however import two passenger steamboats to the lake, and it constructed a private railway from Chapala to the state-owned rail system in Atequiza. Then in the 1930s and 1940s road travel began to flourish, and soon a trip by automobile from Guadalajara took only a few hours instead of days as it did in the past. Although Ajijic remained a sleepy fishing village, tourism promotion of Chapala had begun, and foreign travelers such as Mrs. Ethel Alec-Tweedie[17] and Carl Lumholtz[18] included this locale in their travelogues, forever changing life along the banks of Mexico's largest lake.

The Founder Stage
This second period of development witnessed important changes in the type of visitor to the region, their destinations, and their relationship with the Lake Chapala Riviera. Beginning in the 1920s, artists and writers began to trickle into the area, and while Chapala remained the principal destination for Guadalajaran weekenders and some tourists, this new group of bohemians, intellectual travelers, and artists and writers "chose Ajijic because of the climate, the environment, the isolation, and, as one informant put it, the 'freedom from the social constraints of American society,' and for the 'intellectual stimulation afforded by other artists.'"[19] The subsequent fame of Ajijic as an artist colony was probably due to D. H. Lawrence's visit to Chapala and to the publication of his novel *The Plumed Serpent* in 1926. Other writers and artists followed in his path over the years, and the area became a temporary home to a number of successful and not-so-successful novelists, playwrights, poets, and artists.[20]

One of these, writer Neill James, was particularly instrumental in the development of the foreign community, not so much because of her writing, but more for her interest in the local population and their living conditions. Eventually she donated her home to house both a library for the local children and the headquarters of the Lake Chapala Society, an organization that offered camaraderie to new foreign immigrants while promoting philanthropic support for the local community. Today this society is considered to be the largest of its kind, and it still promotes a number of charitable efforts directed toward the local population, although social groups (e.g., a computer group and a bridge club) far outnumber those charitable efforts. Nonetheless, the interaction between the local and the immigrant communities during the founder stage was positive, and a symbiotic relationship grew out of these early days. The immigrants offered economic opportunity to a subsistence-based local population, and they in turn offered assistance and security to this eclectic bunch of immigrants. Obviously, the approach of this foreign community to its hosts was probably not characteristic of other Western immigrants and foreign communities of the time. However, the relationship led to the formulation of a local culture unique to the region.

The village of Ajijic then was barely noticeable from the road with most of its dwellings oriented along and toward the beach. Foreigners refurbished old Mexican homes within the village or built homes along the lakeshore, a location not preferred by the locals. High walls, a common feature associated with the traditional hacienda-style of construction, hid most of the houses, obscuring the North American presence from the unwanted visitor. The climate encouraged open living areas situated around an interior courtyard, and the walled courtyards afforded the foreign migrants a certain degree of anonymity, while maintaining the natural appearance of the village on the outside. Life in the "early days" was inexpensive (estimated expenses totaled $75 to $200 a month) and unstructured. Impromptu parties were open to all members of this egalitarian foreign community. While most foreign visitors stayed for less than a few months or a year, those who remained became the foundation of the foreign community.[21]

This eclectic assortment of North American and European bohemian travelers forever changed the nature of life along Lake Chapala, and their preference for lakeside property and the establishments they created changed the cultural landscape of the area. In sociocultural terms, these early migrants laid the foundation for a tolerant and egalitarian foreign community that developed an equally interesting relationship with the local community; sexual or social idiosyncrasies were ignored or at least tolerated not only by the foreign migrants but also by the somewhat conservative local community. Many of the local people benefited from the employment opportunities created by the growing foreign community, and in fact, foreign migrants often became part of their workers' extended families. This symbiotic host/guest relationship, the tolerant and egalitarian nature of the foreign community, and the casual and unstructured lifestyle of the community became hallmarks of this area.

The Expansion Stage

From the mid-1950s until approximately 1970, the structure of the foreign community began to formalize, heralding "the emergence of the 'Lakeside' as a social entity."[22] The Mexican government finished paving the Chapala road in the late 1960s, which ushered in the first significant retiree migration. Foreign-owned businesses such as the hotel La Posada and a weaving and embroidery factory started by the first foreign settlers signaled the beginning of a more formal society, and one that offered enough comfort and structure to attract a new type of visitor: middle class, sometimes affluent, and, more importantly, retired. Tour agencies enticed tourists to Lake Chapala to see the textile factories and experience the idyllic climate and natural surroundings in the hopes of luring potential retirees to the area. These early promotions targeted mainly those with a history of extensive travel (e.g., those associated with the military or with other government agencies and international corporations). Formal organizations such as the American Legion and the Lake Chapala Society, and an English newspaper, the *Colony Reporter*, were established during the mid-to-late 1950s and catered to a growing North American immigrant population.

The migrants of this period, however, were more conservative than the early settlers, and they also preferred other locations and living styles.[23] Some of these migrants did not gravitate to the shoreline as previous migrants had, and they seemed more interested in building new homes than in refurbishing older ones. In 1958, Chula Vista, the area's first *fraccionamiento*, or subdivision, was completed. This planned community offered an alternative to life in the village or along the shore. It was the first development that targeted the foreign community specifically and was located on the north side of the Chapala highway, taking full advantage of its view of the lake.[24] Changes in the cultural landscape now became particularly noticeable as brick and concrete replaced adobe, ornamental shrubs and fruit trees replaced native flora, and modern plumbing and electrical services were incorporated into new buildings.[25]

These changes came slowly at first, but were more apparent by the late 1960s. The difficulty of travel along the Chapala highway still deterred less-adventurous visitors, sparing Ajijic from rapid growth. In fact, life in the sleepy fishing village remained generally unchanged until the late 1960s. As the number of foreign residents in Ajijic grew to perhaps seventy-five or eighty, they maintained their solidarity by hosting impromptu parties and gathering at El Tejaban for its Blue Plate Specials on Tuesday nights.[26] Telephone service was almost nonexistent. Those visitors that did venture to Ajijic still resembled those from the founder stage, and the writers and artists among them straddled the transition from the Beat to the hippie generation.[27]

The region grew rapidly in response to a number of guide and retirement books that promoted the benefits of retiring there. The region's low cost of living, its climate, proximity to Guadalajara with its vast array of cultural amenities, and the low cost of household servants there all allowed a style of life that many visitors could not afford in the United States.[28] Chula Vista was billed as an American housing development complete with a 9-hole golf course, a motel, and an interdenominational church. Ajijic, on the other hand, still retained its bohemian and artistic appeal, but its notoriety attracted an influx of "undesirables" there in the mid-1960s. This prompted local officials to round up and escort Ajijic's growing number of transient hippies to the U.S. border.[29] Ajijic's charm was too valuable to squander on "offbeats." Meanwhile, the sleepy Indian village began to show up in tourist guidebooks.[30]

The results of this first wave of retirement promotion were in line with its goals. The Chapala Riviera was no longer a secret, and a market for it had been identified that represented a greater economic input than the previous migrants associated with the founder stage. Development then continued as the presence of the foreign community became more formalized. A social distinction emerged within the immigrant population; the first settlers, who for various reasons had found themselves at odds with their native countries, differed in both their attitudes and their behavior from many of the new retirement wave. These artists, writers, and intellectual bohemians reveled in the area's lack of structure and in their unique relationship with the local population, but the retirees of the new wave of immigration came looking for a higher quality of life at a lower price. Not surprisingly, the pursuit of the new immigrants for a comfortable leisure lifestyle did not always correlate with the previous symbiotic host/guest relationship cultivated by the early foreign residents.[31]

The Established Colony Stage

Stokes conducted her research (1977–1980) during this period, and this led to her observation regarding increases in the social stratification of the area's immigrants as well as increases in the stratification of the foreign or Lakeside community and its host community. She also noted an increased immigration of Canadians and New York Jews to the area, and the movement of foreign interest from Chapala to Ajijic. During this period Ajijic became the center of the Lakeside community; restaurants serving pizza and hamburgers opened, and a supermarket and liquor store catered to immigrant tastes and preferences. Purified water became readily available, and the number of English-speaking individuals offering services from hair styling to architecture increased.[32] The whole community adapted and evolved to meet the demands of the immigrant community, and as a result of that adaptation, the landscape of the community changed also. Gradually a small section of the village located closer to the lake developed as a service center for foreign visitors and residents.

The development of *fraccionamientos* that began in 1958 intensified during the late 1960s and early 1970s, and by 1973 eighteen subdivisions were located along the north- and southwestern edges of the lake.[33] Not all of the developments were successful, however, and many fell short of their desired occupancy quota. Although many of these developments targeted foreign tourists and retirees, La Floresta, which opened in 1973, was geared primarily toward the Mexican tourist and retiree market. Modeled after similar resort-style communities in the United States, it included a yacht club, a trailer park, a hotel, and so forth. Many of the *fraccionamientos* built at this time still exist today, but some have become incorporated into other areas. Nonetheless, this growth dramatically altered the nature of the villages along the Rivera coastal area.

The perception that American retirees increased the value of the areas surrounding their property led to land speculation and investment for resale to future retirees. The location of a building site depended on three primary factors—view, security, and convenience—while cost tended to be of secondary importance.[34] Many foreign residents elected to live close to other foreign residents and within close proximity to the village plaza and its stores. Concurrently, another spatial pattern emerged during this period. While some immigrants sought sites around the village and shore, others migrated to sites along the valley walls. These homes afforded superb views and greater isolation from the traditional Mexican community. This isolation, however, had drawbacks: inadequate telephone service and poorly maintained access roads limited the social life of those along the slopes and hindered their interaction with the rest of the community.

These locational preferences of the foreign immigrants demonstrated, for the first time, the growing geographical and sociocultural bifurcation of the foreign community itself. Some of the immigrants believed that "living in town is the way to enjoy Mexico." They would refer disparagingly to subdivision living, and they dubbed Chula Vista the "Gringo Ghetto." An alternative stance held that to live in a Mexican village was to "live among pigs, dirt and noise."[35] In essence, the egalitarian nature of the foreign community began to show signs of disruption as visitors to the area began to display very distinct housing preferences. Construction styles began to gravitate away from the traditional walled hacienda construction. Ranch-style homes began to flourish along the slopes, further away from the villages and lakeshore. Walled homes were replaced by walled communities, and real-estate agents began to market different areas (e.g., the village versus the upper valley), based on a buyer's desire to reside closer to or farther away from the "Mexican lifestyle."[36] Thus, not only were the foreign community's internal dynamics changing, but the former symbiotic relationship between the host/guest communities was also under pressure.

Life during the 1980s saw some improvements in the area's public services, but as in the past, the speed of delivery and efficacy of these services were always a concern for some and a source of jokes for others. The promise of these improvements, however, helped fuel the publication of books extolling retirement on four hundred dollars a month in "a fashionable residential community filled with upscale restaurants and boutiques."[37] Local residents, however, pointed out that living on four hundred dollars a month, as it was promoted by some writers, was often less than practical, although it was certainly possible.[38] Even with these dynamics at work, however, home prices between twenty thousand dollars and forty thousand dollars were still common, and lots were available from a few hundred dollars to a couple thousand dollars, depending on location. The foreign community's impact on Ajijic's settlement patterns and land values was also offset by fluctuations in economic markets, and a cycle of boom and bust continued until the late 1980s when many immigrants returned to North America, leaving a landscape dominated by *se vende* (for sale) signs.[39] While obvious changes had occurred in the natural landscape during this period, equally dramatic changes in the sociocultural nature of the migrants began to emerge. These changes pertained to the nature of the migrants themselves and their level of commitment to the community at large.

The Modern Stage

The development of the Lake Chapala Riviera during the 1990s initially appeared to be no different than that of the previous era, and periods of boom and bust were complicated or exacerbated by both internal and external economic and sociopolitical events (e.g., the Zapatista uprising in 1994, accusations of political corruption within the Mexican government, and a growing international concern over these issues). An ensuing peso devaluation coupled with growing economic prosperity in the United States had once combined to lure potential retirees to the Riviera.[40] This time, however, other factors were in play. NAFTA by now had significantly altered the economic and retail landscape of many areas of Mexico, and American franchises such as Wal-Mart and Home Depot began to appear on Guadalajara's skyline. North American household products and services were also becoming more available to communities in and around the Guadalajara area. While most foreign residents initially welcomed these conveniences, some expressed nostalgia for the old days when these products were considered contraband and had to be smuggled across the border after a visit to the United States.[41] Many of the long-time residents' concerns over the importation of U.S. brands was due to a concurrent rise in prices and had less to do with the quality or origin of the goods. Also, the relative ease of communication and access to North American television programming via satellite had displaced the need for traditional face-to-face interaction within the foreign community, altering the "sense of community" that had characterized life along Lake Chapala. Most alarming, however, was a rise in violent crime targeted toward North Americans. While some blamed the ineffectiveness of the local police, others suggested that this had to do with the new immigrants' behavior. Anonymity to these new migrants was apparently not a virtue, and many dressed and acted as they would in their home country, wearing expensive jewelry and driving new, expensive SUVs—an openness not so common among previous immigrants.[42]

While NAFTA may not have been the only factor, real-estate sales and rentals during the late 1990s increased dramatically and remain strong today.[43] Many real-estate agents report turning away renters due to a lack of properties, and all agree that the market has become less seasonal and more year-round in nature. Although rentals of four hundred to six hundred dollars can still be found, these prices are still double and triple rental prices from the 1980s and early 1990s. Real-estate sales and the prices of homes in the area have also increased. For example, a house in 1976 that sold for $28,000 might have sold for $70,000 in 1985–1986, and that same house would probably sell for $145,000 or more in today's market. The construction of *spec homes* (i.e., houses built without a specified buyer but on the assumption that the market will provide a buyer) during the late 1990s also grew at a high rate, both in terms of the size and the price of these homes, which often exceeded $150,000—a price unheard of before 1996. Developers from both inside and outside Mexico have responded to the increased prices in the area, although there has been little if any governmental control or oversight. This has resulted in a widening of the shoreline road and the disappearance of rural farmlands along the Riviera. While real-estate booms and busts are not uncommon here, the magnitude and intensity of recent development along the Riviera signals a new era of development—and to some, the end of the Riviera of the past.

A Cultural Landscape Interpretation

The Lake Chapala area has a history of North American immigration and a unique cultural landscape that offers clues to the diffusion or intrusion there of North American culture and the nature of its foreign expatriate and retirement communities. This cultural landscape interpretation touches on three traditional aspects of the cultural landscape: the roads and transportation system, the location and nature of the residential and commercial buildings, and the dwellings and homes in the area. In regard to the last, I have given particular attention to the concept and use of walls and the implications of that concept and use for this community. My interpretation takes into consideration the previous discussion of the development of the Lakeside community, and focuses on changes to this cultural landscape in the late 1990s that reflect or suggest the increasing presence of and impact of recent North American migration.

The Chapala-Jocotepec Highway: A Roadside Perspective

> Roads no longer merely lead to places; they are places. And as always they serve two important roles: as promoters of growth and dispersion, and as magnets around which new kinds of development can cluster. In the modern landscape, no other space has been so versatile.[44]

The road from Guadalajara to the Chapala Riviera today is a smooth, well-maintained four-lane highway that affords easy national and international access from the Guadalajara airport. Cresting the ridge on the approach to Chapala, one first catches sight of Lake Chapala and its shimmering waters nestled in the volcanic depression that created it; the signs of human occupation become more apparent as one descends into the valley. The main highway offers two routes into the basin: the first leads directly into Chapala while the second route bypasses Chapala to the west, merging with the only road that connects Chapala to Jocotepec. Each route offers a different perspective on the region.

The first route gradually changes from a four-lane highway into the congested central thoroughfare of Chapala, and one quickly notices the high percentage of U.S. license plates and roadside signage that reflects the cultural milieu of this lakeside community. The foreign presence is, however, still relatively subtle compared to Mexican coastal resort towns such as Cancún and other popular Mexican vacation areas; there are no signs of U.S. franchise food establishments such as McDonald's or Denny's, for example. The highway narrows and then divides as it comes to the lakefront with its *malecon* (boardwalk), lake-front parks, and restaurants. For many visitors, this is their first opportunity to witness a dying lake.

A closer view of Lake Chapala reveals the effects of years of exploitation of the lake and its source, the Lerma River, for industrial and agricultural uses (see fig. 8.1). The lake supplies hydroelectric power and potable water to the city of Guadalajara and serves as a major source of irrigation for some of the Mexico's most productive agricultural fields. Dehydration and fluctuating rainfall, sediment build-up, high concentrations of heavy metals and phosphorus, and the exacerbating effect of human-introduced aquatic weeds have rendered the lake an inhospitable habitat for many of its indigenous species. The once thriving fishing industry now struggles to survive, and unique native fish species (e.g., the whitefish, the popocha, and the commercially significant charal) are all either in serious decline or on the verge of extinction.[45]

Although the Mexican government has discussed or proposed policies to reverse these trends, a recent review of conditions on the lake suggests little progress. The lake's water levels remain low, and tourists must "take

Figure 8.1.   View of Chapala from the dry lake bed. Photo courtesy of David Truly.

a long walk or taxi ride across a wide expanse of exposed lake bed now surrounding Chapala pier."[46] (During the last few years heavy rains have
partly refilled Lake Chapala, but the underlying environmental issues remain unaddressed). While perhaps not a causal agent, increased development since 1996, particularly around Ajijic and San Juan Cosala, has been
a concern to many because of a lack of development guidelines regarding
water usage. The increasing affluence of today's international migrant has
also meant swimming pools, expansive gardens, and larger homes, all of
which put pressure upon the lake's resources. Although some activists and
local groups such as Amigos de Lago (Friends of the Lake), along with national and international organizations, have begun to raise awareness of
these concerns, the issue of Lake Chapala's health remains unresolved.
The problem is further compounded by other concerns within the foreign
community. For example, some residents of the foreign community feel
that if the lake were cleaned up, it might draw more traditional types
of recreational tourism, and that this then could further increase development.

To the east of Chapala are small native communities offset by Vista Del
Lago, a golf community popular among foreign residents. Except for Vista

del Lago, there are fewer signs of foreign residency along this short stretch of the coastal road because most of the development has shifted west toward Ajijic. On the western edge of Chapala, older hacienda-style homes—many showing signs of disrepair and neglect—give way to the signs of and entrances to any number of Mexican-style *fraccionamientos*. Some of these communities are well marked with guardhouses and modern signs, while others are less demarcated and show signs of deterioration. Small concrete buildings that resemble truncated American strip malls now begin to appear along the highway. Doctor's and dentist's offices share space with furniture and curio shops, and there are occasional signs in English, usually promoting real-estate sales.

Although this highway remains the sole access route for the Riviera, in the past it served as more of a supply road than a central highway. And for the most part, the economic centers of activity remain where they have always been: off the highway, and located near the village plazas and along the lakeshore. Yet, if we peer up the valley walls, we can get a sense of the magnitude and degree of development in the area. The contrast between the housing developments above and the older ones off the main highway is noticeable even from the valley floor. The expansive and modern housing developments perched on the hills above puncture the skyline with Moorish minarets and other modern architectural features that contrast dramatically with the homes and *fraccionamientos* built before the 1990s.

The other route that bypasses Chapala offers greater insights into the hilltop developments seen from the valley floor. These gated communities perched upon the highlands overlooking Lake Chapala are strikingly different from the older developments located below. Billboards and signs enthusiastically welcome visitors to the area, and "Models Open" banners and flags lure potential buyers. These subdivisions blend Mediterranean lines with Mexican colors and boast an array of modern American amenities such as fitness facilities and swimming pools. A manned guard house and security gate await new arrivals, and high walls around the entire compound obscure the views of the lake except for those who live within the confines of the compound. The signage suggests that English, not Spanish, is the lingua franca, at least as long as one remains behind the walls of this foreign enclave.

As one descends into the valley and rejoins the Chapala-Jocotepec highway, roadside vendors appear selling Mexican textiles and furniture indigenous to the area. The roadside strip malls multiply in number as one moves closer to Ajijic, the undisputed center of the foreign community.

The traffic now becomes more congested, and tourist-oriented stores (e.g., curio stores and art galleries) appear more frequently alongside local pharmacies and bakeries. The foreign element is much more noticeable here; North American license plates and late-model SUVs are common sights. Delivery trucks maneuver among the pedestrians and the parked cars that line the highway; at points the road and the sidewalk are virtually indistinguishable, and it is not until one ventures either below or above the highway that the congestion abates. There is little evidence of an idyllic lifestyle from this vantage point, and it is somewhat difficult to understand why this locale—congested and dusty—attracts so much attention from foreign migrants.

As the road moves through Ajijic and towards Jocotepec, the valley widens and there are signs of the more traditional lifestyles that once flourished in this valley. Trellised fields of chayote and a number of other crops are visible along the highway to the north, and natives strategically locate themselves near *topes* (i.e., speed bumps) to sell local fruits and maguey husks (the plant from which *tequilla* is produced), and *pulque*—the undistilled byproduct of the maguey plant indigenous to this region. Yet, interspersed within this traditional landscape are the signs of new developments boasting large ranch-style homes with expansive picture windows that will offer their future owners scenic views of the lake.

The rural character of this stretch of highway is short-lived; a barrage of bulldozers and other heavy equipment appear, lining the highway as workers transform this two-lane highway into a four-lane thoroughfare. This is perhaps the most dramatic indicator of potential change. Once we are past the four-lane construction and into the heart of Jocotepec, the landscape reveals a city much like Chapala, but without Chapala's tourist-orientation toward the lake. These two cities act as bookends for the other more hidden communities that lie along the Riviera. Those communities (Ajijic, San Juan Cosala, and San Antonio), like the *fraccionamientos* that dot the landscape, conceal themselves behind walls and within a maze of narrow cobble-stoned streets. It is those walls, and their locations, that can offer us further insights into the changing nature of the foreign community's presence in the area.

Fraccionamientos and the Home

First time visitors to Ajijic often wonder why so many non-Mexicans have chosen to retire here. They are sometimes critical of the modern housing subdivisions on the outer edges of the village, perhaps failing to realize that many of the best houses are really "behind the walls."[47]

Except for the new construction along the ridge, the views from the main highway offer little evidence of the lifestyle of those who live in this area. Most of the houses are located well off the main highway or behind concrete walls. Walls in themselves are not unique to this landscape and traditionally served as a defense against natives and bandits in earlier times. Yet those traditional walled homes contrast sharply with the more recent walled communities that constitute a modern adaptation of the traditional feature. Large perimeter walls have eliminated the need for walls around the individual houses within the perimeter, and thus the areas within these walls are more characteristic of a typical American subdivision. This is not only an architectural change, because it also implies a shift in the nature of privacy and anonymity. The walls built around individual houses originally afforded the foreign residents of those houses anonymity and helped the early settlers maintain a low profile within the region. The walled community, however, suggests a more collective type of existence—one that caters to the masses, not the individual. Thus, while the walls themselves are not unusual or particularly unique, their function has changed.

These walled or gated communities are part of another tradition that has an equally long history in this area—the *fraccionamiento*. While the design of the *fraccionamiento* may rest initially in the hands of the developer, it is the needs of the residents themselves that will eventually determine that design. For example, the newer gated communities along the valley's ridgeline (e.g., Birds of Paradise or Chula Vista Norte) look appreciably different from the outside because the construction incorporates modern features and untraditional architectural design, and the feeling inside the walls differs dramatically from that of older *fraccionamientos* such as Chula Vista or La Floresta. The newer subdivisions offer modern conveniences and some even have onsite stores and services. They look and feel more like all-inclusive resorts or compounds rather than subdivisions. In fact, it is difficult when touring the model homes and the grounds to gain any sense of one's absolute location (see fig. 8.2).

In comparison, La Floresta, an older subdivision located below the major highway between Ajijic and San Antonio, resembles a southern California suburb with wrought-iron-gated, southwestern-style homes that emulate adobe construction. Originally built as vacation homes for Mexican families, this *fraccionamiento* with its wide streets and manicured lawns extends on both sides of the main highway. This residential landscape is markedly different from that of the village but does not have large walls like other gated communities; instead, the concrete barriers around the development act only as ornamental boundaries. Both foreigners and

Figure 8.2.   New villa construction for retirees in upper Ajijic. Photo courtesy of David Truly.

Mexicans alike reside in this strikingly American-looking subdivision. The *fraccionamientos* along the Riviera, in fact, vary considerably in their design, size, and composition, but most of the newer developments utilize large walls and manned guard houses. In addition, most are located away from the village centers and further up the valley walls. From this vantage point, the views of the lake and the surrounding mountains are spectacular, although somewhat diminished by a sea of satellite dishes that litter the landscape—all pointed towards North American broadcast satellites. For those who reside in these retreats, their safety and culture is assured as is their segregation from the lifestyle along the shore.

Within the village of Ajijic (the area located between the main highway and the lake) the sounds and noises of Mexican children and families create a vibrant atmosphere. In these sections of the city, the walls of the older homes may offer security and privacy, but they cannot block out the sounds and smells of the ethnic milieu. Even in those sections of the village where the foreigners live, the environment is distinctively Mexican. In fact, the focal point of the village remains the plaza, which represented an essential aspect of life in New Spain and other areas affected by the Spanish Conquest, including the southwestern United States. The plaza served as both a gathering place and a reminder of the dual authority of the colonial period: the

Catholic Church and the Spanish government. Those influences are visible in the plazas of Ajijic, San Antonio, and the other villages along the Chapala shore, but the landscape today is equally shared with local meat and produce shops, banks with ATMs, community centers, and an occasional restaurant. While the plaza still serves its traditional role within the native community (e.g., the yearly festival of the patron saint is held in the plaza), it has also become a popular haunt for retirees and visitors. In Ajijic, a Casa de Cultura (House of Culture) sits on the plaza next to a restaurant where one can always find a foreign visitor or retiree. Although the plaza "feels Mexican," it also reflects the foreign residency in this area. In some ways the landscape still reflects a symbiotic relationship representative of earlier times.

Once inside the gates or garden walls of one of the more traditional homes, the luxury of living in an idyllic climate becomes perfectly clear. Many of these homes have an interior garden, and very often the living area opens into it. Some homeowners have modified this style and added windows or French doors but maintained the outdoor environment as part of the house. While this walled, hacienda-style design is still found throughout the valley area, it is concentrated in the urban and village centers in a way similar to areas of the Vieux Carre in New Orleans. Residents of such homes have both their privacy and easy access to the services and bustling lifestyle of the area. For many, this style of living also most closely resembles the original sense of community and place associated with earlier settlement in the Lake Chapala area.

The farther away we move from the core of the village, while keeping parallel to the lakeshore, the more the impact of foreign immigration is noticeable. On the periphery of the village, the contrast between newly built or renovated homes aimed at the foreign market and the simple concrete and wooden shacks of the local natives is obvious. In some parts of the village area, renovations or restorations stand out against otherwise untouched buildings, a clear indication that the demand for new housing is still strong. Although the village houses many foreign immigrants, their presence is often difficult to notice due to the constant pulse of Mexican life that permeates the village area.

Just as we noted in our view of the village from the highway, the streets and the walls of the village reveal little to the observer. For this reason, perhaps, the presence of immigrants here never overwhelms or threatens the native landscape. In many ways the urban landscape of Ajijic reflects the symbiotic relationship that has developed between the local and the foreign community—a relationship characterized by tolerance, mutual interdependence, and a healthy respect for the sovereign authority of the local people. Yet, while the signs of change are unmistakable, the question remains as to the speed and intensity of that change.

A Last Look at the Riviera Region

Landscape can be evaluated in itself as beautiful or ugly, productive or infertile. On the other hand, it is also a clue to a region's human personality.[48]

The landscape of the Lake Chapala Riviera in the late 1990s offers conflicting images of traditional Mexican rural life and modern retirement, secluded residential retreats and garish ranch-style living, beautiful lake vistas and satellite-dish-dotted landscapes, all woven together in an intricate cultural mosaic that has, until now, maintained a certain degree of integrity and equilibrium. Today, the forces that created that mosaic are still at work: the highway has been widened; the development of gated communities has continued; crime is still a serious issue, albeit somewhat accepted now; and the continued influx of new migrants continues to concern those who feel the area is changing for the worse. In fact, some residents suggest that in many ways the Lake Chapala Riviera is more American than it was in the past. The impact of the area's foreign community is more obvious, and forces not readily apparent in the architecture and design of its homes and subdivisions also threaten the symbiotic relationship that once defined life in this region. The combination of these forces may signal significant changes for both the foreign and local communities along Lake Chapala's shores.

The economic boom of the 1990s in North America and the aging of the baby boomer generation have created a large demand for seasonal and retirement homes, and the Lake Chapala Riviera has become highly visible in that market. Local realtors have remarked on the unprecedented nature of this boom period, and the effects upon the landscape are obvious. Large, modern homes are found along the higher slopes of the valley, farther away from the traditional lakeside and village homes that were once the object of foreign interest. Gated communities offering all the amenities and conveniences of similar communities in the United States or Canada continue to sprout up along the shoreline, displacing farmland and traditional Mexican homes. The more private, walled homes that once symbolized this area are now being replaced by ranch-style homes, more typical of the United States, that flaunt large picture windows designed to take full advantage of the view of Lake Chapala—or by housing communities that are separated by high walls from the landscape around them. And as the cultural landscape interpretation above suggests, it is not the mere appearance of the walls in the area that is unusual, it is the manner in which they are being used. Walls no longer reinforce individual privacy and security; now they imply a collective form of isolation that is more characteristic of enclaves and compounds.

Other signs indicate the intensity and speed of development along Lake Chapala. The widening of the coastal road from Chapala to Jocotepec, improved telephone service and Internet access, and the satellite dishes on area rooftops, suggest an increased accessibility and interaction with the outside world. Most importantly, the Mexican government, which has always been a leader in tourism development[49] and recent research,[50] condones the recognition and promotion of retirement-destination development. The government's proactive stance toward this type of economic development, the effects of NAFTA, and the increasing presence of multinational corporations and franchises in the region, along with relaxed immigration controls, all suggest that a different style of development is now underway. Some local North American business owners and observers along Lake Chapala even believe that the area might one day be more similar to fashionable developments such as Las Hadas (a Mediterranean-style tourist destination located on the Pacific coast in Puerto Vallarta), and then will cater only to the very wealthy and sophisticated traveler and immigrant. The issue of the dying lake may also be moot if a deliberate draining of 40 percent of the lake is approved, a proposal that led one author to suggest (sarcastically) building a man-made "Eco-Chapala" complex in the tradition of Disney World.[51] Perhaps more interesting than such speculations, however, is why it has taken so long for these changes to occur, especially in a country renowned for its promotion and development of tourism.

The reason for Lake Chapala Riviera's lack of change over the years can be attributed to its relative isolation, its failed attempts at mass-tourism development, a dying lake, and perhaps more importantly, to a somewhat unique lifestyle that is inherently foreign to North Americans. In fact, this was a lifestyle that evolved from "behind the walls" of the area's villages. From the interviews that I conducted, it is quite apparent that the informal and tolerant nature of day-to-day life along Lake Chapala has had a profound effect on foreign immigrants to the area: they maintain a low profile, preferring to blend into their surroundings rather than to draw attention to themselves, a trait not so common among more recent immigrants. And it should be remembered that those amenities and services that are now considered standard in most tourist and retirement communities were not part of the attraction for previous immigrants to the area. Whether the increased availability of these amenities and services will overwhelm the lifestyle that has been such an attraction for generations of foreign visitors and residents is difficult to predict. It is certain, however, that the attraction of this area is not dependent solely on the area's economic advantages or its climate but also on its unique social nature.

As noted above, many area residents feel that life along the Lake Chapala Riviera today is more American that at any time in the past. The impact of this Americanization over time could be significant; some long-time residents are considering moving, but their age and health may not now allow it; others have moved to smaller villages in the area where the American presence is less obvious; and others will simply stay and weather the booms and busts so common here. In any event, the nature of both the foreign community and the larger community along the Lake Chapala Riviera has changed and will continue to evolve, as perhaps best exemplified by the following anonymous comment:

> I was finalizing the sale of my house in Dallas with my agent and we talked about my moving to Mexico. We laughed a bit when we realized that her dream as a Mexican had always been to leave Mexico and come to the United States. And now she was helping me with my dream to leave here and live in Mexico . . . kinda strange, don't you think?

Notes

1. Neill James, *Dust on my Heart: Petticoat Vagabond in Mexico* (New York: C. Scribner's Sons, 1946), 284.

2. Dane Chandos, *Village in the Sun* (New York: G. P. Putnam's Sons, 1945), 15.

3. June Nay Summers, *Lake Chapala—Villages in the Sun* (Guadalajara: Lake Chapala Society, 1993), 45–46.

4. Norvelle Sannebeck, *Everything You Ever Wanted to Know about Living in Mexico* (Anderson, S.C.: Droke House, 1970).

5. Justin Martin, "Or If You'd Rather, Retire Abroad," *Fortune*, vol. 132, no. 2 (1995): 95–105.

6. Tony Burton, *Western Mexico: A Traveler's Treasury*, 3d ed. (Guadalajara, Jalisco, Mexico: Editorial Agata, 1997), 23–43.

7. Melynda Wilcox and Susan Province, "Retirement Spots That Feel Like Home," *Kiplinger's Personal Finance*, vol. 46, no. 8 (1992): 49–54.

8. Alan Williams et al., "A Place in the Sun: International Retirement Migration from Northern to Southern Europe," *European Urban and Regional Studies*, vol. 4, no. 2 (1997): 115–34.

9. Lorena M. Otero, "US Retired Persons in Mexico," *American Behavioral Scientist*, vol. 40, no. 7 (1997): 914–22.

10. Virgil Harold Holder, "The Migration of Retirees to Mexico: A Survey and Case Study of Guadalajara, Mexico" (PhD diss., University of Minnesota, 1977); Phillip H. Allman Jr., "A New Form of International Migration: The United States Military Retiree in Central America" (PhD diss., Michigan State University, 1977); Boris J. Popov, "American Retirement Abroad: The Costa Rican Experience" (PhD diss., University of Massachusetts, 1979); Eleanore M. Stokes, "La Colonia Extranero: An American Retirement Community in Ajijic, Mexico" (PhD diss., University of New York, Stony Brook, 1981).

11. Charles F. Longino Jr., "Geographical Distribution and Migration, " in *Handbook of Aging and Social Sciences*, ed. R. Binstock and L. George (San Diego: Academic Press, 1990): 45–63.

12. Allan Findlay, "Population Geography," *Progress in Human Geography* 16 (1990): 88–97; P. Taietz, "Sociocultural Integration of Older American Residents in Paris," *Gerontologist*, vol. 27, no. 4 (1987): 464–70.

13. David Truly, "International Retirement Migration and Tourism along the Lake Chapala Riviera: Developing a Matrix of Retirement Migration Behavior," *Tourism Geographies*, vol. 4, no. 3 (2002): 261–81.

14. Carl Sauer, "The Morphology of Landscape," *University of California Publications in Geography* (Berkeley: University of California Press, 1925), 19–54.

15. Donald W. Meinig, ed., *The Interpretation of Ordinary Landscapes* (New York: Oxford University Press, 1979).

16. Burton, *Western Mexico*, 17–22.

17. Ethel Alec-Tweedie, *Mexico As I Saw It* (New York: Macmillan, 1901).

18. Carl Lumholtz, *Unknown Mexico: A Record of Five Years' Exploration among the Tribes of the Western Sierra Madre* (New York: C. Scribner's Sons, 1902).

19. Stokes, "La Colonia Extranero," 49.

20. Michael Hargraves, *Lake Chapala: A Literary Survey* (Los Angeles: M. Hargraves, 1992).

21. Stokes, "La Colonia Extranero," 50.

22. Stokes, "La Colonia Extranero," 52.

23. Stokes, "La Colonia Extranero," 50–56.

24. Dick Tingen, interview with the author, November 10, 1997, Chapala, Mexico.

25. Stokes, "La Colonia Extranero," 55.

26. Dale Palfrey, interview with the author, November 17, 1997, Ajijic, Mexico.

27. Summers, *Lake Chapala*, 56–57; Allyn Hunt, interview with the author, December 10, 1997, Jocotepec, Mexico.

28. Sannebeck, *Everything You Ever Wanted to Know*, 115–23.

29. Louise Harrison, interview with the author, December 6, 1997, Ajijic, Mexico.

30. Terry T. Phillip, *Terry's Guide to Mexico* (Garden City, N.Y.: Doubleday, 1965).

31. Stokes, "La Colonia Extranero," 57.

32. Stokes, "La Colonia Extranero," 59–62.

33. Tingen, interview.

34. Stokes, "La Colonia Extranero," 65–67.

35. Stokes, "La Colonia Extranero," 67.

36. Tingen, interview.

37. John Howells and Emily Merwin, *Retire to Mexico—For a Few Dollars a Day* (New York: Hampton Press, 1994), 135.

38. Hunt, interview.

39. Stokes, "La Colonia Extranero," 68.

40. Tingen, interview.

41. Harrison, interview.

42. Betty Edwards, interview with the author, October 16, 1997, Chapala, Mexico; Hunt interview; Harrison interview.

43. Tingen, interview.

44. John Brickerhoff Jackson, *A Sense of Time, A Sense of Place* (New Haven, Conn.: Yale University Press, 1996), 190–94.

45. Manuel Guzman Arroyo. *La Pesca en el lago del Chapala: Hacia su ordenamiento racional y explotacion*, (Guadalajara: University of Guadalajara, 1995).

46. Tony Burton, "Can Mexico's Largest Lake Be Saved: A Year 2000 Update, The State of the Lake," *Mexconnect Online Magazine* (Chapala, 2000).

47. Burton, *Western Mexico*, 27.

48. Yi-Fu Tuan, "The Eye and the Eye's Mind," in *The Interpretation of Ordinary Landscapes*, ed. D. W. Meinig (New York: Oxford University Press, 1979), 93.

49. Walter Krause, *International Tourism and Development*, with G. Donald Jud and Hyman Joseph (Austin: University of Texas, 1972).

50. Otero, "US Retired Persons in Mexico."

51. Tony Burton. "Lake Chapala—Fish, Farmland or Bungee Jump," *Mexconnect Online Magazine* (Chapala, 2002).

CHAPTER NINE

"To Be Served and Loved:
The American Sense of Place
in San Miguel de Allende"
Nicholas Dagen Bloom

San Miguel de Allende is ceaselessly promoted to American retirees and tourists as an unspoiled colonial gem,[1] but the city's social, physical, and cultural fabric is being modernized at a furious pace. Its exotic cathedral, La Parroquia de San Miguel Arcangel, the seasonal Indian dances, the Mariachi players on the Jardin (San Miguel's central square), and the courtyards of old haciendas certainly lend an air of bygone days to the historic center. These traditional Mexican ornaments should not, however, be mistaken for centrality in the current reality of this undeniably picturesque place. Those who move beyond the marketed version of San Miguel de Allende find that it is not a city untouched by time but a thriving and complex point of contact between the United States and Mexico.

San Miguel de Allende represents the future of many Mexican cities as the U.S.-Mexico border becomes more porous. Many more colonial towns will eventually become tourist and retiree destinations as they are infiltrated by a small and energetic American elite. Similar processes of change along the Lake Chapala Riviera are documented in this collection, but cities such as Guanajuato, Morelia, Patzcuaro, and Zacatecas remain relatively untouched by American influence. The low cost of living and antique charm of these places, however, may make them destinations for growing numbers of American retirees.

San Miguel de Allende's fifty years of American colonization makes the city a provocative urban premonition of what may happen elsewhere—particularly in the historic "silver" cities of Mexico's interior. An ambitious group of Americans have lived in San Miguel long enough to allow the study of significant American influence on a Mexican town. Today, there are an estimated 4,000

Americans[2] who live in San Miguel for extended periods every year, and they are surrounded by approximately 100,000 Mexicans (mostly poor, but some middle- and upper-class Mexicans, too). Americans are comparatively small in number, but they are very powerful.

San Miguel de Allende is important because it is the most earnest and self-righteous of the American colonies. It has done the most to try to uplift and improve its city of choice, and it has the richest institutional matrix of any American colony in Mexico. San Miguel's resident American population has made an intriguing effort to move beyond a "consumption" mode in their lifestyle. This activist stance is a sharp, and self-conscious, contrast to the standard American tourist role in Cancún and other Mexican destinations. Environmental organizations, social-service charities, language instruction classes, art schools, performance series, and theater groups have prospered. Although many of these activities are needlessly showy, reflect aspects of guilt compensation, and seem to be more closely focused on status competition within the American community (rather than just good works), many of them have made a great difference in the lives of local Mexicans. They have also a set a particular tone in the city that attracts well-educated and self-styled "sophisticated" Americans.

It is fair to say that even the large scale of this philanthropy has not been able to cope with the larger social realities that are quickly changing San Miguel, however. Although connections to local conditions seem to be made through philanthropy, the American colony as a whole is increasingly isolated from the vibrant Mexican society growing quickly around it. A "high" white culture in San Miguel de Allende that shops in Americanized stores, enjoys luxury homes, is attended to by servants, and enjoys lush restaurants, spas, art galleries, and charity events contrasts strongly with a boom in mass tourism and a rapidly growing working-class Mexican majority in shanty suburbs that reflect third-world urban conditions.

These parallel American and Mexican societies seem to be able to live in a symbiotic fashion, and their spaces interweave (though not always in an aesthetic or pleasing fashion); this way of living may well become a standard for urban society in the choicest Mexican colonial towns.

A Convincing Start

An element of serendipity catalyzed the process of expatriate community growth in San Miguel de Allende. The colony was founded on an adventurous note with the arrival of Stirling Dickinson in the 1930s. As Lane Simmons, a flamboyant local real-estate agent, explained recently, the "way you are treated is how the first gringo" acted. He notes with some humor that "if it had been Texans [who arrived first], don't get out of the car." Dickinson arrived with greater respect for Mexican culture than most Americans and paired his respect and admiration with active philanthropic and cultural projects.[3]

Dickinson, born in Chicago to a wealthy family, attended Princeton and the Art Institute in Chicago, toured Mexico in 1934, and with a friend authored a guidebook titled *Mexican Odyssey* (1936). When he finally made it to San Miguel in 1937 on the suggestion of Mexican opera star Jose Mojira and in search of a setting for a fictional treatment of the Mexican War of Independence, it took him only ten days to buy a house. At that time, according to Dickinson, San Miguel had only about fourteen thousand residents (all Mexican), no modern roads, and a visitor had to arrive by train. There was only one taxi in the town, with air in three tires and sawdust in the fourth. There were no private automobiles, major stores, tourist shops, or banks.[4] The town certainly had had a distinguished history: established in 1542 by Spanish settlers, it had played a leading role in centuries of silver trade and once had been remarkable for artisanship of great skill in crafts such as weaving and leather working. Although it had fallen into disrepair, it still boasted leading examples of colonial architecture and nineteenth-century stone mansions and churches.

Dickinson enjoyed the exotic life he found in San Miguel, but he was not able to ignore the contrast between the picturesque aspects of the town and its serious humanitarian problems. The poverty then, as now, was severe and highly visible; unlike the case in the United States, poor people were not restricted to a particular neighborhood or district. There were then few social-service agencies, government or otherwise, addressing the general poverty. Like all Mexican towns at the time too, it lacked the modern services (water, gas, electric, paved roads, and sewers) that urban areas had developed during the last century in the United States.

The town embarked on a path to extensive philanthropic commitment in part because of Dickinson's energy. Over a fifty-year period he played a leading role in the creation of the town's two art schools, Belles Artes and the Instituto Allende, the Biblioteca (a library and quasi-Settlement house), the local Red Cross, a hospital, a garden club, a local Audubon society (the first outside the United States), a *club deportiv* (a soccer club for kids), rural libraries, and more. As an upper-class native of Chicago, he was probably familiar with Hull House in Chicago and its famous commitment to social justice through direct action by college-educated reformers, and it was Dickinson, fluent in Spanish and well liked by many Mexicans in the town, who imported this progressive spirit. There is even a street in San Miguel named in his honor.

Dickinson also did his best over the decades to increase American appreciation for Mexican culture and society. He offered unconventional classes and trips to Americans at the Instituto Allende from the 1950s through the 1980s. One former student described his experience in a Dickinson class:

> Most of the classes were excursions into the backcountry where we were introduced to some wonderful albeit strange customs of the *campesinos*. We climbed over pigpens and chicken coops to get to a farmer's house, we drank *pulque* right out of the barrel, we trudged into remote nurseries for rare plants.[5]

Dickinson, through these types of courses, aimed to encourage Americans to understand the power and attractiveness of Mexican life and culture. To what degree he succeeded, and to what degree this curiosity remains a salient part of San Miguel culture, is unclear.

A Growing Colony

More Americans and Canadians dribbled into the town during the 1940s and 1950s. Drawn by the low cost of travel and the exoticism of Mexico, the postwar era initiated an influx of veterans with money to spend from the GI Bill. Other adventurous Americans found their way to the town, too. In 1948, one American admitted that a wrong turn out of Morelia brought him to San Miguel. John Johnson stayed at the Posada del San Francisco, then one of the town's few hotels, and subsequently rented a furnished house for thirty dollars a month. There were still very few foreigners, but according to Johnson, Stirling Dickinson had already become popular with the local population.[6] Canadians Leonard and Reva Brooks, he a painter and she a photographer, established themselves in San Miguel in the 1940s and helped bring a number of other artists, both Canadian and Mexican, to the town.[7]

Life magazine published a misleading article on the town in 1948 that helped build international interest. Dickinson remembered that a postman arrived one day at the Escuela Universitaria de Bellas Artes, then a small art school directed by Dickinson, with an overflowing bag of letters:

> After reading the first of the letters, which, believe it or not, reached a total of 3,600, it became evident that this windfall of correspondence was due to an article entitled "Luxury living on 45 dollars a week." All you had to do was hurry down to SMA [San Miguel de Allende], talk to the first person you met on the street, and then pick up the keys to a lovely home complete with swimming pool, servants and all the trimmings.[8]

Dickinson dryly noted that some of the letters "pathetically revealed the search for a garden of Eden retirement paradise which the article seemed to promise." These are still the notes most often sounded in promoting San Miguel to Americans. Still, at that time many aspiring writers and artists arrived and set San Miguel's early progressive, antiestablishment tone. Americans and Mexicans often fell into each other's arms, and San Miguel developed its own local mixed-nationality population.

Dickinson in the 1940s was directing what is now known as the Belles Artes (an art school run by the Mexican government), but as a result of a controversy involving a David Siqueiros mural project, the school suspended operations. The San Miguel colony had a reputation at the time, only partly deserved, as a center of communist activity, and Siqueiros's presence did not help. As a result, Dickinson and a number of artists found themselves deported in 1950. Although generally tolerated by Mexicans, the small international colony and its unconventional behavior (by both American and Mexican standards of the day) had also made powerful local enemies.[9]

After the Americans were allowed to return in 1950, the creation of what became known as the Instituto Allende, a university-level institution that accepted GI-Bill money, unleashed a flood of American students rather than just pleasure seekers. In 1950 Enrique Martinez, a former governor of Guanajuato state, and his wife Nell Martinez (an American from Arkansas), with Dickinson, restored an old and ruined mansion, adding new studios, hotel rooms, landscaping, and instructors.[10] The Instituto Allende they founded, with Dickinson as director, expanded during the 1950s to five hundred students and thus speeded up San Miguel's Americanization.[11] San Miguel from the beginning attracted not only tourists but also a more adventurous (if also quite mischievous) student crowd. The student partying, including immoderate drinking and sex, according to many accounts characterized the period.

For most visitors in the 1950s, San Miguel, beyond the cheap booze and congenial climate, was more than exotic enough even with the growing numbers of Americans living and visiting there. San Miguel existed a world away from the booming suburbs and modern downtowns of 1950s America; for many visitors, the trip to San Miguel was more than just a trip through space, it was a form of time travel. One long-time resident, Mimi Loomer, who became a columnist for *Atencion*, the local American paper published by the Biblioteca, remembered,

The Indians . . . sat with their backs against the *Parroquia* wall, sombreros tipped down over their eyes, serapes pulled up across their faces to protect them from the chill mountain air. The young blades lingered beneath the barred windows singing love songs to their sweethearts. . . . The Sunday morning market was different then. Everything was outdoors and even noisier than now with burros braying, chickens squawking and dogs barking.[12]

Author Sally Mathews, who came in 1957 to attend the instituto, remembered that chaperones still policed the young people in the Jardin, Mexicans dressed conservatively, and after a bullfight, the bulls' heads were displayed in the Mercado. Nevertheless, she remembered that in 1961 for the first time she "saw Americans driving into town with poodles with big rhinestone necklaces."

Indeed, wealthier visitors to San Miguel could find lodging to their taste by the late 1950s. Americans could take a Pullman to San Miguel from St. Louis (with a number of stops in between) on what was known as the Aztec Eagle that ran to Mexico City.[13] Roads improved during this period, better linking San Miguel to the surrounding towns. The party life for Americans of most social classes had already started. Bars with a mainly American clientele, El Patio and the Cucharacha, drew carousing students and visitors, and three or four inexpensive hotels offered decent accommodations. Costs remained unbelievably low for Americans, and a "fixed income of 100 dollars got one the 'soft life.'" Americans could pay as little as sixteen dollars a month for rent and eight dollars a month for a full-time maid.[14]

During this period the founding of the Biblioteca began the institutionalization of good works in San Miguel. The library, founded in 1954 by American resident Helen Wales with help from Stirling Dickinson and other Americans, first operated in a modest rented house and was primarily targeted to Mexican children. Children's books in Spanish were hard to find, and volunteers made translations of American children's classics. The staff, a combination of tourists and residents, wondered if they would succeed in attracting Mexicans: "Would the children come? Whole families and clusters of them [did] and they have never stopped coming."[15]

The Biblioteca had struck a chord with the local population and it remains popular. Americans had demonstrated that they could be more than just observers and consumers in a Mexican milieu. The governor of the state of Guanajuato donated a former slaughterhouse in 1958 that, after renovation, allowed for expansion of the library, more numerous social-welfare activities, and active cultural events. There were enough permanent residents with attractive homes and enough visitors to justify in 1959 the beginning of home tours that continue today to raise significant money for the library and its many programs. These home tours are packed events in San Miguel de Allende and have a number of functions beyond philanthropy. They are opportunities for wealthy residents to show off their homes and good taste, and they are also ways to advertise real estate and potential rentals (because many residents rent their homes for significant portions of the year).

At the Biblioteca, eager, well-behaved, and adorable Mexican children are still taught English and art by college-educated (mostly retired) Americans; local cultural events for both Mexicans and Americans are frequent and often of good quality; a restaurant within the library brings in money for the philanthropic activities of the library; the local newspaper run by the Biblioteca, *Atencion*, has become the main voice of the American colony; and the library itself, with thousands of both Spanish- and English-language books, serves both Mexicans and Americans. The library has, over the years, extended its reach to provide books for rural schools, and to this day it maintains an impressive scholarship system for local Mexican students. A local Mexican resident explained that it is wrong to believe that the Biblioteca belongs "to the foreign colony. The foreigners have the time to give to this excellent cause, but it is geared in its totality to elevate the culture and standards of all the people of San Miguel de Allende. Should you visit any afternoon you will see it filled with Mexican children and young people studying and making use of its facilities."[16] On one level at least, the Americans seem to have connected with the Mexican population.

Building an Ideal San Miguel de Allende

By far most American creativity in San Miguel is still devoted to philanthropy. Philanthropy is an essential aspect of the guilt compensation that some Americans make for their bargain, luxury lifestyle. Charity is also a familiar part of American life generally, and it provides a focus for retiree activity. In fairness too, it must be said that most Americans are sensitive to the poverty and problems that surrounds them. The initial projects created by Dickinson have grown over the decades, and the town is now an active laboratory of America's associational spirit. These activities are not unique to San Miguel, but in their scale, ambition, and number they are the most impressive of the American communities in Mexico. The degree to which these activities are actually able to shape San Miguel into the kind of community that the residents would ideally like (one with less poverty, ignorance, and pollution) is a matter for debate. The actual realization of such an improved society would also, by making Mexicans less eager to work for very low wages in domestic service, undercut the lifestyle so beloved by the Americans.

Lane Simmons, local real-estate agent and provocateur, perhaps says it best: "Here with so little effort, so much result" can be seen in the Mexican community. He dryly notes, too, that "San Miguel is where the dead sergeant's wife becomes the admiral's widow."[17] The multiplication of philanthropic efforts is indeed impressive, and it covers family planning, an old age home, free food and medical care for Mexican children, scholarships for Mexican students, large-scale environmental efforts (including significant improvements of the intown Parque Juarez as well as environmental reserves surrounding the city), English-language instruction, and informal forms of philanthropy to help with the school tuitions of servants. One can hardly attend an event sponsored by the American community in San Miguel—lecture or movie or concert—that is not a fundraiser for a Mexican-oriented good work in the town. Few events lack this seal of endorsement. Because a list of all the different ongoing events and activities would be tiresome, I cannot wholly convey the scale and ambition of the many projects in this town. These activities, however, are both numerous and constant.

Philanthropy in San Miguel, not surprisingly, has its theatrical side. At an auction of the *Patronato por los niños* I attended, proceeds of which were to be devoted to medical care for children, luxury vacations and goods for sale—all tax deductible as a donation—often sold for thousands of dollars. This event brought well-heeled Texans and summer crowds, social noise, and an aggressive auctioneer and his paddle-wielding assistants. He encouraged his audience to "take another drink and bid one thousand dollars" because it was all "money for the *niños*." The countless cocktail parties for large groups sold at the event would evidently lubricate group bonding among the American, particularly the Texan, elite of the town (one of the items up for sale was lunch with the governor of Texas). The auction the evening that I attended raised over ninety thousand dollars alone, and the items for sale offered an intimate portrait of international travel, cultural power, political connections, luxurious homes, and sociable spaces for those with sizable resources.

Nor are the older sources of philanthropy any less spirited. One resident told me that factions are a way of life in San Miguel, with the formation of duplicate splinter organizations of certain institutions. Battles among factions at the Biblioteca in 2002, for instance, led to arrests, election fraud, and wounded egos during board elections. Some defeated community leaders, including former Biblioteca president Mort Stith, threatened to leave town over the debacle. As many residents told me, in San Miguel there are "too many chiefs, and too few Indians." The attraction of the Biblioteca nevertheless remains strong for many of the retired residents of the colony. It welcomes their presence, offers a variety of events, and even utilizes their lack of Spanish-language skills by offering, as one of its main forms of service, English-language instruction and conversation by Americans.

The opportunity for good works is particularly appealing to American retirees and expatriates because poverty is less hidden in San Miguel than in
the United States. The conditions around their villas are a continuing shock,
and Americans soon discover that they have become first-world elites in an
impoverished land. Americans, however, are not openly made targets of
working-class anger and do not feel that they should be (that many do not
understand Spanish can be a benefit, too, when insults are made on the
streets). Poor Mexicans are not a minority population seeking political
recognition, government goods, or economic progress at the expense of the
Americans, in a way that would be similar to the more common portrayal of
minorities in the United States. In fact, some Americans in San Miguel have
a negative opinion of the people who actually govern the town and country.
Criticism by Americans of the tough ways of wealthy Mexicans is common.
In general too, Americans are not challenged for leadership of the organizations they create. The organizations' administrative staffs are often Mexican
and happy to have good jobs, while most Americans lack the language skills
(and connections) to run an organization in Mexico.

San Miguel's overheated philanthropy is not to everyone's taste. A retired
real-estate broker explained to me that he, like many people in town, would
"rather give directly to people . . . [and] pay for education of people who need
help," and he doesn't "like going to parties for giving money." He has noted
that only when he donated was he invited to many parties and events. The
self-interested side of philanthropy also bothered him: "People vie to be on
boards to have something to do." A number of people I interviewed also
noted that the coldness many Americans see in wealthy Mexicans is a reflection of the fact that extended families are more important than charity in
Mexico and that these families take much better care of their older and sick
members than many of those in the United States do. One resident remarked
at the lack of concern for sickly, old Americans as opposed to the concern
shown for charming Mexican children, and disliked the distinct patter of
"benevolence but superiority" in San Miguel's philanthropic scene.[18] According to another of my informants, volunteers and donors are "not Mother
Theresas" but are simply "guilt-ridden" retirees who feel they must do something to justify their low-cost, luxury existence.[19]

The interesting question here is the degree to which these efforts have
changed the fate and face of San Miguel. The city has grown large (an estimated 100,000), but at its outskirts it has also grown as a primarily un-
planned and poor city. Whole districts, primarily newer ones on the outskirts,
are genuine Mexican districts, with all the vibrancy and poverty one usually
finds in Mexico's *colonias* but very little colonial charm. Like most towns in

the developing world, this massive growth in population has meant an expansion of usually semi-legal, squatter *colonias* around the historic core of the town.[20] Mexican officials have slowly extended urban services to these districts, and they acknowledge the problems:

> The saddest [part of San Miguel's problem] is the existence of what Americans call slurbs, suburban slums—the outlying colonies that lack most if not all of the basic city services . . . we saw a creek of black water that must have harbored every kind of all too possible epidemic. . . on its banks lay piles of garbage, dead animals, junk . . . all of this stinking.[21]

Americans feel much more powerful than they actually are in improving the local environment.

Stirling Dickinson himself had little affection for these new communities on both humanitarian and aesthetic grounds. In 1975 he admitted, "We see the mushrooming of unsightly suburbs where there is rarely enough water, drainage or light. Sewage flows through arroyos . . . a focal point for disease. . . . San Miguel has severe growing pains that threaten to spoil its beauty as one of the real colonial gems of Mexico."[22] As can be seen, the social problems of Mexico far exceed the philanthropic activities of San Miguel's small American population. The Americans of San Miguel may feel that they are transforming the city in which they live into a version of the first world, but this illusion can only be maintained in the historic center of the city. Vast numbers of San Miguel's population remain underemployed or unemployed. On the positive side (from an American point of view), these workers provide a solid and inexpensive labor market for the American population.

These new slums are not scenes of utter devastation (in contrast to the slums in many American cities). Mexicans have a way of making the best of their situation. The growing *colonias* have crept over the surrounding hills, and they have taxed water resources and public services generally, but as they regularize they can become passable with the addition of colorful paint, stone window and doorframes, and even tile roofs. Most of the *colonias* feature an active street life and communal scenes that are increasingly less common in the more gentrified sections close to the Jardin. It is hard to see what influence the American colony's environmental and social efforts have had on these districts (which is not to say that they have had no effect at all). They seem like the *colonias* in Mexico City or at the edge of any Mexican town.

The boom and bust nature of Mexico's economy, and the government's tolerance of partial building, allows even more luxurious areas to have an uneven appearance. Newly planned suburbs, even for the middle class, are not immune to the half-building that occurs all over Mexico. Los Frailes, an otherwise upper-income planned suburban development outside of town, has its "share of instant ruins. The countryside is dotted with unfinished buildings, some that have been there for years, staring with empty windows at the lake below . . . great ugly hunks of brick and masonry. . . . The answer is, of course, that the owner began his building and ran out of money."[23] The frequent economic crises in Mexico, and the tolerance for a slower pace of construction, conspire, with *colonia* sprawl, against the creation of an ideal colonial town.

A Creative Colony

San Miguel's position as an art colony is as important an element of the colony's justification for its existence as is its social conscience. This claim to being a true art colony is debatable, but it provides, in combination with philanthropy, a sense for the Americans that they are not a part of a self-indulgent resort but rather are active participants in a sophisticated, culturally important experiment. It is more accurate, however, to call San Miguel a creative colony rather than an art colony. There is no true "San Miguel" style of art, nor is San Miguel ever likely to be remembered as a cultural center on a par with Montmartre, Soho, or Provincetown when each was at its height. Some active artists have lived in San Miguel (and some artists take vacations there), but the majority of San Miguel's artistic class appear to be arts-related professionals from major cities in America. A large number of art directors, designers, executives, and newspaper professionals have lived in San Miguel over the years. The people of San Miguel are mostly retired professionals who take a serious interest in the arts but are rarely accomplished artists themselves. Attractive watercolors, high participation in art classes and amateur theater, and well-attended art events should not be mistaken for a thriving colony of the arts.

The town's reputation in the arts and its particularly artistic quality have been overplayed over the years, but it has also been bolstered by imported talent, and an institutionalized series of cultural events offer a round of professional activities to even the most jaded visitors. Belles Artes and the Instituto Allende offer regular art classes by professional artists from San Miguel and around the world, and their galleries feature artwork by both Mexican and international artists. The chamber music festival at Belles Artes is perhaps the most notable cultural institution of the town because it brings world-class musicians to the city for both concerts and master classes for Mexican students during the summer.

Norman Loletus, a part-year resident of the town with extensive experience in New York and other major cities, will "only concede part of the artistic reputation. Culture is not at the level people think it is. . . . [San Miguel is]

not New York, Chicago, [or] LA." He does note that "those things indigenous to Mexico are excellent," including Indian dances, the Ballet Folklorico
(which visits), and Flamenco performances.[24] Nor does the kind of criticism
so necessary to artistic growth seem to be in play, in either the local paper or
informally. "One sure way never to be invited back anywhere in San Miguel
is to make a truthful comment at a gallery opening or offer your frank opinion about the poem that was read at the literary corner."[25] *Atencion* has never
offered anything but "good news" in its art reviews.

The attraction of creativity is understandable for retired Americans who
are looking for a more serious cultural scene than that available in a traditional retirement community. A resident explained the active retirement
lifestyle that is so attractive to newcomers: "In San Miguel de Allende unlike
many other places, they have not retired from life. They paint and sculpt and
write. They take classes in poetry and crafts and are creative. They are active
in community affairs."[26] The accent is on maximum feasible participation
rather than on breaking artistic boundaries. Although there were and still are
a few serious artists in San Miguel, they have not set the tone for the rest of
the community. One of the few long-time gallery owners, Sylvia Sameulson,
acknowledged in 1988 that "some people who have retired here think they
are artists because they won a prize back in high school. They are having the
time of their lives, but they dilute the support for the serious young artists."[27]

There are only a few active galleries in San Miguel, and there have been,
until recent times, serious restrictions on the moving of art out of the country. Phil Roettinger, a former CIA agent and professional artist, explained
that he was leaving the town because he couldn't sell art there:

> I know a few artists in San Miguel de Allende who are making a living at the
> game and most of those have turned to teaching. I cannot conveniently enter
> shows which are vital to the development of an artist. . . . I cannot ship paintings
> from Mexico nor for that matter take them out legally by auto. If I do manage to
> get them out and they fail to sell, I have great difficulty in bringing them back.[28]

Although San Miguel "has long been considered an arts center," columnist
Mimi Loomer admitted that "for many years there have been pitifully few
galleries [at which] to enjoy the work of local and national artists."[29]

The same limitation on local professionalism is true in the performing
arts. Residents of the town do stage frequent musicals (with older people con-
vincingly playing young characters) of better than average quality. The
Playreader's Society—staging its performances in a church hall with lights
fashioned from tin cans—offers acting, blocking, costumes, and lighting in a

convincing manner. The society has already demonstrated its commitment to the craft by staging over five hundred plays during its existence. Professional theater is another story and is not part of the cultural life of the community. There is no way for professional actors to support themselves in San Miguel through their art.

The views of some long-term residents illustrate, in part, what makes San Miguel attractive as a cultural destination even if it is not a true art colony. It is the accessibility of the arts, no matter the quality, an accessibility made possible by San Miguel's compact development, that is especially important to one couple, who say that they "trot out like dutiful horses from our house to whatever is available. So I get far more music than we do in LA, are exposed to plays we might ignore otherwise, and see more fresh art."[30] Cecil Smith, former television critic for the *Los Angeles Times* and a frequent columnist in *Atencion*, cataloged his activities in one week in 1989: "[hear] a Pulitzer Prize poet . . . attend two concerts and a ballet, [see] a highly professional production of the musical review 'O Coward' and go to openings at a couple of galleries, and see some of the most exciting paintings and sculpture you'd find anywhere."[31] The list of cultural activities in San Miguel on a weekly basis remains impressive today, but is fed by external sources and is not a reflection of the true passion of the American residents there.

San Miguel may not live up to its art colony reputation, but in comparison to many other American destinations in Mexico, it is impressive for its patrons' commitment to and interest in Mexican folk arts. Not only are the houses on the Biblioteca Home Tours filled with masks, rugs, furniture, and sculpture reflecting Mexican folk art traditions, but San Miguel's galleries and stores are also overflowing with a wide range of folk arts from across the country. San Miguel is an important market for higher-quality contemporary folk arts in Mexico as a whole. In certain cases too, interior designers from both Mexico and the United States have hired traditional artisans to make high-end, often outsized, versions of traditional Mexican craft objects. These objects can be found for sale at some of the chicest boutiques in town; these stores, and the related interior designers, cater equally to Mexicans and Americans. An impressive number of Americans are engaged in high-profile varieties of import and export in San Miguel.

Americans can also enjoy the traditional Mexican qualities of the town. As Jerry Novak, a long-time resident, explained in 1988, "Our town may have grown alarmingly large but a lot of the pleasures that were here when it was a small village are still here. . . . Newcomers to our town are unabashedly delighted by every sound and gesture. I was once, too."[32] For those with a slightly more adventurous spirit, the vegetable and meat *mercados* offer traditional

Mexican foods, displays (Indian women with piles of *nopales*, flowers, etc.), and a kind of character that can be found only in Mexico. One resident, in 1984, loved that "the open street market in San Miguel de Allende surges with life and beauty, colorful vegetables and fruit."[33] Even *campesinos* on burros can still, on occasion, be sighted on San Miguel's streets. The Jardin, while in the mornings filled with gringos and the English language, in the evenings is still dominated by Mexican teenagers and young adults.

The many annual festivals and celebrations in San Miguel, and the large number of churches in nearly continuous operation, still offer at least a vicarious connection to a preindustrial, exotic culture. Looming above the Jardin is La Parroquia, an exuberant neo-Baroque confection. According to local psychologist Mark Taylor, "Something about *La Parroquia* welcomes the infidel," and he believes that one can "see massive Pagan symbolism" in its tower. The church, created during the nineteenth century by an Indian stonemason and architect, Zefereino Gutiérrez, seems muted in its Christian symbolism. In general, the exotic aspects of Mexican Catholicism offer an unthreatening spirituality to even nonreligious Americans. As one resident noted, "Life seems so elemental here . . . in this medieval mountain city, this place thousands of miles away from all homes she had ever loved and nurtured, this make believe world of small donkeys on cobblestone streets, dark eyed children and brilliant blossoms, of street vendors and barking dogs, and the endless droning bells . . . she had come home."[34] Religion, in short, becomes for many an amiable, comforting, and timeless expression of human culture that can even help shape an American's positive sense of self.

My interview with Mark Taylor reminded me that traditional festivals, fireworks at dawn, and peregrinations to repotentiate the saints all offer an "opportunity to connect with origins of civilization" to the few Americans willing to move beyond a pleasing, if superficial, contact with Mexican spirituality. Figures such as Stirling Dickinson, Mort Stith, and Mark Taylor himself have aimed "to invite Americans into deeper understanding of culture." San Miguel, Taylor thinks, is still the "most accessible point of entry into [the] culture of Mexico." San Miguel's connection to the Mexican Revolution, ancient Mexican cultures, and still-vibrant Indian cultures can introduce Americans to the essentials of Mexican life. Seeing a bleeding Jesus, Americans "can't help but be affected."[35]

The Society of the Future, Today

An interest in philanthropy, the arts, and Mexican culture has enhanced the lifestyle of Americans in San Miguel and increased the growing attention given to San Miguel in the international media. This attention has set a tone that sharply contrasts with the tone of a standard resort community. But as illustrated above, the degree to which the arts or philanthropy shape or have transformed day-to-day life in San Miguel is arguable.

Although there is a small group of Americans who speak Spanish, live simply in a Mexican style, and have developed a high level of cultural and social interaction with the Mexican majority, this direct connection to Mexican life seems to be the exception. The growing scale of the American community, the growth in short-term tourism, and the Americanization of Mexico have undermined the connection of Americans to the Mexican town around them. Self-indulgence of a great variety also tends to undermine any American's attempt to make strong connections to his or her Mexican surroundings.

It would be easy to paint a picture of ever-spiraling costs in San Miguel, but the price structure of life in San Miguel still allows a bargain luxury life for most Americans. Costs are far more uneven in San Miguel than in most other Mexican (or American) towns. Not only are local property taxes nominal on even the most expensive homes, but upscale restaurants serve food at reasonable prices, Mexican products are very cheap in stores, and most importantly, servants are still available at low prices. Even art events such as the chamber music festival offer ticket prices that are cheaper compared to similar cultural events in the United States. A further buffer against cost increases are less-fashionable neighborhoods with cheaper accommodations and homes (in hastily constructed *colonias*), a number of inexpensive city *mercados* offering inexpensive food, bargain bus service, free local entertainment and festivals, and the central Jardin "sitting room" that keep this quasi-colonial paradise affordable for even the lower stratum of American retirees. Such Americans do, however, have to be willing to go "Mexican," and to be savvier about costs than those in the luxury group.

The popularity of San Miguel with Mexicans, combined with increasing numbers of visiting Americans, has certainly distorted the price structure in the town. A house in an Americanized district will be comparable in price to many middle-class homes found in leading urban areas of the United States; an American-style meal or shopping trip will be similar in cost to that in the United States; and a car costs nearly the same as comparable vehicles in the United States. Those unwilling to go the Mexican route will find remarkably few cost savings beyond prescription drugs. Most distressing for some of San Miguel's lower-income residents are the increasing costs of many of the local English-language events. Because so many of these events are billed as combination cultural events and fundraisers, the cost for a film or talk can near American prices, though it will seldom exceed that. Irene Rose came for the better prices of the 1970s, but in 1993 she worried that "there are now more things than ever whose prices match their counterparts in the US. Real estate is booming. Rents are up. . . . One dollar for a cup of coffee at a moderately priced restaurant?"[36] Those on fixed retirement incomes have been hit by price inflation. As in much of the United States, there is a growing gap between the wealthy retirees and those on fixed incomes.[37]

Many Americans, with too much time on their hands, can become obsessed with comparative "bargains." *Atencion* has frequently run comparisons between the cost of American products stateside and the same goods for sale in San Miguel; such comparisons fill the time for some, but they should not automatically be taken as an indication of real economic problems on the part of the Americans in San Miguel. As one resident put it, "After observing the self-deluding, quixotic, the peso pinching, guilt compensating attitude of most of the foreigners here . . . [one remembers that] the rich have an interest in bargains as keen as it is pointless."[38] Almost all Americans in San Miguel are better off than the Mexicans around them. Most have pensions, investments, or forms of government support that go far in the town. Frequent devaluations of the peso have also taken the edge off price increases directed at the American colony. As one resident noted in 1982, "While the Mexicans are in deep trouble due to the devaluation of the peso, those of us who are in possession of dollars are embarrassingly rich. For us all the prices have dropped dramatically."[39] This consistent devaluation creates periods during which services and local goods are extraordinarily inexpensive—although these low prices do not last long.

Self-indulgence remains surprisingly cheap. There are reportedly thirteen different Alcoholics Anonymous (AA) groups in town, and many social and cultural events feature free or inexpensive alcohol. Many of the women and men here are also preoccupied with the aging process, diets, and facelifts. Mark Taylor offered some insights into the effect of this low-cost luxury lifestyle, suggesting that time freed from housework and other drudgery was not necessarily devoted to local cultural activities. "My impression is that alcohol is extraordinarily accessible, cheap," he told me, in part as a result of the fact that "in a town where matters of a spiritual nature [are] so in your face," even the unreligious have "a longing for spirituality," though they discover that they can only "connect through [an] altered state." He thought that those who lack "direct involvement with cultural life" can find themselves "isolated and lonely" although this is often masked "under [a] surface of gala parties and substance abuse."[40]

One of the best bargains in San Miguel is cheap Mexican labor, and it is a cornerstone of the luxury life and self-indulgence advertised to potential residents. If Americans were forced to take care of their homes and survive independently in Mexico, fewer would come to stay. A local realtor illus-trated this luxury life to newcomers in one of the many free "Living in San Miguel de Allende" informational sessions offered around town, explaining that maids can still be had for ninety-five dollars a week and a cook for fifty dollars a week. He explained, with some pride, that "I never lift a finger," and that he lived "like a king even if I can't afford it."[41]

A revealing portrait of what inexpensive and abundant servants mean to local residents was given in 1977 by a resident who divided his time between San Miguel and St. Louis:

> From the moment you arrive at your front door with your luggage until the mo-ment you depart you are not allowed to do anything for yourself. . . . No gro-cery shopping, no cooking, no dishes, no cleaning, no washing or ironing, no work whatever. Meals are a delight, perfectly prepared, beautifully served, epi-curean in taste. . . . The cook plans, shops, prepares and serves every meal. The lady of the house doesn't even have to think about it.

He contrasted this to the United States where the "dinner party with the hostess leaving the table between courses is not gracious living."[42] Women, traditionally responsible for housework among these retired couples, reap the rewards of so much female help. One woman wrote to the paper, "Living as we do in this wonderland of affordable servants, you would think we women would sport the most beautiful fingernails in the world. We seldom wash a dish, we never dust, mop or launder even our dainties."[43]

The fact that so much cheap labor is available does not mean that Amer-icans can enjoy this lifestyle without worry. There is much talk of servants camping out in houses while the homeowners are gone, even moving their whole families in; there is a great deal of concern that servants are taking ad-vantage of their American employers. "In any gathering of our foreign colony . . . at least one of three topics will inevitably be heard . . . the servant prob-lem, amoeba, and experiences with customs."[44] An annoyed dog walker spread word in *Atencion* about the dangers of servants walking dogs: "Don't let your servants or their children exercise your dogs. I see many dogs yanked by their collars, kicked and dragged by unfeeling 'walkers' about which I am sure the owners know nothing."[45]

The hottest topic in San Miguel, as in most American communities, is real estate. It is a barometer of the community's attractiveness (and some Ameri-cans are engaged in realty or other forms of real-estate promotion), and it is also a potential source of income because houses are rented on a regular basis to winter visitors, or "snowbirds," while their owners return for short periods to the United States to visit families, renew their tourist visas, and so forth.

Real-estate offices are numerous in the historic center and offer orientations to many newcomers that are really sales pitches for buying in the city.

Real estate, by Mexican and even American standards, has become expensive in the fashionable center and hillside districts, but by luxury standards, prices are still reasonable. By the 1980s, the boom was on. "A recent [1981] survey of 5 prominent real estate agencies in town proves that what we all think is happening is happening. Prices of houses, lots, and undeveloped land have soared in the last 2–3 years. . . . One house that sold for 55,000 US two years ago is 125,000 today." Nor can Americans alone be blamed for the run-up in prices: "Buyers are now coming from Europe, France, Germany, Holland and from England, they are trickling in from South America. They continue to come in ever increasing numbers from the United States and Canada . . . retired and professional people who want to move their families out of the smog and noise of Mexico City." The influx of affluent Mexicans, in particular, can be seen as a positive sign: "Happily this could save us from ourselves, from being a town full of gringos."[46] Joe Persico, a well-known writer and part-time resident, worried in 1989 that "soaring costs, lack of reasonable housing, an influx of affluent visitors may be making San Miguel de Allende less an art and literary center than a more conventional resort and retirement community. I saw it happen in Carmel and former other art colonies."[47]

While affordable homes can still be found in the primarily Mexican districts of town, those houses in the Hillside and central historical zone start at 200,000 dollars (for a very small house) and quickly rise upward, sometimes into the millions of dollars for the most grand and important edifices and haciendas. The wealthy, however, get a great deal for their money, and super-luxury homes are still significantly cheaper in San Miguel than they would be in cities such as Santa Fe or Aspen (especially in light of the minimal property-tax rates and low wages for gardeners and other servants). Houses can also be rented at handsome prices as a way to pay for upkeep. The nicest homes in San Miguel have not only elaborate tile and brickwork throughout, but also colonnaded courtyards with fountains, *boveda* ceilings, pools, terraces with magnificent views, glass-curtain walls, maid's quarters, massive old doors, extensive acreage (for those on the edge of town), and water systems specially designed to create the illusion of American-level services. Most of these houses are designed to maximize views of the leading historic structures of the city and the vast plain that begins below. The houses now constructed for Americans appear to be modeled on a blend of colonial styles, Moorish accents, and American modernism. Bright colors, expanses of glass, and lush gardens make these homes very pleasant indeed.

Most distinct in terms of American styles of life are the gated, or at least separate, suburban districts growing around the town (see fig. 9.1). It would be easy to condemn these communities for reflecting only a retreat from Mexican life, and they *are* physically distant, but even in the central, historic districts, the better homes are actually walled, *cantera* block compounds that are forbidding in their own way. In fact, these new districts offer luxury housing that is probably cheaper by the square foot than most housing in the historic center, and their gates are often decorative; but the massive scale of these houses and the generous amounts of land they occupy still make them expensive. Many Mexicans also live in these districts, and the districts are similar to the Americanized, gated, suburban communities found around many of Mexico's larger cities. A retired American real-estate broker in Atascadero, a suburban villa community that is not gated, explained that "even in a neighborhood like this, [one finds] 30 percent Mexicans," and he notes that other Mexican "people walk by and [are] poor and needy compared to you. You don't see this in [American] suburbia." The suburban lifestyle of San Miguel could, in theory, lead to more contact between the new North American suburbanites of Mexico and average Mexican life, because encroaching around many of these new suburban districts are average *colonia* shantytowns, but in practice this contact can be minimized by a gated and auto-oriented existence (see fig. 9.2).

Figure 9.1.   Upscale gated development on San Miguel's outskirts. Photo courtesy of Nicholas Dagen Bloom.

Figure 9.2. View from a new villa on the San Miguel outskirts. Photo courtesy of Nicholas Dagen Bloom.

Gentrification of Mexican districts such as Colonia San Antonia has accommodated the demand for affordable housing for Americans. Middle-class Americans can find affordable new homes in these areas, and some builders have built on speculation for the Americans and for middle-class Mexicans. Americans do have to be willing to adapt to Mexican standards of life if they live in these areas, but many seem willing to tolerate the additional noise and activity prevalent in Mexican districts in order to have their own homes. Thus even the middle class can enjoy a luxury lifestyle in less-fashionable districts.

For Americans, the villa fantasy, even in a working-class neighborhood, can become an island existence. At the point when many older couples would need less space, they are in fact building or buying their dream homes in San Miguel. These big houses seem far too large and dangerous for the many older Americans that buy them. Hard and slippery tile floors, complex and unpredictable stairways, and multiple living levels are forbidding for even the most agile. The houses are such a good bargain, however, that few can resist the temptation to buy big. And the fact that many of these Americans come from cities such as New York, where conditions are cramped, makes large, inexpensive spaces even more enticing.

Making life easier for these Americans are the comforts of home now available in San Miguel and the surrounding communities. Many of those who live in these communities could walk easily to town, but most of them have cars. These communities are also convenient to a new Gigante supermarket and adjoining shopping center where the main road heads to Queretaro. Auto trips to Queretaro's Sam's Club and Wal-Mart have become frequent. Isolation from the "real" Mexico is possible for Americans in both the historic center and the new suburbs (see fig. 9.3).

Figure 9.3. Shopping American-style at Gigante. Photo courtesy of Leanne Bloom.

The combination of cable television, a Blockbuster video store, English-language cultural events, and a fairly segregated English-language social and benevolent circle means that very few Americans have achieved any degree of Spanish-language fluency.[48] Many Americans even have local contacts, usually their maids or servants, who shop for them and get better deals at local stores. Linguistic self-indulgence is noticeable. Mexicans cannot afford to ignore English, but Americans can easily afford to flaunt their lack of Spanish. At local coffee shops and restaurants, it is not uncommon to hear American music and loud conversations in English.

There are many schools teaching Spanish, and Americans must of course learn some survival Spanish in order to interact with servants and shopkeepers, but if San Miguel's expatriate community is learning and speaking Spanish, they are keeping it a secret from their neighbors. In my month in San Miguel, I never once witnessed those who appeared to be American speaking Spanish among themselves, and most of the Spanish used in the stores by Americans was rudimentary. The structural isolation possible in the community contributes to what is often perceived as cultural insensitivity, but the advanced age of the population, too, makes language acquisition that much harder; many of these Americans had never learned a second language before coming to Mexico, and San Miguel's attraction was more aesthetic, cultural, or climatic than linguistic. In addition, many Mexicans are eager to learn English in order to prepare for emigration to the United States.

Many Americans have complex reasons for leaving San Miguel—often involving disapproval of San Miguel's overdevelopment or Americanization—but the most common and plausible reason is declining health. San Miguel remains an ideal environment for those in active retirement, but the narrow sidewalks, cobblestones, growing traffic, and language confusion are quickly compounded by the lack of American-level health care in Mexico. There is near universal agreement among the Americans here that Mexican hospitals and doctors fall short of American standards. Frequent trips to the United States for medical care and long-term care often lead to departure from Mexico. One sees very few truly infirm older Americans in San Miguel. As one might expect, too, there are many more older women than older men in San Miguel, and many older women tell me they were drawn to San Miguel because it has a reputation as being a town open to single women. As they age, however, life in San Miguel can become more difficult. As one long-time resident told me, "older women [had started] leaning on her" for rides and favors, and "most of the little old ladies are alcoholics or drinking a lot over a long period of time." Their befuddled state makes them "easy prey" for crime and scams, although they "rarely file a complaint."[49] Pressure from their families back home also will force many older residents of the colony to move stateside.

Rude Awakening

The American colony of San Miguel has worked to preserve and enhance the town's historical attractiveness, but modern Mexican culture (a blend of American, Mexican, and European elements) has done as much or more to change San Miguel. Customized cars, diesel buses, modern clothes, cement-block houses, fast food served on the street, popular music, mass sports, mass-produced crafts, and professional wrestling are not what most of San Miguel's American elite imagine when they say they respect and value Mexican culture—but plenty of Mexicans enjoy these urban pleasures and activities both on vacation and on a daily basis. Much of San Miguel is devoted to these modern, international activities. Mexico has become an industrialized society with a strong connection to global culture and styles of life. These ways of living contrast strongly with the vision of primitive Mexico so beloved by Americans who have settled here. Modern Mexico is not always closely tied to the values of the San Miguel American colony that emphasize handmade folk or studio art, indigenous or classical music, live theater, genteel drinking, historic preservation, environmentalism, and good works.

Also annoying to many of San Miguel's American residents has been the growth of the mass-tourism industry in the town that has begun to overwhelm the central historical district. The Jardin is considered by most Americans to be the central public space of the American and Mexican community, but its ability to serve this role is being undercut by tourism. One of the best summaries of the function of the Jardin was given in 1982 by a long-time columnist in the city, Connie Moore, who compared her hometown of Los Angeles to San Miguel:

> One of the biggest differences between the two places has to do with street life: there is virtually none in LA. The *Jardin* here strikes me as the town living room with all the streets corridors leading to it. We have electric people-vibes here, human energy waves different from anything I have known elsewhere. To walk two blocks to the post office and encounter 16 humans who are involved in your life is in some way a heady experience and one can never duplicate in LA or any other part of the world the smile and warmth of the truly caring Mexican trades person.[50]

In 1987, long-time resident Phil Hammerslough wrote of the Jardin that "it never disappoints: the shade trees, the gazebo in the center, the wonderful iron benches facing the church and the clock tower . . . the reality is as fresh as ever"[51] (see fig. 9.4).

Some residents find the flood of tourists innocuous, and tourists do tend to arrive in waves; weekends and evenings are the times of heaviest tourism in San Miguel. For sensitive residents, however, the growth in tourism is an annoyance that complicates the sense of retreat from modernity they are seeking. Gary Jennings expressed his frustration in a 1977 column:

> As soon as 10 years ago San Miguel was still a colonial town that took pride in its antiquity. It then welcomed foreign settlers attracted by its colonial atmosphere (and who could be expected to help preserve same). . . . Nowadays, the short-timers—vacationers, weekenders, students, caravanists—have become San Miguel de Allende's underlying raison d'etre. The town caters to them, truckles to them, and even changes its character and ambiance for them.

Jennings was aghast that "within 50 meters of the *Parroquia* . . . are 3 tourist hungry nightclubs deafening worshipers, sightseers, and promenaders." Many of the American visitors arrived "in shepherded packs" and refused to eat in local restaurants.[52] A humorous suggestion for cultural regulation underscores these changes: "Every foreign male when appearing in public has to wear a *serape* and a *sombrero*. Every woman has to wear a *rebozo*. This place

Figure 9.4.   The scene in the Jardin: talk and time matter. Photo courtesy of Leanne Bloom.

will finally look authentic again."[53] And the crowds have continued to swell, giving the Jardin a Disneyland feeling.

The growth of Mexican and American daytrippers, with the improvement of bus and road service, added during the 1970s and 1980s to the pressures on what is a very diminutive town. By 1989, 175,000 tourists were visiting San Miguel on a yearly basis, and of these, 120,000 were Mexican.[54] One of my interview subjects estimated that a couple hundred Americans were involved in some way with the retail, restaurant, realty, and hospitality industries of the town. Most of these Americans, if they have survived in business, have benefited from the booming tourism industry. New tourist businesses have also played a role in reducing Mexican unemployment. San Miguel in the mid-1970s, for instance, still suffered from nearly 50 percent unemployment with another 20 percent underemployed; local tourism industries employed approximately two thousand workers in local bars and restaurants. As one local official put it, "In spite of everything we cannot look on the tourist industry as a cause of all the evils."[55] San Miguel is still dependent on the tourism industry; there is no other major source of employment in the city, and the industry stimulates activity in services, construction, and government.

Mexican government officials visiting the town have been unimpressed with the benefits of tourism here, and they chastised town leaders as early as 1978 because "the traffic has become insupportable so that the tranquility of the city is a myth. The architectural harmony has been broken owing to the indifference or incompetence of previous administrations."[56] Traffic has grown since this report, and the city is full from dawn to dusk with loud and dirty cars and buses, but the city has in recent decades worked hard to increase historic preservation with now noticeable improvements in the care of older buildings and parks. These improvements, however, are likely to draw even more visitors.

Cities such as San Miguel, Guanajuato, and Zacatecas are important national and cultural symbols for much of Mexico, and so they attract crowds, particularly of middle-class Mexicans from Mexico City, or *chilangos*, year-round. Americans in San Miguel have generally negative opinions of the *chilangos* and tend to believe that they share this opinion with the local Mexican population. It is these tourists who are most responsible for the abundant t-shirt shops, discos, restaurants, and manufactured crafts and furnishings that have been slowly converting the historic center of the town into a tourist zone. The Mexican tourists, however, are known for being more open-handed with their money than the American tourists and the resident Americans, who have a reputation for being tightfisted (and of being constantly suspicious that they are being cheated).

San Miguel, in spite of the growing numbers of tourists, has not become a homogeneous tourist environment. Tourism development here, in contrast to Acapulco or Cancún, is of the less-intrusive variety. Conversions of older family compounds into hotels, and of old stores into coffee shops, internet cafes, t-shirt emporiums, galleries, and restaurants, has been matched by a growing interest in historic preservation that has prevented some of the more invasive types of development found elsewhere. There are no blaring neon signs, no American fast-food restaurants, and still no traffic lights in the town center. This less-intrusive tourism development has become so pervasive in certain streets adjoining the Jardin that over time it has displaced almost all of the stores serving the daily needs of San Miguel's residents. The increasing density of these courtyards converted into mini shopping malls, even if the malls are primarily Mexican-owned, is appealing (because it has led to the preservation and enhancement of older structures) and at the same time overwhelming, because so much of the older city has been converted to tourist uses.

Long-term American residents cannot be held solely responsible for the growing scale of the city and its tourism; and many of them are uncomfortable with these changes. They are, however, powerless to direct this growth. Americans in cities like these simply have to make their peace with these changes, or better yet, find some way to profit from them.

In the end, the Americans in San Miguel wish to be served *and* loved. This combination makes the American community so complex. If the Americans were simply desirous of servants and a luxury lifestyle, it would be easier to condemn them as the sort of colonizers or boorish tourists found in places such as Cancún. But Americans are not only exploiters of labor in San Miguel. They have also made genuine attempts to improve the life of the average Mexican in this city, and they are engaged in the arts. But the Americans in San Miguel are small in number, and their impact is far more noticeable in the luxury lifestyle they have carved out for themselves. The waves of Mexican urban growth in the city, and the city's independent Mexican culture, further complicate the question of influence and impact.

One point, however, should not be overlooked. The path carved out in the early years for San Miguel by figures such as Stirling Dickinson has been well trod, but in a rather superficial way. Dickinson and others certainly did initiate cultural and social institutions, but they also advocated a more direct connection to Mexican life because they respected the culture, learned the language, lived rather simply, and did not want to create an American village in the Mexican highlands. Their spirit of philanthropy and cultural activity is still alive here, but the general spirit of the American community's social and cultural engagement with Mexico seems to be dwindling. External factors, such as the globalization of American culture, have contributed to this process, but the bargain, luxury, Americanized way of living pursued by Americans here is equally responsible. San Miguel de Allende, an odd blend of self-indulgence and public spirit amid Mexican squalor, will likely be but the model for further American residential growth in the old colonial towns of Mexico.

Notes

1. This article is primarily based upon a close reading of approximately thirty years of *Atencion*, the weekly English-language newspaper of the American community. Bound editions can be found at the *Atencion* office in the Biblioteca. Other material was drawn from attendance, observation, eavesdropping, and participation in a variety of cultural and social activities in San Miguel de Allende in July 2002 and from approximately twenty interviews of long-time and new residents of the community. Published accounts such as Charles Smart's *At Home in Mexico* (Garden City, N.Y.: Doubleday, 1957), and more recently, Tony Cohan's *On Mexican Time* (New York: Broadway, 2001), also proved helpful in setting the context for this article.

2. This population figure is solely an estimate given to me by an official, Paula Ramirez, at the American Consular Agency in San Miguel de Allende. It is based on the fact that there are eight thousand permanent American residents registered in the states of Guanajuato and Michoacán (for which the agency has responsibility), of which she estimates half are in residence at San Miguel de Allende. A frequent number given in town, also unofficial, is five thousand American residents. Because a sizable, but undocumented, number of Americans stay in Mexico on tourist visas, these numbers are mere estimates.

3. Lane Smith, interview with the author, July 20, 2002, San Miguel de Allende.

4. Zelda Kosh, "50 Golden Years," *Atencion*, February 2, 1986.

5. Jerry Novak, "And Then," *Atencion*, September 23, 1988.

6. John Johnson, "A Wrong Turn Brought Us to San Miguel de Allende," *Atencion*, August 15, 1975.

7. For more details on the Brooks story, see John Virtue, *Leonard and Reva Brooks: Artists in Exile in San Miguel de Allende* (Montréal: McGill-Queen's University Press, 2001).

8. Stirling Dickinson, "Write Me a Letter, Please," *Atencion*, December 5, 1975.

9. See Virtue, *Leonard and Reva Brooks*, for the complete story of the expatriate's political and social problems during this period.

10. Kosh, "50 Golden Years."

11. Zelda Kosh, "Spotlight on People," *Atencion*, February 2, 1986, and September 30, 1977.

12. Mimi Loomer, "Those Were the Good Old Days," *Atencion*, November 6, 1979.

13. Harold Black, "Remember the 1950s," *Atencion*, March 22, 1991.

14. "Dean Remembers from 1952, "*Atencion*, November 6, 1979.

15. "From Helen's Library to *Biblioteca Publica*," *Atencion*, July 18, 1975.

16. "An Open Letter," *Atencion*, March 31, 1981.

17. Smith, interview.

18. Norman Loletus, interview with the author, July 19, 2002, San Miguel de Allende.

19. Gretchen Roberts, interview with the author, July 19, 2002, San Miguel de Allende.

20. "Gil Flores Speaks Out on Tourism," *Atencion*, November 11, 1977.

21. Gilberto Flores, "My Turn," *Atencion*, February 11, 1977.

22. "Patronatos," *Atencion*, August 29, 1975. From Stirling Dickinson, Summary of Community Comments on August 20, 1975.

23. Cecil Smith, "A proposito," *Atencion*, July 20, 1990.

24. Loletus, interview.

25. Stuart Harris, "21 Ways to Survive in SMA [San Miguel de Allende]," *Atencion*, May 26, 1989.

26. "Adios con amor," *Atencion*, June 11, 1976.

27. "Busybodies," *Atencion*, May 6, 1988.

28. Phil Roettinger, "Un poquito de todo," *Atencion*, June 4, 1982.

29. Mimi Loomer, "My Turn," *Atencion*, September 20, 1985.

30. Connie Moore, "Moore platica," *Atencion*, August 20, 1982.

31. Cecil Smith, "A proposito," *Atencion*, March 10, 1989.

32. Jerry Novak, "And Then," *Atencion*, November 11, 1988.

33. Dar Simms, "Random Shots: Patience is a Virtue," *Atencion*, March 9, 1984.

34. Connie Netherton "Homecoming," *Atencion*, October 5, 1984.

35. Mark Taylor, interview with the author, July 18, 2002, San Miguel de Allende.

36. Irene Rose, "Rambling Rose," *Atencion*, October 8, 1993.

37. Connie Moore, "Moore platica," *Atencion*, December 12, 1975.

38. Pat Kelly, "Letter to the Editor," *Atencion*, December 4, 1987.

39. Phil Roettinger, "Un poquito de todo" *Atencion*, September 10, 1982.

40. Taylor, interview.

41. Real-estate presentation, July 22, 2002, San Miguel de Allende.

42. John Windsor, "Commuting To and From Mexico," *Atencion*, January 28, 1977.

43. Clairus Grevenson, "Hard as Nails," *Atencion*, June 25, 1982.

44. Phil Roettinger, "Un poquito de todo," *Atencion*, May 1, 1979.

45. M. Von H. Charlton, "Letter to the Editor," *Atencion*, July 1, 1977.

46. Pat Gehlert, "Surreal Estate," *Atencion*, March 3, 1981.

47. Joe Persico quoted in Cecil Smith, "A proposito," *Atencion*, March 10, 1989.

48. Smith, interview.

49. Roberts, interview.

50. Connie Moore, "Moore platica," *Atencion*, August 20, 1982.

51. Phil Hammerslough, "Walking through San Miguel de Allende," *Atencion*, February 20, 1987.

52. Gary Jennings, "My Turn," *Atencion*, November 4, 1977.

53. Harold Black, "Doing Well in SMA," *Atencion*, March 13, 1992.

54. "Much Tourismo," *Atencion*, February 2, 1990.

55. "Gil Flores Speaks Out on Tourism," *Atencion*, November 11, 1977.

56. Eduardo Morreno Laparade, "Should SMA Be Declared a National Monument?" *Atencion*, originally printed in *Heraldo de Mexico*, March 17, 1978.

Further Reading

Historical research that treats Americans in Mexico includes Diana Anhalt, *A Gathering of Fugitives: American Political Expatriates in Mexico, 1948–1965* (Santa Maria, Calif.: Archer, 2001); Deborah Baldwin, *Protestants and the Mexican Revolution: Missionaries, Ministers, and Social Change* (Urbana: University of Illinois Press, 1990); William H. Beezley, *Judas at the Jockey Club and Other Episodes of Porfirian Mexico*, 2d ed. (Lincoln: University of Nebraska Press, 2004); Janet Bennion, *Desert Patriarchy: Mormons and Mennonite Communities in the Chihuahua Valley* (Tucson: University of Arizona, 2004); Helen Delpar, *The Enormous Vogue of Things Mexican* (Tuscaloosa: University of Alabama Press, 1992); Paul Dosal, *Doing Business with the Dictator: A Political History of United Fruit in Guatemala, 1899–1944* (Wilmington, Del.: Scholarly Resources, 1993); Gene Hanrahan, *The Bad Yankee: American Entrepreneurs and Financiers in Mexico* (Chapel Hill: University of North Carolina Press, 1985); John Mason Hart, *Empire and Revolution: The Americans in Mexico since the Civil War* (Berkeley: University of California Press, 2002); Robert Herr, *An American Family in the Mexican Revolution* (Wilmington, Del.: Scholarly Resources, 1999); Tullis F. LaMond, *Mormons in Mexico: The Dynamics of Faith and Culture* (Logan: Utah State University Press, 1987); Taylor D. Littleton, *The Color of Silver: William Spratling, His Life and Art* (Baton Rouge: Louisiana State University Press, 2000); Joan Mark, *The Silver Gringo: William Spratling and Taxco* (Albuquerque: University of New Mexico Press, 2000); David Pletcher, *Rails, Mines, and Progress: Seven American Promoters in Mexico, 1867–1911* (Ithaca, N.Y.: Cornell University Press, 1958); Andrew F. Rolle,

The Lost Cause: The Confederate Exodus to Mexico (Norman: University of Oklahoma Press, 1965); Ramón Ruiz, *The People of Sonora and Yankee Capitalists* (Tucson: University of Arizona Press, 1988); and William Schell Jr., *Integral Outsiders: The American Colony in Mexico City, 1876–1911* (Wilmington, Del.: Scholarly Resources, 2001).

The research on border dynamics is extensive and includes Tom Barry, *The Great Divide: The Challenge of U.S.-Mexico Relations in the 1990s* (New York: Grove, 1994); Claire Fox, *The Fence and the River: Culture and Politics at the U.S.-Mexico Border* (Minneapolis: University of Minnesota Press, 1999); Rosa Fregosa, *Mexican Encounters: The Making of Social Identities on the Borderlands* (Berkeley: University of California Press, 2003); Lawrence Herzog, *Where North Meets South: Cities, Space, and Politics on the U.S.-Mexico Border* (Austin: Center for Mexican American Studies, University of Texas, 1990); Lawrence Herzog, *From Aztec to High Tech: Architecture and Landscape across the Mexico-United States Border* (Baltimore: Johns Hopkins University Press, 1999); David E. Lorey, *The U.S.-Mexican Border in the Twentieth Century: A History of Economic and Social Transformation* (Wilmington, Del.: Scholarly Resources, 1999); Oscar J. Martínez, *Border People: Life and Society in the U.S.-Mexico Borderlands* (Tucson: University of Arizona Press, 1994); Oscar J. Martínez, ed., *U.S.-Mexico Borderlands: Historical and Contemporary Perspectives* (Wilmington, Del.: Scholarly Resources, 1996); Jóse Saldivar, *Border Matters: Remapping American Cultural Studies* (Berkeley: University of California Press, 1997); David Spencer, ed., *The U.S.-Mexico Border: Transcending Divisions, Contesting Identities* (Boulder, Colo.: Lynne Rienner, 1998); and Andrew Grant Wood, *On the Border: Society and Culture between the United States and Mexico* (Wilmington, Del.: Scholarly Resources, 2004).

For a general introduction to modern tourist theory, see Barbara Kirshenblatt-Gimblett, *Destination Culture: Tourism, Museums, and Heritage* (Berkeley: University of California Press, 1998); Dennis R. Judd and Susan S. Fainstein, eds., *The Tourist City* (New Haven, Conn.: Yale University Press, 1999); Dennis R. Judd, ed., *The Infrastructure of Play: Building the Tourist City* (Armonk, N.Y.: M. E. Sharpe, 2003); Dean MacCannell, *The Tourist: A New Theory of the Leisure Class* (New York: Schocken Books, 1976); Chris Rojek and John Urry, eds., *Touring Cultures: Transformations of Travel and Theory* (New York: Routledge, 1997); and John Urry, *The Tourist Gaze* (London: Sage Publications, 1990).

The origins of tourism are documented in a number of books, including Michael Foss, ed., *On Tour: The British Traveler in Europe* (London: O'Mara, 1989), 197. See also Jeremy Black, *The British Abroad: The Grand Tour in the*

Eighteenth Century (New York: St. Martin's, 1992) and Black, *Italy and the Grand Tour* (New Haven, Conn.: Yale University Press, 2003); James Buzard, *The Beaten Track: European Tourism, Literature, and the Ways to Culture, 1800–1918* (New York: Oxford University Press, 1993); Brian Dolan, *Ladies of the Grand Tour* (London: Harper Collins, 2001); Christopher Hibbert, *The Grand Tour* (London: Thames Methuen, 1987); and John Stoye, *English Travelers Abroad* (New Haven, Conn.: Yale University Press, 1989).

American tourism history has also become an active field. See Cindy Aron, *Working at Play: A History of Vacations in the United States* (New York: Oxford University Press, 1999); Warren Belasco, *Americans on the Road: From Autocamp to Motel, 1910–1945* (Cambridge, Mass.: MIT Press, 1979); Dona Brown, *Inventing New England: Regional Tourism in the Nineteenth Century* (Washington, D.C.: Smithsonian Institution Press, 1995); Catherine Cocks, *Doing the Town: The Rise of Urban Tourism in the United States* (Berkeley: University of California Press, 2001); Karen Dubinsky, *The Second Greatest Disappointment: Honeymooning and Tourism at Niagara Falls* (New Brunswick, N.J.: Rutgers University Press, 1999); Christopher Endy, *Cold War Holidays: American Tourism in France* (Chapel Hill: University of North Carolina Press, 2004); John Findlay, *Magic Lands: Western Cityscapes and American Culture after 1940* (Berkeley: University of California Press, 1992); John Jakle, *The Tourist: Travel in Twentieth-century North America* (Lincoln: University of Nebraska Press, 1985); Hal K. Rothman, *Devil's Bargains: Tourism in the Twentieth-century American West* (Lawrence: University Press of Kansas, 1998); John F. Sears, *Sacred Places: American Tourist Attractions in the Nineteenth Century* (New York: Oxford University Press, 1989); Marguerite Shaffer, *See America First: Tourism and National Identity, 1880–1940* (Washington, D.C.: Smithsonian Institution Press, 2001); Richard Starnes, ed., *Southern Journeys: Tourism, History and Culture in the Modern South* (Tuscaloosa: University of Alabama Press, 2003); and William W. Stowe, *Going Abroad: European Travel in Nineteenth-century American Culture* (Princeton, N.J.: Princeton University Press, 1994).

On the loss of regional character in the United States, which partly inspired Mexican tourism, see Nicholas Bloom, *Suburban Alchemy: 1960s New Towns and the Transformation of the American Dream* (Columbus: Ohio State University Press, 2001); Nicholas Bloom, *Merchant of Illusion: James Rouse, America's Salesman of the Businessman's Utopia* (Columbus: Ohio State University Press, 2004); Robert Fishman, *Bourgeois Utopias: The Rise and Fall of Suburbia* (New York: Basic Books, 1989); Owen Gutfreund, *Twentieth Century Sprawl: Highways and the Reshaping of the American Landscape* (New

York: Oxford University Press, 2004); Jeffrey M. Hardwick, *Mall Maker: Victor Gruen, Architect of an American Dream* (Philadelphia: University of Pennsylvania Press, 2004); and Kenneth Jackson, *Crabgrass Frontier: The Suburbanization of the United States* (New York: Oxford University Press, 1987).

More general suburban analyses include Andres Duany, *Suburban Nation: The Rise of Sprawl and the Decline of the American Dream* (New York: North Point, 2001); Delores Hayden, *A Field Guide to Sprawl* (New York: Norton, 2004); Jane Holtz Kay, *Asphalt Nation: How the Automobile Took Over America, and How We Can Take It Back* (Berkeley: University of California Press, 1998); and James Howard Kunstler, *Home From Nowhere: The Rise and Decline of America's Man-Made Landscape* (New York: Free Press, 1994).

Index

About the Contributors

Diana Anhalt, a freelance writer and resident of Mexico City, is the author of *A Gathering of Fugitives: American Political Expatriates in Mexico 1948–1965* (2001). She has reviewed books for the *Texas Observer*, and her articles have appeared in magazines and anthologies in both Mexico and the United States.

Dina Berger is assistant professor of history at Loyola University, Chicago. She completed her PhD at the University of Arizona in 2002. She is the author of *The Development and Promotion of Mexico's Tourism Industry: Pyramids by Day, Martinis by Night* (2006).

Nicholas Dagen Bloom received his PhD from Brandeis University. He is the author of *Suburban Alchemy: 1960s New Towns and the Transformation of the American Dream* (2001) and *Merchant of Illusion: James Rouse, America's Salesman of the Businessman's Utopia* (2004). He is currently writing a history of public housing in New York for the University of Pennsylvania Press.

Michael Chibnik is professor of anthropology at the University of Iowa in Iowa City. He is the author of *Crafting Tradition: The Making and Marketing of Oaxacan Wood Carvings* (2003) and *Risky Rivers: The Economics and Politics of Floodplain Farming in Amazonia* (1994).

Drewey Wayne Gunn is emeritus professor of English at Texas A&M University. He is the author of *The Gay Male Sleuth in Print and Film* (2005) and *American and British Writers in Mexico, 1556–1973* (1975).

Janet Henshall Momsen is professor of geography in the Department of Human and Community Development at the University of California, Davis. She has authored four books, edited six, and is editor of the International Studies of Women and Place series for Routledge. She has carried out field-work in the Caribbean, Latin America, South Asia, West Africa, Hungary, and China.

Rebecca M. Schreiber is assistant professor of American studies at the University of New Mexico. Her current book project, *The Cold War Culture of Political Exile: U.S. Artists and Writers in Mexico, 1940–1965*, forthcoming, examines the cultural and political history of U.S. exile communities that developed in Mexico City during the 1940s and 1950s.

Rebecca Torres is assistant professor of geography at East Carolina University. She has conducted research in Mexico and Cuba and worked in the field of rural development in Peru. Her research has appeared in *Annals of Tourism Research* and the *Annals of the Association of American Geographers*, among other scholarly journals.

David Truly is associate professor in the Department of Geography at Central Connecticut State University, where he also serves as the Director of Tourism and Hospitality Studies. His research interests include international retirement migration to Latin America, sustainable tourism development and management, and the diffusion of popular music.

Richard W. Wilkie is professor of geography at the University of Massachusetts, Amherst. He is author of *Latin American Population and Urbanization Analysis* (1985), coeditor of the *Historical Atlas of Massachusetts* (1991), and author of many articles and chapters as well as numerous photographs in books, magazines, and newspapers. Travel has taken him to more than eighty countries, including Mexico, Switzerland, Argentina, and Singapore.